Business of Tourism

Dr. K.N. Patel

AKHAND

AKHAND PUBLISHING HOUSE
NEW DELHI (INDIA)

Published by
AKHAND PUBLISHING HOUSE
L-9 A, IST FLOOR, STREET NO. 42
SADATPUR EXTENSION
DELHI-110094 (INDIA)
CELL- 0-9013387535, 0-9968628081

Business of Tourism

Edition 2010
ISBN 978-81-910525-7-2

Printed in India
at Asian Offset Printers, Delhi

Preface

The tourism industry in India is substantial and vibrant, and the country is fast becoming a major global destination. It is one of the most profitable industries in the country, and also credited with contributing a substantial amount of foreign exchange. Several reasons are cited for the growth and prosperity of India's travel and tourism industry. Economic growth has added millions annually to the ranks of India's middle class, a group that is driving domestic tourism growth. Thanks in part to its booming IT and outsourcing industry a growing number of business trips are made by foreigners to India, who will often add a weekend break or longer holiday to their trip. Foreign tourists spend more in India than almost any other country worldwide.

The Tourism Ministry has also played an important role in the development of the industry, initiating advertising campaigns such as the 'Incredible India' campaign, which promoted India's culture and tourist attractions in a fresh and memorable way. The campaign helped create a colourful image of India in the minds of consumers all over the world, and has directly led to an increase in the interest among tourists. The tourism industry has helped growth in other sectors as diverse as horticulture, handicrafts, agriculture, construction and even poultry. Both directly and indirectly, increased tourism in India has created jobs in a variety of related sectors.

Written for a diverse audience, this book explores travel and tourism comprehensively—examining the travel sectors, promotional strategies, economic influences and business principles that govern the industry. It will be a comprehensive reference tool for students looking to make careers in travel and tourism as well as industry professionals already there.

Author

Contents

1

Tourism Business in India

Tourism is the largest service industry in India, with a contribution of 6.23% to the national GDP and 8.78% of the total employment in India. India witnesses more than 5 million annual foreign tourist arrivals and 562 million domestic tourism visits. The tourism industry in India generated about US$100 billion in 2008 and that is expected to increase to US$275.5 billion by 2018 at a 9.4% annual growth rate. The Ministry of Tourism is the nodal agency for the development and promotion of tourism in India and maintains the "Incredible India" campaign.

According to World Travel and Tourism Council, India will be a tourism hotspot from 2009–2018, having the highest 10-year growth potential. The Travel & Tourism Competitiveness Report 2007 ranked tourism in India 6th in terms of price competitiveness and 39th in terms of safety and security. Despite short- and medium-term setbacks, such as shortage of hotel rooms, tourism revenues are expected to surge by 42% from 2007 to 2017.

It is boom time for India's Tourism and Hospitality sector. A 5,000 year history, culture, religion and alternative medicine fascinate both budget and luxury travellers alike. The Department of Tourism's resolve in promoting Indian tourism has strengthened as it recognises its potential. Tourism in India is the third largest foreign exchange earner, accounting for 2.5 per cent of GDP. It also makes a direct contribution to economy with significant linkages with agriculture, horticulture, handicrafts and construction. The outlay on tourism development rose to Rs 7,860 million in 2005/2006, from Rs 3,500 million in 2003/2004, and continued to focus on the "Atithi Devo Bhavah" campaign, targeted at the inbound foreign tourists in the country. Translated literally this means "Guest is God".

1.1. Drivers of Tourism Growth

Commencing with a slow growth at the start of the millennium, the Indian tourism industry has performed quite well in the last couple of years. The Indian tourism industry has out performed the global tourism industry in terms of growth in the volume of international tourists as well as in terms of revenue.

According to World Travel and Tourism Council (WTTC) the Travel & Tourism Industry contributes 2.1 per cent to India's GDP. The industry employed an estimated 24,349,000 people in 2006.

The key driver for this growth in the Indian tourism industry has been a fast growing economy for the last 3-4 years. Despite lagging in the basic infrastructure that supports the tourism industry, Indian tourism industry has been showing an impressive double-digit growth. In order to sustain this growth and meet the expectations, it is essential for the Government of India to invest in infrastructure such as transport and accommodations. According to global hotel and hospitality consulting firm, HVS International, the strong performance in tourist arrivals in 2005 can be attributed to a strong sense of business and investment confidence in India inspired by:

- India's strong GDP performance
- Strengthening of ties with the developed world, and
- Opening of sectors of the economy to private sector/ foreign investment.

The efforts made by the Ministry of Tourism & Culture in the last few years have had a salutary effect on India's tourism industry.

- Foreign tourist arrivals witnessed a growth of 78 per cent in 2006 over 2001.
- Growth in foreign exchange earnings was of the order of 122 per cent during this period.
- As per estimates on an average, about 3.1 million additional jobs per year have been created directly and indirectly in the tourism sector in the last four years.

India is fast emerging as one of the most enticing destinations for the global leisure traveller. The Readers Travel Awards 2006, conducted by Condé Nast Traveller has recently placed India at number four among the world's must-see countries, up from number nine in 2003. The Incredible India campaign has also been a huge success. As an engine for economic growth, the tourism and hospitality sector cuts across the rural-urban divide, and bridges economic boundaries. The sector grew at a rate of 8.4 per cent in 2006 and is expected to grow by 8 per cent per annum, in real terms, between 2007 and 2016.

1.2. The Hotel Industry

The Hotel Industry comprises a major part of the Tourism industry. Historically viewed as an industry providing a luxury service valuable to the economy only as a foreign exchange earner, the industry today contributes directly to employment and indirectly facilitates tourism and commerce. Prior to the 1980s, the Indian hotel industry was a slow-growing industry, consisting primarily of relatively static, single-hotel companies. However, the Asiad, held in New Delhi in 1982, and the subsequent partial liberalisation of the Indian economy generated tourism interest in India, with significant benefits accruing to the hotel and tourism sector, in terms of improved demand patterns.

The euphoria of the early 1990s prompted major chains, new entrants and international chains to chalk out ambitious capacity additions, especially in the metropolitan cities. However, most of these efforts were directed towards the business travellers and foreign clientele. In recent years, the hotels sector has grown at a faster rate than GDP. As a result, the share of hotels & restaurants in GDP at current prices has increased from 2.1 per cent in FY2000 to 1.5 per cent in FY2005. In constant prices, the GDP from hotels and restaurants has increased from Rs. 222.65 billion in FY2000 to Rs. 335.49 billion in FY2005. As a result, the share of hotels and restaurants in total GDP at constant prices has increased from 1.24 per cent in FY2000 to 1.40 per cent in FY2005.

1.2.1. Structure

Hotels in India are broadly classified into 7 categories (five star deluxe, five-star, four star, three star, two star, one-star and heritage hotels) by the Ministry of Tourism, Government of India, based on the general features and facilities offered. The ratings are reviewed every five years. As of December 2005there are following number and category of hotels.

Table 1. number and category of hotels in India

Star Category	*No. of Hotels*	*No. of Rooms*
5-Star Deluxe	82	18764
5-Star	92	11332
4-Star	132	9401
3-Star	704	31039
2-Star	587	19031
1-Star	212	695
Heritage	83	2216
To be classified	50	5127
Total	1934	103973

1.2.1.1. Premium and luxury segement

This segment comprises the high-end 5-star deluxe and 5-star hotels, which mainly cater to the business and upmarket foreign leisure travellers and offer a high quality and range of services. The segment accounted for 29 per cent of the total hotel rooms in the country in December 2005.

1.2.1.2. Mid-market segment

This segment comprises 3 and 4 star hotels, which cater to the average foreign and domestic leisure traveller. This segment also caters to the middle level business travellers since it offers most of the essential services of luxury hotels without the high costs since the tax component of this segment is lower compared with the premium segment.

1.2.1.3. Budget segment

These comprise 1 and 2 star hotels referred to as 'Budget Hotels'. These categories do not offer as many facilities as the other segments but provide inexpensive accommodation to the highly price-conscious segment of the domestic and foreign leisure travellers.

1.2.1.4. Heritage hotels

In the past four decades, certain architecturally distinctive properties such as palaces and forts, built prior to 1950, have been converted into hotels. The Ministry of Tourism has classified these hotels as heritage hotels.

1.2.1.5. Others

At any point in time, applications for classification are usually pending with the Ministry of Tourism because of which such properties remain unclassified. The number of hotel rooms pending classification has declined from historical 15-20 per cent to 5 per cent of the total rooms available in the recent past.

1.2.2. Key Consumer Segments

The market for the hotel industry can be divided into the following key consumer segments based on purpose of visit:

1.2.2.1. The business traveller

The Business Traveller is a businessman or a corporate executive travelling for business purposes. This segment includes corporates, both domestic and foreign, who open offices in the hotel premises during start-ups, corporate executives who make extended stay either for long duration projects or while waiting for permanent accommodation and convention arrivals. While the senior executives usually stay in 5 star hotels, the middle level executives, who are much larger in number, stay in the budget hotels. This segment offers better realisations, as they demand relatively smaller discounts on room rents use more of facilities such as PCs, fax multi-media, conference halls. Also, the Food & Beverage revenues are better as they usually eat in the hotel itself due to their busy schedules.

1.2.2.2. The leisure traveller

The Leisure Traveller could either be a foreigner or a domestic traveller whose primary purpose of visit is holiday and site seeing. Among non-business foreign tourists the primary motivation for visiting India is largely cultural attraction followed by conferences and conventions, tourist attractions like beaches, wild life, hill resorts etc. The margins offered by leisure travellers tend to be lower because of two reasons. Firstly, they seek higher discounts and also provide less F&B revenues as they usually eat out. The business offered by this segment is highly seasonal and tends to peak in the September to March period.

1.2.2.3. Airline cabin crew

Airline Cabin Crew forms another important segment because of the repetitive and guaranteed nature of the business that they provide. Usually, these are a part of an annual contract whereby, in return for a fixed rate, a certain number of rooms are provided on demand for cabin crews. With discount rates in the range of 40 per cent and 50 per cent, this represents a low-yield segment for hotels in general.

1.3. Demand and Supply Scenario

1.3.1. International Tourist Traffic

The foreign tourist arrivals in India increased at CAGR of 5.5 per cent from 2.29 million in 1996 to 3.92 million in 2005. Significantly, the bulk of international arrivals into India, both in 2004 and 2005, have been business travellers. Main reason for this increase has been following fundamental factors:

— India's strong GDP growth.

— Opening of sectors of the economy to private sector/ foreign investment.

— Strengthening of ties with the developed world.

— Reforms in aviation sector which led to better connectivity with many countries and created additional capacity on existing routes. Also, introduction of low cost airlines also contributed to the demand.

— Development of infrastructure by the Government

— India's emergence as an outsourcing hub.

— Success of "Incredible India" campaign and other tourism promotion measures.

— India's growing recognition as an exciting place to visit has helped boost its image as a leisure destination.

Table 2. Foreign tourist arrivals in India during 2007

	Foreign Tourist Arrival (Nos.)			Percentage Change	
Months	*2005*	*2006*	*2007*	*2006/05*	*2007/06*
January	385977	444260	514453	15.1	15.8
February	369844	407198	462578	10.1	13.6
March	352094	390824	443976	11.0	13.6
April	248416	309775	334558	24.7	8.0
May	225394	258527	271454	14.7	5.0
Total	1581725	1810584	2027019	14.5	12.0

1.3.2. Supply Scenario

According to estimates by HVS International, around 10,856 hotel rooms in Delhi, 9,318 rooms in Mumbai, 7,794 rooms in Bangalore and 7,408 rooms in Hyderabad are expected to be added by 2011.

1.3.3. Major Players

The Hotel Industry mainly has following major players:

1.3.3.1. Hotel chains

They comprise major players including Indian Hotels Company Limited and associate companies, EIH Limited ITC Hotels Limited Indian Tourism Development Corporation and Hotel Corporation of India. Most of these chains had an established presence in one or more metro cities prior to the tourism boom of the 1980s. Subsequent to the tourism boom, these chains aggressively expanded their presence in other locations.

1.3.3.2. Small chains

They are companies that have come up after the tourism boom of the 1980s and 1990s. Due to lack of prior experience in the hotel industry, these players have preferred to opt for operating/management arrangements with international players of repute. Some of the companies in this category are Hotel Leela Venture. Asian Hotels Bharat Hotels. As late entrants, most of these hotel companies have fewer properties, compared with the big chains. However most of these players have initiated expansion plans during the late 1990s.

1.3.3.3. Public sector chains

ITDC and HCI, boast of some of the best locations in major cities but are relative underperformers, as compared with their private sector counterparts.

1.3.3.4. International hotel chains

They are also looking at India as a major growth destination. These chains are establishing themselves in the Indian market by entering into joint ventures with Indian partners or by entering into management contracts or franchisee arrangements. Some of the players who have already entered or plan to enter the Indian market include Marriott, Starwood, Berggruen Hotels, Emaar MGF. Most of these chains have ambitious expansion plans especially with a strong focus on the budget segment and tier II cities.

1.3.3.5. Localised hotel companies

They are mainly comprise early entrants who have an established localised presence and who preferred not to expand during the tourism boom but focus on building and catering to a loyal customer base.

1.3.3.6. The Indian Hotels company

The Indian Hotels Company and its subsidiaries are collectively known as Taj Hotels Resorts and Palaces, recognised as one of Asia's largest and finest hotel company. Incorporated by the founder of the Tata Group, Jamsetji N Tata, the company opened its first property,

The Taj Mahal Palace Hotel, Bombay, in 1903. The Taj, a symbol of Indian hospitality, completed its centenary year in 2003.

The company has had a long-standing commitment to the continued development of the Indian tourism and hospitality industry. From the 1970s through the 1990s, the Taj played an important role in launching several of India's key tourist destinations. Working in tandem with the Indian government, the Taj developed resorts and retreats while the government developed roads and railways to India's hidden treasures.

1.3.3.7. ITC/ Sheraton corporation

ITC's Hotel division was launched on October 18, 1975, with the opening of its first hotel - Chola Sheraton in Chennai. ITC - Welcomgroup Hotels, Palaces and Resorts, is today one of India's finest hotel chains, with its distinctive logo of hands folded in the traditional Namaste is widely recognised as the ultimate in Indian hospitality. The design concept and themes of these dynasties play an important part in their respective style and decor.

With more and more hotels being added at strategic destinations, the group has joined hands with the Sheraton Corporation to strengthen its international marketing base. A successful marketing franchise for almost 25 years now, there are currently 10 ITC - Welcomgroup Sheraton hotels, and more in the pipeline.

1.3.3.8. The Leela Group

Founded in 1957 by Capt. C.P. Krishnan Nair, the Rs.4.5 billion Leela Group is engaged in the business of ready-made garments and luxury hotels and resorts. The Leela Kempinski, Mumbai and The Leela, Goa are two of the best hotels in India, and have also won considerable international acclaim.

Recently in 2001 Capt. Nair fulfilled his longstanding dream of constructing a palace hotel in the garden city of Bangalore. The Leela Palace Kempinski, Bangalore is built in art deco style recreating the grandeur of The Mysore Maharajas Palace. It is set amidst 8 acres of landscaped garden and waterfalls. Its 254 rooms are opulently furnished and are befitting royalty. The newest addition The Leela Kovalam is Kerala's largest resort, built on a rock face cradled between two wide sweeping beaches with a stunning view of the famous Kovalam coastline.

1.3.3.9. The Bharat Hotels Group

The Bharat Hotels group is a major player in India's tourism and hotel sector. It operates its hotels under 'THE GRAND' banner and its present portfolio of hotels incorporates FOURTEEN luxury hotels in the five-star deluxe segment. These include InterContinental 'The Grand' hotels in New Delhi, Mumbai, Goa & Srinagar and The Grand Ashok Bangalore, The Grand Laxmi Vilas Palace Udaipur and The Grand Temple View Khajuraho.

1.3.3.10. The EIH Ltd (The Oberoi Group)

Asian elegance is the key to running hotels, if you ask EIH. The company owns and operates about 20 luxury hotels, about 10 mid-range hotels, and two inland cruises; The Oberoi Group operates primarily in India, but also in Australia, Egypt, Indonesia, Mauritius, and Saudi Arabia. Most of the company's luxury properties bear the Oberoi banner. The company in 2004 joined forces with Hilton International to rebrand most of its mid-range hotels as Trident Hiltons. The Oberoi Group also operates luxury cruises of the Nile River and India's Kerala region.

1.3.3.11. India Tourism Development Corporation (ITDC) / The Ashok Group

India Tourism Development Corporation (ITDC) was established in 1966 as an autonomous public sector corporation, entrusted with the task of helping develop tourism infrastructure and promoting India as a tourist destination.

The ITDC Ashok Group of hotel chains manages some of the best five star and luxury tour hotels in the Indian hospitality industry. The hotels run by the ITDC Ashok Group of hotel chains may be divided into different categories, these are elite hotels, comfort hotels and classic hotels. The ITDC Ashok Group of hotel chains manages 33 hotels in 26 different tourist destinations all over India.

The Ashok Group of hotel chains boasts of running some of the best hotels in the Indian hotel industry. The hotels that are a part of the elite and classic category of the ITDC Ashok Group are the Ashok Hotel in New Delhi, the Kovalam Ashok Beach Resort in Kovalam, Kerala, the Agra Ashok in Agra, Hotel Jaipur Ashok in New Delhi and the Qutab Hotel in New Delhi. Most of the hotels managed by the ITDC Ashok Group have had the privilege of playing host to several international and national dignitaries.

1.3.3.12. The Hotel Corporation of India (HCI)

The Hotel Corporation of India Limited (HCI) is a public limited company wholly owned by Air India Limited and was incorporated on July 8, 1971 under the Companies Act, 1956 when Air India decided to enter the Hotel Industry in keeping with the then prevalent trend among world airlines. The objective was to offer to the passengers a better product, both at the International Airports and at other places of tourist interest, thereby also increasing tourism of India.

1.3.3.13. Jaypee Hotels Ltd.

Jaypee Hotels Limited primarily engages in the ownership and operation of hotels in India. The company owns three Five Star Deluxe Hotels, namely Jaypee Palace Hotel at Agra, and Jaypee Vasant Continental and Jaypee Siddharth Hotel at New Delhi. It also manages the operation of the hotels Jaypee Residency Manor at Mussoorie and Jaypee Green Resorts. The company is headquartered in New Delhi, India. Jaypee Hotels Limited is a subsidiary of Jaiprakash Associates Limited.

1.4. Policies and Initiatives

Tourism being a concurrent subject under the Indian constitution, both the central and state governments regulates the hotel industry. The regulations include statutory and regulatory sanctions from the Central and State departments or agencies. This includes license to operate a restaurant, a hotel license license from police and a bar license.

1.4.1. Tourism Policy

In order to develop tourism in India in a systematic manner, position it as a major engine of economic growth and to harness its direct and multiplier effects for employment and poverty eradication in an environmentally sustainable manner, the National Tourism Policy was formulated in the year 2002. Broadly, the "Policy" attempts to:

— Position tourism as a major engine of economic growth
— Harness the direct and multiplier effects of tourism for employment generation, economic development and providing impetus to rural tourism
— Focus on domestic tourism as a major driver of tourism growth
— Position India as a global brand to take advantage of the burgeoning global travel trade and the vast untapped potential of India as a destination
— Acknowledges the critical role of private sector with government working as a pro-active facilitator and catalyst
— Create and develop integrated tourism circuits based on India's unique civilisation, heritage, and culture in partnership with States, private sector and other agencies
— Ensure that the tourist to India gets physically invigorated, mentally rejuvenated, culturally enriched, spiritually elevated and "feel India from within".

The Government's major policy initiatives include:

— Liberalisation in aviation sector
— Pricing policy for aviation turbine fuel which influences internal air fares
— Rationalisation in tax rates in the hospitality sector
— Tourist friendly visa regime
— Immigration services
— Procedural changes in making available land for construction of hotels
— Allowing setting up of Guest Houses

The Indian Ministry of Tourism has identified 31 villages across the country to be developed as tourism hubs. The states in which these villages have been identified include Himachal Pradesh, Gujarat, Maharashtra, Bihar, Karnataka, Madhya Pradesh, Andhra Pradesh, Kerala, Tamil Nadu, Orissa, Assam, Sikkim, Rajasthan and West Bengal.

1.4.2. Government's Open Skies Policy

The Government's Open Skies policy, permission for domestic airlines to commence international flights, start-up of various low-cost carriers, and fleet expansion by domestic players has created a huge incentive for domestic travellers to explore far-off destinations within and outside India. The numbers, according to the Ministry of Tourism, speak for themselves:

— The number of domestic and international passengers has increased fifteen-fold to 73.34 million in 2005/06 since 1970.

— Domestic air passenger traffic grew by 16.8 per cent in 2005/06 compared to 2004/05.'

— International passenger traffic observed a growth of 16.9 per cent in the same period.

— Private airlines accounted for 77.0 per cent of the total domestic traffic.

1.4.3. Foreign Trade Policy

The Foreign Trade Policy announced in April, 2006, offered following incentives to the hospitality industry:

Hotels and Restaurants are allowed to import duty free equipment and other items including liquor, against their foreign exchange earnings under the Served from India Scheme. As in previous years, this entitlement is 5 per cent of previous year's foreign exchange earnings for hotels of one-star and above approved by the Department of Tourism and other service providers in the tourism sector registered with it. The stand-alone restaurants will be entitled to duty credit equivalent to 10 per cent of the foreign exchange earned by them in the preceding financial year.

Service exports in Indian Rupees, which are otherwise considered as having been paid for in free foreign exchange by RBI, will now qualify for benefits under the Served from India Scheme. Also, foreign exchange earned through International Credit Cards and other instruments as permitted by RBI for rendering of service by the service providers shall be considered for the purposes of computation of entitlement under the Scheme. The measure aims at supporting the

Group service companies not earning foreign exchange in getting access to the international quality products at competitive price and providing services of international standards. This new initiative allows transfer of both the script and the imported input to the Group Service Company. The earlier provision allowed transfer of imported material only.

1.4.4. FDI in Hotel and Tourism Sector

100 per cent FDI is permissible in the sector on the automatic route. The term hotels include restaurants, beach resorts, and other tourist complexes providing accommodation and/or catering and food facilities to tourists. Tourism related industry include travel agencies, tour operating agencies and tourist transport operating agencies, units providing facilities for cultural, adventure and wild life experience to tourists, surface, air and water transport facilities to tourists, leisure, entertainment, amusement, sports, and health units for tourists and Convention/Seminar units and organisations.

For foreign technology agreements, automatic approval is granted if:

— up to 3 per cent of the capital cost of the project is proposed to be paid for technical and consultancy services including fees for architects, design, supervision, etc.

— up to 3 per cent of net turnover is payable for franchising and marketing/publicity support fee, and up to 10 per cent of gross operating profit is payable for management fee, including incentive fee.

1.4.5. Other Government Initiatives

Government has undertaken following initiatives to attract both inbound and outbound tourists:

— *Incredible India* - Under this program the Government promotes India through various integrated marketing programs.

— *Atethie devo bhava* - Under this program the Government create awareness among Indian people who come in contact with the tourist.

— Various Infrastructure building initiatives

— Encourage religious tourism for instance promote various places in India as Buddhist abodes.

— Other projects are the Rs. 5,400 million National Highways Development Project, the 5,846 km Golden Quadrilateral and the 7,300 km north-south and east-west corridors.

1.5. Opportunities and Challenges

1.5.1. Opportunities

Considering India's size and unparalleled diversity - natural, geographic, cultural and artistic, there is vast room for growth in tourism industry. As travellers surge into India, the demand for rooms, across segments, has skyrocketed. Anticipating this demand, around 10,856 hotel rooms in Delhi, 9,318 rooms in Mumbai, 7,794 rooms in Bangalore and 7,408 rooms in Hyderabad are expected to be added by 2011, according to estimates by HVS International.

The expected growth of the industry in future has provided its players with an opportunity to invest in new technologies such as CRM tools and latest security systems, and to venture into niche tourism segments like Medical, Religious, Cruise, Casinos, MICE etc. India can also develop infrastructure to host international conferences and trade shows, thus increasing its share of tourist traffic from such activities

1.5.1.1. Health Tourism

India is gradually gathering popularity as a health tourist destination. At its current pace of growth, healthcare tourism alone can rake over USD 1.7 billion additional revenues by 2012. Medical tourism is now a USD 299 million industry, as about 100,000 patients come each year. The country needs to exploit the cost advantage it can offer to a health tourist, the study said. The biggest driver for healthcare tourism is the disparity in costs.

— A heart surgery in the US costs USD 30,000 as compared to USD 6,000 in India.

— A bone marrow transplant in the US costs USD 250,000 and USD 26,000 in India.

With yoga, meditation, ayurveda, allopathy, and other systems of medicine, India offers a unique basket of services to an individual that is difficult to match by other countries.

1.5.1.2. Critical success factors

The key success factors for the Hotel Industry are mentioned as follows:

1.5.1.2.1. Site and location

This can be considered the most critical factor in determining the success of a hotel property. In addition to identifying a city, the site location within the city also assumes significance and issues like distance from the Central Business District and connectivity assume importance.

1.5.1.2.2. Positioning

Equally important is the positioning of the hotel according to the target guest segment.

1.5.1.2.3. Financial Flexibility

Development of hotels is a highly capital intensive activity and new hotel properties, typically, have a high break-even point. Therefore, financial flexibility is essential, especially during early years of operations.

1.5.1.2.4. Brand equity

Branded hotels can be further classified into chain hotels and independent hotels. Chain hotels would typically be affiliated to one of the large national or international hotel chains. Association with a hotel chains allows the property to be branded with one of the chain brands. This way the property is able to attract tourists from areas where a independent hotels may not be able to reach effectively.

1.5.2. Challenges

India's poor domestic tourism infrastructure is leading to a threat of loosing foreign tourists to other competing countries. India is highly prone to prevailing socio-economic and political conditions. Like terrorist strikes, riots, epidemics, political uncertainty, slowdown in reforms etc. The growth in the Indian tourism sector is accompanied by the imminent destruction of local ecology and an increase in pollution, which, in the long run, is going to negatively impact the tourism industry of India.

The biggest challenge in the Indian tourism sector is that of entry of new players, the country's growing economy has attracted a host of new players, the number of which is expected to increase further. Aman Resorts, Shangri-la Hotels, Four Seasons Hotels and The Hilton group are some of the international players that are at various stages of establishing presence in India. Remarkably, unlike earlier, many new entrants are reportedly considering entry into the mid-market segment, which is currently dominated by non-chain properties.

1.6. Future of Indian Tourism Industry

The Indian Hospitality sector is expected to show a healthy growth in the medium term. Strong economic growth, increased FDI, greater emphasis on tourism development, favourable Government policies, impending 2010 Commonwealth games, 2011 Cricket World Cup and other international events, will be the major drivers for the growth. There exists a lot of scope for growth in tourism sector.

By 2020, the Government of India expects travel and tourism to contribute Rs 8,500 billion to GDP, almost four times the value in 2005. With successive Governments committed to reform, a strong manufacturing sector and a private sector that already has a critical mass that is needed to drive growth, it is unlikely that the strong growth in GDP is likely to be reversed. The rising middle class is also becoming increasingly affluent, mobile, Internet savvy and more sophisticated in terms of what is demanded in terms of tourism products and services, and more importantly the price they are willing to pay for it. But ICRA expects the shortage in rooms to remain for next five years leading to higher occupancy levels and increase in Average

Room Rates (ARR). Currently, according to industry estimates, there are only 1,05,000 hotel rooms in India while in China the figure is much higher at 7,65,000 rooms.

The annual growth rate of hotel rooms in India is only 6 per cent, compared to 22 per cent in China, 18 per cent in Thailand and 15 per cent in Malaysia. Economic growth in tier II and tier III cities have put these on the hospitality industry map. ARR are likely to harden in these cities in next 2-3 years due to shortage of room. Niche areas like health tourism and spiritual tourism are emerging as lucrative business opportunity for the industry. The growth for hotels is also likely to come from proliferation of Special Economic Zones.

Major impediments to the growth are sensitivity to business cycles and adverse political and social events high rate of tax, high land price, bureaucracy, and poor infrastructure. For instance, the effective rate of taxation on tourism in India is 21 per cent as compared to 7 per cent in Thailand, 4 per cent in Malaysia and 1 per cent in Hong Kong. Furthermore, owing to high land prices, there are more five star hotels than budget hotels, making India a high cost deluxe destination. The existing visa process is cumbersome and comparatively more expensive than other destinations. Yields are expected to be low in coming years on account of continuing price-cutting and discounts.

The Government is planning to grant infrastructure status to all budget hotels and convention centres set up in Delhi and National Capital Region till 2010 Commonwealth Games. This will enable them to enjoy a 10 year tax holiday as in case of other infrastructure projects such as roads, ports and power.

REFERENCES

Costa, Frank J. and Allen G. Noble. 1999. "Sustainable Tourism: An Overview," in Allen G. Noble and Frank J. Costa, editors, *Preserving the Legacy: Concepts in Support of Sustainability*. Boulder, CO: Lexington Books.

Gardiner, Rosalie. 1998. *A Review of Codes of Practice for Sustainable Tourism.* London: UNED-UK.

Honey, Martha. 1999. *Ecotourism and Sustainable Development: Who Owns Paradise?* Covelo, CA: Island Press.

Sitarz, Daniel, ed. 1993. *Agenda 21: The Earth Summit Strategy to Save Our Planet*. Boulder, CO.

2

Travel and Tourism Infrastructure

As part of the growing impact of globalisation in Asia and the Pacific, international tourism is dependent on efficient, reliable and cost-effective transport infrastructure and services to support continued growth and development. At the same time, transport policies and infrastructure development influence the quality, capacity, extensiveness and efficiency of transport, which contributes to the competitiveness of national tourism industries.

Transport infrastructure provides the backbone of transport systems, both within and between countries through networks of airports, highways, railways and ports. Tourism will benefit from the work being done by countries and areas of the region at the national and regional level to provide a framework for internationally agreed routes and infrastructure standards. In countries where the infrastructure policy environment is forward-looking in support of growth and safety, social and economic needs can be met along with the demands of the tourism industry.

2.1 Infrastructure Policy Environment

An infrastructure policy environment that includes consideration of tourism development would have to address:

(1) constraints to sector development;

(2) which infrastructure sectors to prioritise;

(3) how to strengthen international and/or cross border linkages; and

(4) the complexity of relations between tourism development,

environmental sustainability, geographic location of expanded infrastructure and related socio-economic changes.

According to data gathered by the World Bank for 118 airport projects with private sector participation worldwide between 1991 and 2006, a total of 25 airport infrastructure projects were carried out in low and middle income countries of East Asia and the Pacific and 8 projects in South Asia. The total value of private investment was US$ 4,281 million in East Asia and the Pacific, of which US$ 3,130 was for projects involving runway and terminal construction, US$ 881 million for terminal construction only and US$ 270 million for runway construction only.

The total value for 33 projects that meet private sector participation criteria in both Asian subregions (US$ 7,707 million) accounted for 30 per cent of total investment of US$ 25,552 million in low and middle income countries worldwide. For about the past four years, the travel industry in Asia and the Pacific has been undergoing a dynamic change, and the growth of low cost carriers has been cited as the single most important factor currently shaping the region's airline industry.

According to the Official Airline Guide (OAG), more than half of the world's new low-cost flights were in Asia and the Pacific. There were more than 22,000 additional low-fare services within the region during January 2007, representing a 67 per cent increase year on year. At the same time, the aviation industry has had to adjust its strategic marketing and understanding of consumer behaviour in the region.

In Malaysia, 40 per cent of the flights and 59 per cent of the seats were on low cost carriers. In a recent study of the tourism industry worldwide, the World Economic Forum (WEF) developed the travel and tourism competitiveness index (TTCI) to provide a fairly comprehensive tool for measuring the factors and policies that help in assessing the comparative strengths and weaknesses of 124 countries and areas, including 26 in Asia and the Pacific, in their ability to develop travel and tourism.

According to WEF, its assessments of the travel and tourism environments can be used by all stakeholders to work together to improve the industry's competitiveness in their national economies, thereby contributing to national growth and prosperity. The term national competitiveness must be used carefully, however, The notion of national competitiveness is controversial, although it is one way to start asking about the appropriate role and extent of government policy. Given that it is firms that compete, according to the Asian Development Bank (ADB), from the national point of view the real question would be about how government policies might ensure that firms are competitive. Despite arguments about whether or not nations compete, governments play a critical role in shaping the competitive environment and behaviour of firms through a variety of policies and activities. The overall rank is composed of three dimensions of travel and tourism:

(1) regulatory framework,

(2) business environment and infrastructure and

(3) human, cultural and natural resources.

Within each dimension there are several factors that are measured by a number of variables.

The business environment and infrastructure dimension showed one of the highest positive correlations with the overall index by 96 per cent, according to further analysis done for WEF. This tends to confirm the argument that a country seeking success with its tourism industry must give direct attention to the impact of transport infrastructure policies and plans.

The rank of Azerbaijan on overall competitiveness is generally parallel to its rank on the dimension of business environment and infrastructure. However, when comparing the two component factors of air transport and ground transport infrastructure, Azerbaijan's rank of 77 out of 124 countries on air transport infrastructure is about the same as the two rankings already discussed. The relatively higher ranking of 49 on ground transport infrastructure suggests the importance of this factor for tourism accessibility. In the case of China, much higher rankings for air transport and ground transport infrastructure when compared to the overall competitiveness ranking suggests that these two transport factors generally contribute to the strength of the national tourism industry. India achieved higher rankings for both air and ground transport infrastructure factors relative to its rank for overall competitiveness.

Malaysia's high score on overall competitiveness and on the business environment and infrastructure dimension outranked some high income countries with major tourism industries.The rankings for Pakistan varied widely and showed a low rank of 103 out of 124 countries for overall travel and tourism competitiveness. However, on the dimension of business environment and infrastructure its ranking moved to 75th. Within this dimension, Pakistan's ranking on the ground transport infrastructure factor moved up to 52.

For a country with a large geographic area such as the Russian Federation, a high ranking on air transport infrastructure contrasts with lower rankings for ground transport infrastructure and overall travel and tourism competitiveness. This underscores the dominance of air transport in quantitative terms for the Russian Federation. However, these rankings contrast with one of the lowest rankings for the government of the Russian Federation giving priority to the travel and tourism industry.

Thailand had a rank of 43 on overall competitiveness, but moved up strongly to 25th for the air transport infrastructure factor and 28th for the ground transport infrastructure factor. This was the best result among the seven Asian and Pacific countries classified in the lower middle income group. Among the selected Asian and Pacific countries and areas, Hong Kong, China was assessed as having the strongest travel and tourism competitiveness overall, followed closely by Singapore.

When the Asian and Pacific countries and areas are assessed within groups defined by the World Bank income categories, nine were found to have ranked in the top 10 of their respective groups. That is, Malaysia ranked third among the uppermiddle income group. Thailand ranked second and Indonesia ranked tenth within the lower-middle income group. India ranked first, China second, Viet Nam fourth, Mongolia fifth and Cambodia ninth within the low income group.

• 2.2. Transport Network

According to WEF, domestic transport network refers to the national transport network consisting of domestic flights, buses, trains, taxis and so forth. Data about the selected Asian and Pacific countries as a group showed that their average score on the quality of road infrastructure was 3. 60 which was below the average score of 3. 70 for all countries surveyed worldwide.

However, the averages of the Asian and Pacific group for railroad infrastructure and domestic transport network were considerably higher than the respective world averages.Results for the quality of road infrastructure highlight the fact that 10 of the 26 selected countries had scores higher than the world average. Six of these countries were from the high income group; Malaysia and Turkey were from the upper middle income group; and China and Thailand were from the lower middle income group.

Results for the quality of railroad infrastructure show that 15 of the 26 countries in Asia and the Pacific had scores above the world average of 2. 90, including all six high income countries, two upper middle income countries five lower middle income countries and two low income countries. Such scores must be viewed in the context of how much railroad infrastructure exists in the country and whether constraints of size, geography and history, among others, influence the role of such infrastructure, especially for the tourism industry.

Results for the quality of the domestic transport network show that 12 countries had scores above the world average of 4. 60. This included all six of the high income countries and three upper middle income countries two lower middle income countries and one low income country. For seven of the 12 countries, such high scores may be connected to their above-average scores on the extent to which the government prioritises the travel and tourism industry.

However, five of the 12 countries had below average scores on the government priority given to tourism. At the same time, eight countries with high scores for giving due consideration and priority to the tourism industry had below average scores on the quality of their domestic tourism network. Such results suggest that there may be a more complex linkage and related conditions involving an efficient and accessible domestic transport network and giving priority to tourism development.

Table 1. Comparing country scores on government priority given to travel and tourism with selected infrastructure variables

	Government prioritisation of travel and tourism	*Quality of air transport infrastructure*	*Quality of railroad infrastructure*	*Quality of road infrastructure*	*Quality of domestic transport network*
Australia	5.30	6.00	4.60	5.20	5.80
Azerbaijan	3.90	5.10	3.80	3.30	4.80
Bangladesh	3.20	2.50	2.30	3.10	3.50
Cambodia	5.90	3.90	1.50	2.90	4.00
China	4.80	3.70	3.80	4.00	4.50
Georgia	4.80	3.40	3.00	2.89	3.20
Hong Kong, China	6.00	6.70	6.30	6.30	6.70
India	4.70	5.10	4.70	3.20	5.30
Indonesia	5.10	4.10	2.40	2.10	4.20
Japan	3.60	6.40	6.60	6.10	6.60
Kazakhstan	3.90	4.10	3.30	2.30	4.50
Kyrgyzstan	4.60	3.10	2.00	1.90	4.30
Malaysia	5.90	6.00	5.00	5.70	5.80
Mongolia	4.50	2.80	2.50	1.80	3.50
Nepal	4.80	3.30	1.20	2.20	3.70
New Zealand	5.80	5.70	3.70	4.40	5.70
Pakistan	3.50	4.60	3.60	3.50	4.40
Philippines	4.50	4.00	1.70	2.60	3.80
Republic of Korea	3.90	5.50	5.20	5.20	5.60
Russian Federation		4.30	3.90	2.20	4.60
Singapore	6.00	6.90	5.70	6.70	6.60
Sri Lanka	5.30	4.10	2.50	2.70	3.50
Tajikistan	4.50	2.90	2.80	2.10	3.80
Thailand	5.60	5.50	3.60	5.00	5.40
Turkey	4.40	4.70	2.30	3.70	5.50
Viet Nam	4.70	3.80	2.20	2.50	4.20
Average for selected countries of Asia &Pacific	5.08	4.55	3.47	3.60	4.75
Average for 124 countries	4.50	4.50	2.90	3.70	4.60

Developing routes by land and air in order to link existing tourism centres or open new areas in less developed regions are important mechanisms for spreading benefits to areas that might have not directly benefited from tourism development. Route development clearly requires planning and cooperation among a number of partners to create a network of tourist activities, attractions and support services that are structured to provide the maximum socio-economic benefits. Such cooperation also requires coordination in order to understand the tourism product in a systematic way and seek appropriate marketing channels.

A number of ESCAP-member countries have supported the opportunities for shared benefits to the tourism industry at the regional and subregional level from transport infrastructure development. For example, the Asian Highway project is a cooperative undertaking among member countries aimed at improving highway systems throughout Asia. The system is expected to facilitate access to tourism destinations. It is one pillar of the Asian Land Transport Infrastructure Development (ALTID) project with the aim of expanding and standardising roadways in the region. The Intergovernmental Agreement on the Asian Highway Network was adopted in November 2003 and entered into force on 4 July 2005.

There are 55 Asian Highway routes, which have been identified among 32 countries covering a total of about 141,000 km. According to a recent ESCAP publication, member countries, multilateral and bilateral donors have committed to investing about US$ 26 billion in the construction, rehabilitation and upgrading of some 37, 000 km of the Asian Highway network. Almost US$ 18 billion in investment was still required as of 2005 to implement 121 priority road projects for upgrading some 26,000 km of the Asian Highway in 25 member countries. Central and South-West Asia required about US$ 7. 3 billion followed by South-East Asia at US$ 4. 6 billion. At the same time, ESCAP has identified tourism attractions and suggested various activities at the national and regional levels to promote tourism, especially through cooperative efforts.

The Trans-Asian Railway is a second pillar of ALTID that represents the potential for sharing benefits from tourism. The Intergovernmental Agreement on the Trans-Asian Railway Network was signed at Busan in November 2006. Along with the Almaty

Programme of Action of August 2003, which was designed to address the special needs of landlocked developing countries within a new global framework for transit transport cooperation, it is recognised as an example of successful regional cooperation. The Busan Declaration adopted by the Ministerial Conference on Transport in November 2006 resolved that government authorities would develop and implement transport policies at the national, subregional and regional levels that would meet the challenges of globalisation.

In 2001, ESCAP organised the Seminar on the Promotion of Buddhist Tourism Circuits. This resulted in a publication covering Buddhism as part of cultural and heritage tourism in nine countries in South and South-East Asia. Several countries identified the importance of providing connections via air, rail and road infrastructure for the tourist destinations along the Buddhism circuit. Reports indicate that the cruise industry has emerged as one of the fastest growing and popular segments of the worldwide travel and leisure industry. Between 1999 and 2005, passenger levels for conventional cruises have expanded from about 8. 5 million to 13. 9 million.

During the same period, the Asian and Pacific region accounted for from 5 per cent to 8. 6 per cent of the worldwide cruise market. Singapore; Hong Kong, China; and Australia are well-established destinations, as well as home bases, for cruise ships due to the capacity of their port infrastructure. Within the cruise industry, Asia and the Pacific is seen as a region with great potential given the opening of new routes and the diverse cultural attractions. Destinations that aim to attract the cruise industry must focus on port facilities, and ancillary services, according to cruise industry officials. One cruise line has already added Cambodia as a destination that involves travelling from Thailand to Hong Kong, China with destinations in at least four ports in Viet Nam. Another cruise line starts in Bangkok, Thailand and ends in Mumbai, India with stops in Cambodia, Viet Nam, Singapore, Malaysia and Sri Lanka. A new cruise ship terminal developed in Shanghai was expected to open in 2007 and cover 160,000m² with a length of 850m, which would accommodate three large cruise liners or four standard-sized passenger ships at one time.

The possibilities for developing tourism opportunities based on inland waterways transport has been recognised by ESCAP-member countries as recently as 1999, when the Commission included tourism development in Resolution 55/1 on sustainable development of inland water transport in the Asian and Pacific region adopted at the fifty-fifth session. Navigable rivers run through large areas of the country in many riparian Asian countries, including the Yangtze and Pearl Rivers in China, the Greater Mekong River in six countries, the Buriganga River in Bangladesh, the Ganges River in India, the Ayeyarwady River in Myanmar and the Chao Phraya River in Thailand, among others.

Subregional cooperation is an important element for tourism development along the Mekong River. In 1995, the Governments of Cambodia, the Lao People's Democratic Republic, Thailand and Viet Nam signed the Agreement on the Cooperation for the Sustainable Development of the Mekong River Basin and identified tourism as one of the areas of cooperation. The Greater Mekong Subregional Economic Cooperation Programme was established with financing from the Asian Development Bank (ADB) in 1992 among Cambodia, China Lao People's Democratic Republic, Myanmar, Thailand and Viet Nam with the aim of strengthening economic linkages, including tourism. In March 2005, it was reported that the ADB had appropriated $US28 million for infrastructure in the Mekong Tourism Development Project in the context of tourism-related infrastructure improvements. This financial support covered 11 subprojects in Cambodia, Lao People's Democratic Republic and Vietnam, which included, among others, construction of river piers and feeder roads to tourist destinations.

A tourist route in the Lancang-Mekong River border areas of China, Lao People's Democratic Republic, Myanmar and Thailand has been taking shape. A commercial navigation route from Simao in Yunnan Province to Luang Prabang, Lao People's Democratic Republic was officially opened in 2001. In 2006, the capacity along the Lancang-Mekong River was upgraded so that ships with loading capacity below 300 tonnes can cruise the river throughout the year.

One tourism organisation at the prefecture level in Yunnan Province offers trips along the river that start from Xishuangbanna and travel to Lao People's Democratic Republic, Myanmar and Thailand via Jinghong. An efficient transport infrastructure has been considered as a key component that directly influences the competitiveness of a country's travel and tourism industry. As suggested by WEF, the importance of various factors and variables that make up travel and tourism competitiveness is likely to vary depending on each country's stage of development. Determining the dynamics of building up infrastructure as well as the air and ground transport network in different development and geographical contexts could be based on systematically comparing economies in various stages of development, identifying specific key success factors and learning lessons that can be applied for particular groups of countries.

2.3. Role of Government in Tourism Business

Government intervention may be necessary to enhance the contribution of tourism to socio-economic development and poverty reduction. One of the principal roles of Governments is to set policy and legislative frameworks for tourism. Two main reasons why governments should formulate tourism development strategy are:

(1) the tourist industry has many negative externalities, in particular negative social and environmental impacts that need to be regulated and managed at national or local levels, and

(2) tourism can offer major opportunities for local economic development, which can enhance the positive effects of tourism on local socio-economic development and poverty reduction.

Real progress can be facilitated by using a wide range of instruments. A number of these have been identified by the World Tourism Organisation and the United Nations Environment Programme and are categorised into measurement instruments command and control instruments economic instruments voluntary instruments and supporting instruments. The precise mix of policies and instruments will vary depending on the situation, objectives and government structures.

As tourism moves up the national agenda, the government departments dealing with tourism may need to be upgraded and strengthened. In order to achieve sustainable management of tourism, tourism ministry staff need coordination, networking and support of colleagues in other ministries and in a range of subnational administrations. These needs emerge because the administration and governance of tourism takes places in localities where tourists and host communities interact, while regulations and incentives are applied within a framework laid down at the national level.

Tourism ministries have to be alert to the impact of institutional fragmentation on the governance of tourism. Major decisions about planning, management of cultural and natural assets, labour regulations, environmental impact assessments, financial incentives and taxation policy are often the responsibility of other ministries, where there might not be enough awareness about the impact on tourism policies and plans.

For example, air transport has changed considerably in recent years due in part to policy initiatives, such as deregulation of air services, adding a substantial number of new routes and allowing operations by low-cost carriers; all of which would aim to increase the number of tourists.

Tourism ministries can provide the government and its agencies with good quality, systematic data, particularly about the effects of different types of tourism on local socio-economic development. Provision of such data can help to substantiate the contribution of tourism and convince policy makers.

2.4. Tourism Plans

Tourism master plans are useful tools for identifying areas with tourism potential, determining tourism strategy and structuring the provision of infrastructure, investment promotion and financial and other incentives. Governments need to ensure that master plans and tourism development strategies address local economic development goals, the geographic distribution of tourism activities and poverty reduction.

Many governments have been increasing their efforts to identify and plan tourism development located in areas that can help poor communities. In addition to planning based on inventories of natural and cultural assets, information about the spatial distribution of poverty should also be used when planning tourism infrastructure and related tourism development projects. Plans based on clustering assume that tourists need a range of complementary tourism services and attractions supported by infrastructure to make the area accessible.

2.4.1. Empowerment of Poor Communities

Government agencies can promote the empowerment of communities in planning and managing tourism assets by initiating partnership approaches that include poor people. Engaging the poor is particularly important in order to identify opportunities that fit their livelihood strategies and overcome barriers to employment and enterprise. Policy makers need to consider the appropriate mix between promoting the formal and informal sector as this is a key variable for maximising local economic development and poverty reduction.

In Viet Nam, provincial and district-level governments have been given greater responsibility for tourism planning and development in line with the overall decentralisation of governance. Provincial and district governments have the statutory duty to consult and collaborate with other government agencies, as well as with other tourism stakeholders, such as businesses and local communities. Overall, this decentralised and a more integrated approach to tourism planning is a significant step towards enhancing opportunities for incorporating poverty reduction and other local development priorities into tourism development.

2.4.2. Legislation and Regulations

Several areas of legislation have an impact on the capacity of small-scale producers to develop tourism-related enterprises. These include access to credit, business licensing, employment legislation, environmental health, and health and safety regulations as well as the regulation of micro, small and medium-sized enterprises.

2.4.3. Training, Capacity-building and Certification

The needs and existing capacity of local people have to be assessed to ascertain where training interventions would be most useful. There is a need to strengthen informal learning methods and in-place on-the-job training. The certification of guides has been used in several places to control quality and supply, and to ensure minimum standards of service and knowledge. At Keoladeo National Park, in India, local rickshaw drivers are registered with the park to take tourists around the site. The government is often required to play the lead role when issues of women's participation and empowerment in the tourism industry are involved. One example is the government-run TRPAP in Nepal. TRPAP has been running different empowerment schemes for women and has emphasized their participation in various tourism activities. The programme has given training to local women on craft skills to make souvenir items. In such a case, TRPAP can help provide financing to increase capacity as well as training. National and local governments can provide incentives, pre-employment training and continuing education programmes to promote employment of local people in private tourism enterprises.

2.4.4. Taxes and Levies

Taxes on goods, services and transactions, which provide funds for government at the local or national level can be used specifically to support either poor communities or the environments that provide their livelihood.

Government policies on tourism taxation must be evaluated and designed in ways that are comprehensive and integrated in order that the necessary revenues are balanced against the affect on tourism markets and the profits of tourism businesses.

2.4.5. Microfinancing

The poor have limited access to the tourism market for several reasons, including lack of business skills, low educational levels, demanding regulations, inability to escape severe poverty, poor health and social exclusion. Governments can reduce the bureaucracy that small enterprises face, and create advisory services on business development, provide seed-funding for entrepreneurs, develop business linkages with established operators, assist micro, small and medium-sized enterprises to form production or marketing cooperatives and provide educational, technical and professional training programmes to improve quality and business standards.

2.4.6. Marketing

Destination marketing is increasingly the remit of the private sector, privatepublic sector partnerships or clusters. This means that micro, small and medium-sized enterprises and poorer producers may be excluded from the formal marketing processes and distribution channels. They can also encourage the organisation of marketing campaigns to promote responsible tourism practices and suppliers, and give preferential marketing terms to suppliers that adopt sustainable, responsible, poverty alleviation practices.

Tourism market analysts have identified a number of market trends which should inform the strategies and marketing decisions of policy-makers and investors in Asia and the Pacific. One important trend is that tourists are increasingly willing to travel long distances for longer periods and to take more frequent holidays. There is growing demand for nature, adventure, activity and health-related holidays, with more emphasis on individualism and flexibility.

The market is becoming more demanding in standards of service, product and accommodation. Tourists are making greater use of the internet for researching destinations and booking holiday travel and accommodation, often based on growing awareness of the environmental and social impacts of tourism.

While keeping up with market trends in international tourism, much can be done through careful marketing to alleviate the uneven geographic distribution of tourists and to spread the benefits of the industry. For instance, the Nepal Tourism Board has given particular promotional emphasis to areas of the country that traditionally receive fewer visitors, such as the Chitwan Hills.In other countries, unique experiences have been developed and marketed as a tourism niche market.

References

Schlentrich, U., 1992, "The world of hospitality", *Hospitality*, Dec/Jan, pp. 14-16.

Teare, R., Olsen, M.D., 1992, "*International Hospitality Management: Corporate Strategy in Practice*", Pitman and John Wiley, London.

Tsartas, P., 1996, "*Tourists, travels, landmarks: Sociological approaches in tourism*", Eksanta, Athens.

United Nations, 1994, "*Recommendations on* Tourism *Statistics*", Department for Economic and Social Information and Policy Analysis and World Tourism Organization, United Nations, New York.

3

Managing Tourism Workforce

The importance of tourism and hospitality employment in both developed and developing countries is attested to by the World Travel and Tourism Council (WTTC), who suggest that travel- and tourism-related activities account for over 230 million jobs, or 8.7 per cent of jobs worldwide.

However, whilst thc quantity of jobs is unquestionable, the *quality* of many of these jobs is of great concern to academics and policy-makers alike. Despite the rhetoric of policy-makers and business leaders that people are the industry's most important asset, many remain unconvinced that such a view is borne out by empirical evidence. For example, Douglas Coupland, the notable cultural commentator, has for many captured the *zeitgeist* when he talks pejoratively of 'McJob' which he describes as, 'Alow-pay, low-prestige, low-dignity, low-benefit, no-future job in the service sector.' Frequently considered a satisfying career choice by people who have never held one'. Such a situation leads labour analysts to ask what kinds of jobs are being produced and who is filling them. This point is also true for the tourism and hospitality industry and it is important at the outset of this book to add a caveat about the generalisability of the conditions of tourism and hospitality employment worldwide.

Organisations and managers in the tourism and hospitality industry face real challenges in recruiting, developing and maintaining a committed, competent, wellmanaged and well-motivated workforce which is focused on offering a high-quality 'product' to the increasingly demanding and discerning customer.

Many academics, industrialists and policy-makers have attempted to define the nature of the tourism industry – and the place of the hospitality sub-sector within this broader conceptualisation – yet there is still no one commonly accepted definition. Hence, there are inherent problems seeking to define what is a large and diverse sector, which means many of the activities may overlap, and could be described as encompassing tourism and hospitality. This characterisation of the HCTS recognises that, in reality, many jobs in hospitality and tourism, 'share common attributes and are associated with both hospitality and tourism activities'. Clearly, then, we should recognise the potential for a lack of precision in describing the tourism and hospitality industries.

In an attempt to avoid too much imprecision and, at the same time, capture the diversity of the sector this book uses the framework offered by People 1st, which is the Sector Skills Council (SSC) for the hospitality, leisure, travel and tourism sector, to exemplify the broad range of activities that may be seen in the HCTS. SSCs are employer led and amongst other things aim to be the voice of industry on skills matters and encourage best practice approaches to employment Therefore, People 1st suggest that the sector as a whole is made up of 14 sub-sectors:

— hotels;
— restaurants;
— pubs, bars and night-clubs;
— contract food service providers;
— membership clubs;
— events;
— gambling;
— travel services;
— tourist services;
— visitor attractions;
— youth hostels;
— holiday parks;
— self-catering accommodation;
— hospitality services.

Moreover within this broad classification of travel, tourism and hospitality there is massive diversity in the types of jobs generated, in relation to their technical and skills' demands, educational requirements, terms and conditions and the type of person that is likely to be attracted to employment in them. A person buying package holiday is likely to interact with:

— the retail travel agent;
— insurance companies;
— ground transport to and from the airport;
— at least two sets of airport handling agents;
— airport services;
— the airline on all legs of the journey;
— immigration and customs services;
— local ground transportation;
— the hotel or apartment;
— tour services at the destination;
— companies and individuals selling a diversity of goods and services at the destination
— emergency services at the destination
— service providers on return

Baum characterises all of these possible intermediaries, and the interactions they will have with the holiday maker, as crucial in 'making or breaking the tourist experience'. Thus while the physical product is important, for most tourists the quality of their experience is likely to be also reliant to a large degree on the interactions they will have with the variety of front-line staff in the travel, tourism and hospitality industry. These so-called 'moments of truth' are therefore crucial for organisational effectiveness, success, competitiveness and profitability. Indeed, within an industry that is characterised by diversity and heterogeneity in terms of the purpose, size, ownership and demands of the enterprise, the only real point of homogeneity is delivering service to customers and the need to manage people in such a way that they offer a quality service. The reality however is that often such staff have the lowest status in the organisation, are the least trained, and are the poorest paid employees of the company.

In recognising the diversity both of the range of sub-sectors and types of jobs they are likely to generate, this book cannot consider all of these aspects in detail. Indeed, more is known about employment in certain sub-sectors than others. Unsurprisingly, then, the commercial hospitality industry is well served with extensive research on the nature of employment and HRM strategies.

On the other hand, little has been written on the events industry or the nature of HRM in youth hostels, for example. As a consequence many of the examples drawn on in this book are from the commercial hospitality industry, although, where possible, illustrations of organisational practice from travel and tourism organisations are also used.

Thus, how does the experience of an airline flight attendant differ from that of a pot washer in the kitchen in a small restaurant to a receptionist in the front desk of an international hotel or to a tour rep working on an 18–30-type holiday? Afurther issue to consider is the manner in which the sector is heterogeneous in terms of the predominance of small- and medium-sized enterprises (SMEs). People 1st note that within the UK hospitality, leisure, travel and tourism sector 76 per cent of establishments employ fewer than ten people and 50 per cent fewer than five. For example, full service carriers in the airline industry are likely to have very different approaches to HRM compared to low-cost airlines.

The same is true for the hospitality sector, which may range from first class and luxury hotels providing extravagant, full 24-hour service to the more homely comforts of a bed and breakfast establishment; from fast food restaurants to Michelin starred restaurants.

3.1. Tourism and Hospitality Workforce

The International Labour Organisation in their wide-ranging report on the global tourism and hospitality industry provides evidence that suggests that the industry globally is largely reliant on what Wood has described as so-called 'marginal workers', such as women, young workers, casual employees, students, relatively high numbers of part-timers and migrant workers.

More specifically, the hospitality sub-sector is indicative of the broader sector in having a higher proportion of part-time employees than most other industries with the all industry figure being 25 per cent. Young people are also prominent within the hospitality, leisure, travel and tourism sector. For example, 37 per cent of the total UK workforce is under 24 years and 58 per cent under 34 years. Related to this last point a significant part of the tourism and hospitality workforce consists of student, seasonal and migrant workers. They are prepared to work for low wages and be flexible in their working patterns, creating what Curtis and Lucas describe as a 'coincidence of needs' between employers and students.

The number of ethnic minority workers in the broader hospitality, leisure, travel and tourism sector is 11 per cent, slightly higher than the all industry figure of 9.6 per cent. With regard to qualifications only 12 per cent of employees in hospitality, leisure, travel and tourism have a degree or equivalent compared to an all industry figure of 29 per cent, with 15 per cent of the workforce having no qualification compared to 11 per cent of the total workforce.

Having briefly considered the nature of the hospitality and tourism industry and the characteristics of its workforce attention now turns to understanding HRM and the increasingly important role it is felt to play in organisational success.

3.2. Human Resource Management (HRM)

There have been many attempts to define what exactly HRM might be and indeed Heery and Noon recognise that it is a subject of considerable academic analysis and that, ultimately, 'there is no common agreement on what HRM means'. Resultantly, they offer 10 definitions, which they feel capture the complexity and dynamism of HRM as a subject of academic study:

— *A label* HRM is seen as simply being another name for personnel management and there is nothing distinct or special about HRM.
— *A convenient shorthand term* that allows for the grouping together of a whole series of sub-disciplines that are broadly concerned with people management.
— *A map* to help guide students and practitioners to understand the concept and ideas associated with the management of people.

— *Aset of professional practices* suggests that there are a range of personnel practices that can be integrated to ensure a professional approach to managing people. In this view a potentially key role is likely to be played by the Chartered Institute for Personnel and Development (CIPD), which is the professional association for those entering the HR and personnel profession.

— *A method of ensuring internal fit* again sees the need to co-ordinate approaches to people management, but here the co-ordination needs to be with other areas of the organisation.

— *A method of ensuring external fit* where HRM activities have to be fully integrated with the demands of the external environment.

— *A competitive advantage* where HRM is the means by which an organisation can gain competitive advantage, a view best captured by the cliché of 'our people are our greatest asset'.

— *A market-driven approach* is that decisions will often be market driven and the needs of the business determine the manner in which employees are treated; some may be treated well, others less so well.

— *A manipulative device* sees it as inherently exploitative and manipulative.

— *A hologram* captures much of the above discussion in recognising the fluid identity of HRM and the fact that it has multiple meanings.

Clearly what the above discussion points to is that HRM means many things to many people, depending on whether you are a manager, an employee or an academic and there is no one definition that will adequately capture the potential complexity of the topic.

As well as providing the concise definition utilised above, Storey also provided one of the earliest and most enduring attempts to recognise different approaches to HRM. These different approaches are captured by the idea of hard and soft HRM, each of which are now briefly described. The hard version is seen to be an instrumental and economically rational approach to HRM. This approach is quantitative and calculative and labour is a commodity/resource, the same as any other. The focus is on HRM. On the other hand the soft version is seen to be much more about adopting a humanistic and developmental approach to HRM. As a result an organisation's people management approach is likely to be more consensual and based on a high level of managerial commitment to employees, which is intended to lead to mutual high commitment from employees, high trust, high productivity and so on.

What hard and soft approaches to HRM point to is that employers will vary their people management strategies. Clearly as well there are likely to be a number of external influences as HRM in practice 1.1 suggests. These external influences will reflect a variety of political, social, economic and technological aspects which will have an effect on HRM policies and practices. Asimilar attempt to recognise that there may be different approaches to HRM is also seen in the debate over whether organisations should aim to achieve 'best fit' or 'best practice'.

Boxall and Purcell suggest that attempts to understand the way in which organisations approach the management of their HR can be seen with regard to whether they aim for 'best fit' or 'best practice'. On the one hand, the best fit school argues for an approach to HRM, which is fully integrated with the specific organisational and environmental context in which they operate.

One of the earliest and most influential attempts to develop a model that recognised the need for a fit between the competitive strategy and HRM was that offered by Schuler and Jackson. The type of needed role behaviours within Schuler and Jackson's model was contingent on the overall strategies that an organisation could adopt to seek competitive advantage and the HRM approached adopted to sustain this.

First, there is an innovation strategy, where organisations seek to develop products or services that are different from competitors, such that the focus here is on companies offering something new and different. Resultantly, the employee needed role behaviour in such a scenario is characterised by things like a willingness to tolerate ambiguity and unpredictability, the need to be creative and risk taking.

Given these characteristics the type of HRM strategy flowing from this approach is based on having a large number of highly skilled individuals who are likely to enjoy high levels of autonomy. Second, is the quality enhancement strategy wherein firms seek to gain competitive advantage by enhancing the product and/or service quality.

These practices include the encouragement of feedback systems, teamwork, decision-making and responsibility being an integral part of an employee's job description and flexible job classifications. The intent of these practices is to create needed employee behaviour such as co-operative, interdependent behaviour and commitment to the goals of the organisation. The characteristics of firms seeking to pursue this strategy are tight controls, minimisation of overheads and pursuit of economies of scale, in the pursuit of increased productivity.

In following such a strategy organisations may use higher number of part-timers, seek to simplify and measure work via narrowly defined jobs that encourage specialisation and efficiency, and offer shortterm results oriented appraisal. Needed employee behaviours include, repetitive and predictable behaviour, low-risk taking activity and a high degree of comfort with stability.

This support for the importance of HRM practices 'fitting' the organisations own strategically defined market segment to create a fit between the functional areas of marketing, operations and HRM is also seen in the work of Lashley and Taylor. Lashley and Taylor describe four basic archetypes within which tourism and hospitality organisations can be potentially located. These archetypes are the service factory, the service shop, mass service and professional services.

The service factory is relatively low labour intensity and low customisation. The service factory is most obviously exemplified by fast food operators, especially McDonald's. The service shop involves more customisation, but relatively low labour intensity. The defining difference to the service factory lies in the degree of standardisation within the process. Lashley and Taylor draw upon the example of TGI Fridays to argue that although there are high levels of standardisation in the tangible aspects of the organisation, such as the menus, layouts, décor and staff uniform, there is also some scope to customise the customers' eating and drinking experience.

The next classification is mass service where service processes involve a relatively high degree of labour intensity, though a limited amount of customisation. Lashley and Taylor assert that the Marriott hotel brand typifies a mass service organisation, as their four star offering is similar to others in relation to the tangibles reflecting the highly competitive nature of the mid to upper segment of the hotel market. As a result of this convergence of the tangibles the key lies in the intangibles and the scope available to organisations to differentiate themselves on the basis of service quality. The final grouping is professional services where there is a high level of service to individual customers and a high degree of labour intensity, as exemplified by hospitality management consultants.

The key point which emerges from the work of Lashley and Taylor is the likely relationship between the service operation type adopted by the organisation and the style of HRM which best fits it. For example, it is apparent that in the four star hotel sector a broadly soft approach to HRM, as exemplified by high discretion in relation to the intangibles, moral involvement and a moderate trust culture, is suggested as being important to sustain a high quality, total quality management (TQM) based approach to the service offering. At the other end of the spectrum, McDonald's are suggested as exemplifying a command and control style which is characterised by things such as low discretion for employees, limited responsibility and autonomy, and scripted service encounters.

Whilst arguments for best fit advocate a close fit between competitive strategies and HRM, those in favour of best practice approaches to HRM suggest that there is a universal 'one best way' to manage people. By adopting a best practice approach it is argued that organisations will see enhanced commitment from employees leading to improved organisational performance, higher levels of service quality and ultimately increases in productivity and profitability, Usually couched in terms of 'bundles', the HRM practices that are offered in support of a high commitment and performance model are generally fairly consistent. For example, Redman and Matthews outline a range of HR practices which are suggested as being important to organisational strategies aimed at securing high-quality service:

— *Recruitment and selection:* Recruiting and selecting staff with the correct attitudinal and behavioural characteristics.

- *Retention:* The need to avoid the development of a 'turnover culture', which may of course be particularly prevalent in tourism and hospitality.
- *Teamwork*: The use of semi-autonomous, cross-process and multi-functional teams.
- *Training and development*: The need to equip operative level staff with team working and interpersonal skills to develop their 'service orientation' and managers with a new leadership style which encourages a move to a more facilitative and coaching style of managing.
- *Appraisal*: Moving away from traditional top down approaches to appraisal and supporting things such as customer evaluation, peer review, team-based performance and the appraisal of managers by subordinates.
- *Rewarding quality*: A need for a much more creative system of rewards and in particular the need to payment systems that reward employees for attaining quality goals.
- *Job security*: Promises of job security are seen as an essential component of any overall quality approach.
- Employee involvement and employee relations: By seeking greater involvement from employees the emphasis is on offering autonomy, creativity, co-operation and self-control in work processes.

In simple terms best practice is likely to entail attempts to enhance the skills base of employees through HR activities such as selective staffing, comprehensive training and broad developmental efforts like job rotation. Additionally, it also encourages empowerment, participative problem-solving, teamwork as well as performance-based incentives.

3.2.1. Models or Reality

Of course ideal types and academic models may not always reflect the complex reality of what really goes on in tourism and hospitality organisations. Schuler and Jackson, for instance, freely admit the description of their three competitive strategies as pure types often does not reflect the reality of, for example, organisations pursuing two or more competitive strategies simultaneously. The same point can also be made with regard to hard and soft HRM; it is not uncommon for organisations to vary their approaches to employees depending on any given practice. A further issue is the predominance of SMEs in tourism and hospitality. It is often suggested that their small scale means that they are unlikely to have the necessary means to employ the kind of HRM expertise to develop sophisticated soft approaches, for example. Nevertheless, they are still likely to require HR policies that require at least some thought with regard to their business circumstances.

Whilst some understanding of debate about soft and hard and best fit and best practice are important to place HR practices within a broader theoretical context, in reality, regardless of these various ideal types all organisations have to manage employees on a day-to-day basis.

Whilst a number of the functional aspects of HRM are unlikely to differ, the manner in which organisations actually develop their overall strategy will. In these circumstances models that allow for recognition of differing strategic intent in HRM are still useful in allowing us to appreciate why and how companies differ in their approaches to HRM in tourism and hospitality. It would be naïve to imagine we could talk in very broad terms about HRM in tourism in hospitality.

3.2.2. Pessimistic Views of HRM in Tourism and Hospitality

Generally tourism and hospitality has often struggled with negative perceptions about employment practices and conditions and this perception has often been matched by the reality. Keep and Mayhew for example in their review of the skills issue in the tourism and hospitality industry suggest the industry has a number of personnel problems, including:

- generally low wages, unless skill shortages act to counter this;
- unsocial hours and shift patterns that are not family friendly;
- overrepresentation of women and ethnic minorities in low-level operative positions, with better paid, higher status and more skilled jobs filled by men, pointing to undeveloped equal opportunities policies in the sector;

— poor or non-existent career structures and use of casualised seasonal employment;
— over reliance on informal recruitment methods;
— lack of evidence of good practice personnel/HRM practices;
— little or no trade union presence;
— high levels of labour turnover;
— difficulties in recruitment and retention of employees.

Recognising this reality of poor employment practices, Riley et al. argue that economics is the key determining factor for HRM policies and practices in tourism and hospitality. That is not to say that organisations and managers in the industry are not well aware of new managerial thinking on HRM. However, they also find themselves wrestling with 'traditional problems', which are underpinned by 'fundamental labour economic imperatives. Importantly, these problems limit managerial actions and this leads Riley et al. to argue the behaviour of managers is determined 'by the structures and forms under which they live'. An obvious impact of this is that HRM concerns of tourism and hospitality organisations are constantly directed to short-term responses to issues such as recruitment, selection and basic training, rather than more long-term areas which could conceivably offer more development and career progression for existing employees.

Another reason for continuing pessimism is the general attitude of employers and particularly the extent to which they are willing to recognise the extent of the HRM problem in the sector. The DfEE registers with some incredulity the awareness of low pay, for example, existing alongside the naïve view of employers of tourism and hospitality as a 'good' employing sector. Thus, although in a number of locations labour shortages were clearly reflective of an unwillingness of employers to offer competitive pay and terms of conditions of employment, the DfEE notes how, 'We were struck by the extent to which employers described pay and working conditions as "reasonable" or even "good" while at the same time reporting extensive recruitment problems, skills gaps and labour turnover.'

This inability by industry to recognise the most glaring of issues is long standing and can also be seen in relation to things like a degree of hostility and opposition from the employers associations in the industry, such as the British Hospitality Association (BHA), to governmental initiatives such as the minimum wage and working time directive. The BHA still remains unsure of the benefits of such initiatives, despite support from others who argue these initiatives are likely to have a potentially positive impact on the industry.

For example, McGunnigle and Jameson surveyed a selected number of hotels from the top 50 hotel groups ranked by ownership of bedroom stock, which were considered to be most likely to exhibit good practice HRM. Despite this they concluded, 'This study suggests that there is little adoption of HRM philosophy in corporately owned hotels in the UK sample .... has a long way to go before it can claim that it is encouraging a "culture of commitment"'. Similarly, Kelliher and Perrett, drawing explicitly on Schuler and Jackson's typology, develop a case study analysis of a 'designer restaurant'.

However, although the restaurant had moved to a more sophisticated approach to HRM in areas like planning, training and development and appraisal, and ostensibly sought an 'innovation' strategy, 'there was little real evidence that human resources were seen as a source of competitive advantage'. Instead, the HRM approaches adopted by the restaurant were much more reflective of immediate environmental constraints, such as the difficulties in recruiting and retaining staff.

In sum, any number of reasons may account for poor personnel practice in the tourism and hospitality industry. Economic determinism, the predominance of SMEs, a low-skills base, employer antipathy to a more progressive approach to HRM, labour market characteristics, organisations ensuring best fit HRM practices to support a high volume, low-cost strategy. That said, it would be equally wrong to paint a wholly pessimistic picture.

Some of the most important work to emerge in recent years on the question of the extent of good practice in the HCTS is the work of Hoque. Based on his work on the hotel sector, he argues that arguments which portray the industry as backward and unstrategic are now outdated, at least where larger hotel establishments are concerned. Indeed, he suggests that 'it is perhaps time researchers stopped highlighting the example of "bad management" and branding the industry as under-developed or backward, and started identifying approaches to hotel management capable of generating high performance'.

Based on this research he discusses three key issues. First, the extent to which hotels have experimented with new approaches to HRM. Secondly, the factors that influence HRM decision-making and whether these factors are any different in the hotel industry compared to elsewhere. Finally, he reviewed the relationship between HRM and performance in the hotel industry. Hoque is able to claim that, compared to a sample of over 300 greenfield-site manufacturing establishments, the hotels in his sample where utilising a number of practices that were very similar to best practice.

Hoque's work remains useful in offering a description of organisational practices that support a professional, high-quality approach to service. That said, there are a number of criticisms that can be levelled at the research. As Hoque himself recognises his sample of hotels is large by industry standards, averaging 125 employees per unit compared to an industry 'standard' of 81 per cent of establishments employing fewer than 25 people, and thus as Hoque himself recognises 'patently unrepresentative of the industry as a whole'. Furthermore his reliance on city-centre hotels with a high proportion of corporate clients is equally unrepresentative. Lastly, the reliance on managerial voices in his research, to the exclusion of those on the receiving end of many of the initiatives described may be considered an important omission. To be fair, Hoque's exclusive reliance on managerial voices is not unique and is shared by much of the literature on HRM. The key point emerging from the work of the likes of Redman and Matthews and Hoque is what good practice HRM is likely to look like in the tourism and hospitality industry.

References

Baum, T. 1995. *Managing Human Resources in the European Hospitality and Tourism Industry – A Strategic Approach*, Chapman and Hall.

Cheng, A. and Brown, A. 1998. 'HRM strategies and labour turnover in the hotel industry: a comparative study of Australia and Singapore', *International Journal of Human Resource Management*, 9(1), 136–154.

D'Annunzio-Green, N., Maxwell, G. and Watson, S. 2002. *Human Resource Management: International Perspectives in Hospitality and Tourism*, Continuum.

4

Global Tourism Marketplace

Many entrepreneurs fail to understand the nature of the tourist industry as a marketplace, and assume that because they have an authentic and exciting tourism product, clients will find them. Many donors and policy makers also make the same mistake, funding conservation projects expecting that tourism will generate sufficient revenues for the long term survival. The challenges mentioned here apply in the majority both to sustainable and non sustainable tourism products.

Poor market research, which is often the result of limited data availability coupled with unrealistic expectations of occupancy levels in low and shoulder seasons, cripple small business start-ups. These businesses tend to have limited understanding of consumer behaviour, particularly for international markets.

There are many examples of sustainable tourism products that are not viable because the supplier has failed to understand market needs, often through a failure to engage the industry in product development. This is sometimes the result of agencies working with host destinations that have suffered the negative impacts of unsustainable development, and then fail to involve operators, on whom marketing success often ultimately depends.

Resource based instead of market led. Sustainability means authenticity, which in turn suggests that the tourism product should not be changed just to please tourists. But in doing so tourism products often do not take into account the expectations of tourists and the needs of tour operators.

Targeting international markets. Too many businesses expect international markets to become the key source of income. This should be balanced with filling a good percentage of the capacity with domestic and short haul regional markets.

Sustainability as unique selling proposition. Marketing on the basis of sustainability is not going to suffice for most tourist segments and products, even when sustainability could be at the core of the product itself, and could be one of the determining attributes that the tourist looks for. For the vast majority of consumers, sustainability will only be a consideration when other criteria, such as price, choice of accommodation and availability of activities have all been satisfied.

Sustainability as part of quality. In the past, too many sustainable products in tourism and elsewhere, have performed worse in the basic quality attributes. Tourists are willing to purchase sustainable once the basic attributes of product quality are met. The win-win products in the sustainable, organic, fair trade sectors are those that provide added value.

4.1. Consumer Product Knowledge

If a tourist market knows the product well, the type of promotion can emphasize characteristics of the product or place that are meaningful to the tourist, whereas first time tourists will need more information about the product as prior knowledge cannot be assumed. Also repeat tourists are more likely to buy directly from suppliers that first time tourists.

Inexperienced product users. Tourists that buy a certain type of holiday for the first time are more open to education, but it is also less likely that their behaviour will be in-keeping with that of locals. First time tourists on a package such as trekking, diving or homestays have specific awareness raising and education needs before and during their experience, that will mark their behaviour for future trips.

Price sensitive first time visitors. Many tourists experiment with destinations, visiting just once, making it hard for the service providers to communicate product quality, and relying on price alone to secure sales. Information sources that can be trusted such as travel guides and signs of quality for example are good vehicles to reinforce such messages.

Repeat clients encourage sustainability. Repeat clients are more likely to appreciate the unique characteristics of a place, usually related to sustainability. Lack of loyalty to destinations often means service providers do not see a short term benefit from providing the required services of quality, as those tourists leaving will not come again, and others just as gullible will follow.

4.2. Risk Perception

Tourists often do not want to book directly with service suppliers because they perceive risk. Small firms are perceived as more risky because they do not have strong brands to support them, and for this reason they will need to work in partnership to ensure purchases. Sustainable tourism should tackle the following:

Risk of the unknown. A large volume of internet sales at present are repeat sales once the client knows the business, and they are mainly for airline tickets, car rental and hotel rooms in global companies with standardised products. This increases when travelling to countries for the first time, particularly when these countries are very different to the country of origin of the tourists.

Risk of fraud. Secure purchasing systems that can give confidence to clients are necessary for small tourism firms to sell directly. At the moment a large percentage of direct sales are with large firms. The perception of potential fraud from giving credit card details to companies outside the tourists' home country is high, also raising concerns about data protection and the possibility of identity theft.

Risk of virtual companies. Tourists are less likely to want to book with small companies because of the perceived threat that these might not be real companies, the client has paid in advance for the service but once they arrive at the destination the company does not exist. Retailing through a link at the national tourist board, or having the backing of consumer organisations can provide the kind of quality assurance that will increase bookings.

Risk of no consumer protection. Purchasing directly from tourism suppliers means that clients will not have the same legal protection as when they purchase a product from a tour operator in their own country. This is clearly the case in Europe, where the Travel

Packages Act places responsibility for the quality of the product including health and safety on the tour operator. There is little regulation and only very limited consumer protection against false claims made on the internet by direct suppliers.

4.3. Current Practice and Prospects

The tourism marketplace is made up of a large number of tourism service suppliers trying to reach a multiplicity of tourist markets. They do so targeting the tourists directly, developing positive messages about their product through promotion channels, and working with intermediary distribution channels that will sell a range of services tailored to the market's needs. There are two commercialisation strategies:

Business to consumer (B2C). Tourism service suppliers can use a range of direct marketing channels such as database and internet marketing to attract tourists. The advantage is having a greater control over the message sent and the type of tourist attracted. The disadvantages are that this is done at a greater financial risk, with potentially high start up costs.

Business to business (B2B). Tourism suppliers benefit from outsourcing the cost and risk of marketing. The advantages are diversification of markets that reduce risk, a potentially secure level of business, and fixed commissions that facilitate financial planning.

Most often, tourism suppliers combine the two: direct (B2C) and via distributors (B2B). In the latter case, intermediaries are used to provide a baseline level of business that ensures minimum occupancy rates or load factors, which provides a contribution towards fixed costs of capital repayment and salaries. Direct marketing is used to capture repeat visitors, particular market segments and for specific promotions. The balance between the two types of marketing is determined by how entrepreneurial the company is, the availability of knowledge and funds, and the interest of intermediaries to work with it.

While eight distribution and communication channels are reviewed here, some of these are much larger than the others, whereas some of them only have an impact on a niche market, or are highlighted here because of their potential for the future.

4.4. Destination Management Organisations (DMOs)

DMOs are agencies or marketing consortia that promote a 'destination' to outbound tour operators and both domestic and foreign consumers through a variety of media, and provide information on local products and suppliers. Sometimes, suppliers receive preferential treatment.

The challenge for destinations is to identify the environmental constraints and impacts of tourism development, and to then engage local destination suppliers, buyers and all visitors in embracing sustainability as a key element of the tourism proposition.

Some destinations have marketed themselves as being totally sustainable, although in reality this often reflects an emphasis on natural heritage, rather than indicating product sustainability. Tourism New Zealand's campaign "100% Pure New Zealand" is a good example of this approach, where this DMO concentrates on presenting a consistent message to position New Zealand as a sustainable destination.

There are examples of tourist boards giving additional promotion to firms that have met certain standards of sustainability. Places as far apart as Scotland and Costa Rica are promoting companies certified as sustainable, either by highlighting certified suppliers with an additional logo in their promotional material or by creating a separate dedicated brochure for sustainable products.

The challenge for DMOs is often less about marketing sustainable tourism products, but more about raising awareness of what the sustainable development of tourism means for suppliers, which in turn will help to ensure the more sustainable development of tourism products. Remarking that the term "'responsible tourism' is more meaningful to suppliers", Oman's Dr Aziz stated that the development of "the responsible tourism sector is one of the guaranteed ways of achieving sustainable development for the Sultanate of Oman." Oman is working to achieve this outcome through a programme of training and awareness raising, and by offering preferential terms to suppliers that adopt more sustainable practices. The former will be achieved through a national training programme, primarily targeted at tourism SMEs, whilst the latter will involve a schedule of discounts on marketing activities, including attendance at international tourism fairs.

There can be other priorities that DMOs must tackle before they can even begin to focus on sustainability issues, but such circumstances can bring benefits, allowing DMOs to approach product development as a 'blank canvas'. Although it has a tremendous product, Yemen has been the subject of much negative publicity in recent years and has been considered by tour operators and consumers alike to be too outlandish a destination for mainstream tourism. Yemen to highlight the sustainability of its products, adding real value to the destination. This involves all the usual marketing activities, such as organisation of familiarisation visits for journalists and tour operators, production of promotional media in paper and electronic formats and attendance at major international tourism fairs.

With a particular emphasis on cultural and nature-based tourism, the main themes being promoted are 'ecotourism' and activity tourism, especially diving, deserts, mountains and climbing, which are attractive to tour operators. With 70% of visitors coming from the MENA region the Yemen Tourism Promotion Board (YTPB) is focusing on several key foreign markets and plans to develop a new multi-lingual website. This will be in Arabic, English, French, German and Italian and in the future also in Japanese and Russian, in order to communicate directly with the consumer. According to the YTPB's Director, "sustainable tourism is fundamental, because it helps the economy of Yemen through the creation of jobs and investment; tourism is Yemen's future".

Marketing sustainable tourism is not simply a marketing exercise, but requires integration across all social and economic sectors. Thus, echoing the approach of Oman's Ministry of Tourism, Yemen's General Authority for Tourism Development (GATD) is focused on the sustainable development of tourism. Observing that Yemen's tourism product is essentially its "environment and culture", the GATD stated that the challenge is to keep this "intact", because "if changed, then Yemen loses". However, since there is limited understanding of 'sustainable tourism', the GATD puts a lot of energy into engaging key stakeholders, especially community representatives, to promote the principles of sustainable tourism. It will support those communities that choose tourism as a development strategy, but critically, it will also respect those that choose to resist tourism.

Natour Communications has run a series of short online campaigns to change the negative perception of Venezuela as a tourist destination, using a database of over 8,000 e-mail addresses of travel agents, operators, media interested in the natural world and tourism. The campaign consisted of between 8 and 10 issues over three months depending on the specific messages, to promote the country's natural attractions and activities, and generating interest for a familiarisation trip for 24 international media and operators Familiarisation visits bring invited press and selected operators to destinations to sample the product. Tourist boards tend to sponsor and support these, and in some instances run them. Typically a fam trip takes 8 to 12 weeks to set up because it requires targeting participants, raising awareness, organising logistics and tailoring the trip to their particular needs. Natour Communications run a fam trip to the Caribbean island of Trinidad coinciding with the 3rd annual Shandy Carib Adventure Festival to showcase adventure, nature and cultural opportunities.

4.5. Tour Operators

These are organisations that sell holidays and travel products to consumers, taking a commission or margin on the product sold, which they have purchased from suppliers or are selling on behalf of suppliers. Additional income is gained through the sale of other travel-related products, such as travel insurance and foreign currency. In some cases, they will establish a 'partnership' relationship with their suppliers, working collaboratively with them on destination management, product development and direct marketing activities.

The key tool for tour operators is the 'service agreement', the contract between operator and supplier, whether an airline, accommodation or excursion provider or ground handler. It defines the service standards, including quality as well as health and safety requirements.

Some tour operators are starting to introduce environmental standards, but with only limited consumer demand, few are yet willing to link these to contractual obligations and financial penalties. The general approach is one of encouragement, with operators identifying key suppliers that might need to improve their environmental performance and are consequently offered mainly training and advice, and in fewer instances financial incentives.

A large proportion of the work done by large tour operators to improve the sustainability of their service providers is by promoting the economic advantages of reducing water, waste and energy costs through being more environmentally friendly. For many specialist tour operators, sustainability is part of the product quality sought by tourists. In this case there are few examples for supplier development, but usually because a minimum sustainability requirement was part of the selection criteria.

Most tour operators are not likely to pay a higher price to their suppliers for sustainability. Generally they argue that sustainability is an element of the expected quality, and that it will also bring major cost savings.

Supplier development initiatives are generally voluntary, with few examples of tour operators making them mandatory. Several large tour operators have reported that between 10 and 25% of suppliers have met the voluntary 'sustainability related' standards. Tour operators are most successful in convincing long-term suppliers, and those that are owned or managed by the same parent company. Few tour operators highlight those suppliers that are more sustainable in their brochures.

The Reiseanalyse 2002 survey in Germany showed that tourists demand such information, but it is likely that many tour operators will not want to do so until a certain volume of their products have met the necessary standards, and they can send a positive reassuring message to the market.

The large German tour operator LTU Touristik distributed 16,000 environmental management manuals to accommodation suppliers in German, English, French, Italian, Spanish, and Greek. Impacts are rated by time and cost required to make a significant improvement. Hotels implementing this manual best are those managed by LTU itself and those where LTU brings a high percentage of their business.

Hello Tuscany promotes to young people a positive experience of sustainable tourism: the Summer Camps in Tuscany. Summer camps seem to be a very pleasant experience, since they combine the attraction of natural parks, a real interaction with a beautiful environment, and with local people with their own historical traditions.

Kel 12 is a small Italian tour operator specialising in adventure holidays mainly in Africa, even though their presence is now widespread everywhere from the Sahara to China to South America. It promotes the marketing of sustainable tourism products by working with destination agencies that share the same philosophy, including sustainability as purchasing criteria, running conservation and community projects in the field, and engaging consumers in projects.

The Dutch Tour Operator Association ANVR requires members to appoint and train a responsible tourism coordinator; develop and implement a responsible tourism policy; report annually to ANVR on at least one sustainability measure per each of five areas; and not offer travel products that are forbidden according to the developed list of irresponsible travel products. Similar requirements are being introduced in the UK through the Federation of Tour Operators.

4.6. Guidebooks

Most guidebooks are produced by independent commercial publishers. Although some guides might be openly commissioned as marketing tools by individual travel companies, guidebook publishers are generally independent of the travel industry. They identify products and destinations, giving objective opinions and are sold to consumers, including conventional tourists and business travellers. Additional revenue can be earned from advertising and the production of associated online editions, but the most trusted guidebooks keep their information independent from commercial ties.

Freelance travel writers are commissioned to write individual books. In general, the appointed writers receive a very specific brief by the guidebook editing team, which outlines the guide, the structure to follow, including the characteristics of the companies to be included in the guide. The authors also receive all the information collected on the country and in particular on hotels and tourism services that they will have to personally review.

These writers research hotels, restaurants and attractions following the criteria of the travel guide according to their market positioning and unique selling proposition. Many guidebooks emphasize unique, exciting and interesting products that are aligned to the principles of sustainable tourism, although few will use explicit criteria for the selection of what towns and companies are to be included, and the final decision depends on space and a balance between different destinations and types of product. Sustainability is often referred to as far as it is part of the exciting and unique attributes that the independent tourist is seeking.

The companies publishing traditional guidebooks are evolving to produce customised guidebooks, spin-off guides and unique travel information, licensed use of web engine or travel information, and to selling photographs. Travel information is now not only coming in the typical guidebook form, but also increasingly in electronic form, whether on websites or in phone/PDA formats. All of these provide new niche opportunities for tourism companies and destinations.

Highly professional guidebooks are now also being produced by non-governmental organisations and campaign groups, for which the motivation is development assistance, rather than commercial profit. The focus is increasingly shifting to the consumer, since publishers are discovering that these publications meet a market need, giving objective advice on obscure community-led tourism products, offering consumers access to 'authentic experiences' with less of the more negative aspects of tourism.

As in the case of travel media, the ability to be included in a guidebook depends on whether the product can be presented as being exciting, quirky and unique. Sustainability is sometimes the reason why a product is interesting, but the message has to be tailored with the tourist experience as the centre of attention.

Over 100,000 Lonely Planet travellers use the electronic Thorn Tree travellers' bulletin boards on a regular basis, where travellers can exchange information on destinations and experiences, and plan their next adventure. This makes Lonelyplanet.com a vibrant heavily trafficked global travel resource. Lonely Planet also sends a monthly email newsletter to thousands of readers.

Lonely Planet's Shoestring guides have a large readership amongst young people travelling for the first time. These guides include extensive information on responsible behaviour in their travels, and the choices of places to visit reinforce this philosophy. Lonely Planet has however been questioned for publishing a guide that encourages tourism to Burma, despite their claims that the guide raises awareness and supports the type of firms that will least support financially the oppressive regime.

Sustainability is at the core of Lonely Planet, although this has so far happened more intuitively than strategically. The company is now examining how they formalise their commitment to sustainability. In their own forecast they estimate that in 10 years, 40 to 50% of the products listed in their guides could have verified sustainability credentials.

Tourism Concern, which "campaigns for ethical and fairly traded tourism" is currently planning the third edition of its The Good Alternative Travel Guide. Working through its large international network of tourism stakeholders, known as the 'Fair Trade in Tourism Network', it is able to identify a wide range of sustainable tourism products, including community-based tourism initiatives primarily and responsible tour operators. Products that pass a preliminary review are sent a questionnaire which is used as the basis of assessment and to determine which products meet sufficient criteria of fair trade and responsibility to be included. There is no fee for inclusion, although there is some income from advertising, and those that are rejected are offered advice and guidance on best practice, since "the objective is to change the industry". Two hundred products were included in the guide's second edition, of which 10,000 copies have been sold, and which is supplemented by promotion at trade fairs and online listings. Tourism Concern's website receives 9,000 unique site visits each month, making this a highly effective medium.

According to Tourism Concern, the guide is particularly valued by suppliers, because the organisation "shares information across its network", promoting best practice and contributing to the development of 'fair trade in tourism'. Whilst for consumers, who are "a bit more socially responsible" and "want to take a different kind of holiday", its value is that it is "not just a marketing tool", but is "effectively a certification scheme". Insofar as the guide is a tool for normalising sustainability and promoting best practice, Tourism Concern describes the guide's contents as "tourism that's developed in the context of sustainable development".

4.7. Media

Media includes the travel section of mainstream newspapers and consumer magazines, as well as dedicated travel magazines. Most income comes from advertising revenue, whilst the content primarily consists of stories, reviews and features about particular destinations and products. Newspapers also offer commercial opportunities through affiliate marketing initiatives. The travel pages of newspapers are the key promotional channel for specialist tour operators other than word of mouth.

But, just as the point of newspapers is to sell news, the point of travel journalism is to promote travel. Therefore, according to The Independent, sustainability is "not an issue", because ultimately "people want to go on holiday, even if they want to travel more thoughtfully". The newspaper has certain values, which means that it will tend to encourage community-led tourism and promote small guest houses, cycling and public transport, but it also has a commercial need to gain advertising revenue, which cannot be constrained by considerations of sustainability, on which there is no specific policy.

Travel pages of newspapers have a small team of staff editors that commission the work from freelance editors, who have to pitch ideas that are original, new, interesting and also good ideas for holidays. Freelance writers look for ideas that will sell. Funnelling interesting stories from the tourism provider and the travel media is the gap. Training tourism companies on how the media operates, and how to identify the relevant freelance journalists with the right stories is crucial.

Original, quirky, interesting stories of exciting and unique places to go and things to do have the greatest potential to be featured in the travel pages. The emphasis sought by freelance journalists and travel editors is on why these are good holidays. Giving money to charities, investing in schools, saving turtles all play a part in the feature, but not in the opening paragraphs. A feature on the importance of responsible tourism per se would only be a story once, while this way there is a way to keep communicating the underlying principles.

Tourism firms need to plan the message to be communicated, emphasising first why it is exciting and unique. They require thinking from the point of view of the consumer, and not focusing first on conservation, and they first have to make an interesting travel proposition.

Messages need to be newsworthy, so products are easiest to be featured when they are new. For products that have been on the market for some time, companies need to think of ways to reinvent messages in the public relations tradition to ensure their products have maximum exposure. For example, the UK project promoting bicycle routes 'Sustrans' had already received extensive exposure for their work in the 1990s, and yet they are being featured again for introducing public artwork along their routes to attract more families to cycling.

Several newspapers run travel awards that highlight good practice and have become great marketing methods for the few companies winning. The Times dedicated four pages to the winners of their Responsible Tourism Awards. Many independent tour operators use their winning status to promote themselves, and a number of sustainable tourism products have dramatically increased their bookings and reputation through winning one of these awards.

The Guardian newspaper in the UK runs a monthly column called The Green Light, featuring responsible holidays, based on market research that identified a gap in the market. "Go diving with octopuses" was the incentive to read about an Earthwatch project in Costa Rica monitoring octopuses and their habitat.

The tour operator Discovery Initiatives was featured in two mainstream UK television travel programmes, The Holiday Programme and Wish You Were Here. In both cases the productions were well received and stimulated a great deal of interest.

4.8. Certification Schemes

Certification schemes highlight sustainable tourism products. They have a dual function of helping tourism suppliers to raise their sustainability standards, and providing market mechanisms to increase trade gained from having the brand of the ecolabel. There are over 60 initiatives, targeting mostly the accommodation sector, and mainly in Europe. Most of them have started since the mid 1990s, with 20 more in development at present.

These schemes have the dual role of increasing industry performance by providing guidelines on how to be more sustainable, directing applicants towards sources of help and in some cases providing advice directly, and at the same time providing marketing benefits.

However, there are too many labels, with few certified products each, to have an impact on the market. Consolidation of current labels for international recognition, and repositioning of the labels as being an extension to traditional product quality are obvious avenues forward. In only a few instances will sustainability be a unique selling proposition that can be meaningfully branded.

The certified product is not meaningful to the consumer for two reasons: firstly, lack of awareness, and secondly, the perception that it does not have significantly different attributes. Consumers cannot tell from the available information whether a certified product is better than the average product, on the points that matter to the tourist. The small number of certified companies, and the fact that the basic quality attributes are very different means that choosing providers based on an ecolabel is not likely. This is partly attributed to the fact that certification programs have no in-house marketing or communications specialists.

VISIT is the acronym for 'Voluntary Initiatives for Sustainability In Tourism', the result of 10 ecolabels uniting forces to raise standards across Europe and to benefit from the economies of scale of joint marketing and lobbying.

The EU funded project Tourlink supports tour operators to standardise their sustainability checklists with those of certification programmes.

Green Travel Market offers tour operators a tool for receiving reliable, up-to-date information on more sustainable tourism products currently available on the market, screened for quality and sustainability. Amongst others it includes over 1000 certified accommodation providers in Europe.

The Sustainable Tourism Certification Network of the Americas aims to make sustainable tourism firms more competitive by providing market advantages through certification. The goal is to involve 175 enterprises in certification by 2007. This effort is being implemented in four pilot countries by Rainforest Alliance-Costa Rica, Alianza Verde in Guatemala, the Ecuadorian Ecotourism Association (ASEC),and Programme for Belize.

FTTSA (Fair Trade in Tourism South Africa) has developed a certification scheme. It is relatively new and has so far only certified seven products, which are mainly accommodations, but it also includes a game reserve and a township tour. Ten more products are currently under review. Tour operators have indicated that the scheme needs at least twenty products to gain critical mass, and FTTSA expects to have certified twenty-five by May 2005. Products are assessed against criteria in eight areas. These are business information, human resources, procurement, community initiatives, social initiatives, environmental initiatives, business policies and the motivation for applying for FTTSA certification.

Some foreign tour operators are encouraging their suppliers to register, which will provide additional revenue and contribute to critical mass. FTTSA is involved in a lot of B2B marketing activities to promote products to foreign tour operators and to promote the scheme to regional tourist boards - and thereby reach more products. The website is currently only in English, but FTTSA also has plans to include basic information in Dutch, French, German and Swedish.

4.9. Consumer and Trade Fairs

Travel and tourism suppliers ranging from individual products to national tourist boards use fairs to present their goods and services to travel trade buyers and consumers, including prospective tourists and business organisations. Key sectors of the fairs market include leisure tourism, independent travel and MICE. The number of specialised fairs addressing the topic of sustainable, eco and responsible tourism is increasing, while traditional national fairs are developing these themes as well by offering specific events or pavilions and forum of discussions. Individual companies are unlikely to attend many fairs, particularly small providers, for cost reasons. Learning about the market is useful, particularly at the early stages of developing a company.

Business travel, as evidenced by the MICE sector, has traditionally not been considered particularly relevant to sustainable tourism, but this is changing. With the growing importance of 'corporate governance' in business and the associated shareholder exposure to corporate risk, buyers are increasingly seeking out suppliers that have strong sustainability credentials, and are asking to see companies' environmental policies and evidence of 'corporate social responsibility'. The Centre for the Promotion of Imports for Developing Countries, an agency of the Netherlands' Ministry of Foreign Affairs, sponsors community based tourism and NGO's under certain conditions and provides marketing assistance prior, during and after the Vakantiebeurs' Fair in Utrecht, Netherlands, such as brochure and website design and negotiation skills, as well as organising meetings with relevant tour operators.

Reisepavillon is the alternative travel fair running annually in Hanover, Germany, attracting 250 stands from 50 countries in 2004. There is a high exhibitor turnover, with 39% of new exhibitors, and 20% of non returns. GTZ supports the fair by organising the industry networking and training event, Tourismus Forum International (TFI), and also bringing 20% of the stands by showcasing developing ecotourism projects from developing countries.

Consumer fairs such as Chicago and New York have rebranded from specialist adventure shows to more mainstream to attract a broader public and companies. In doing so they have attracted first time buyers for specific product types such as adventure and eco tourism because the fairs showcase products not usually found in travel agencies, with actual sales made on the show.

The activity holidays and shortbreak tour operator Inntravel organises a day long travel fairs where suppliers from all over Europe are invited to the UK to meet directly with customers. The fairs are held every three years in different parts of the country, with the most recent in December 2004 in North Yorkshire. About 120 suppliers presented their products and services to 1000 customers and potential customers. Attendance is by ticket only because of the high demand, although tickets are free. Inntravel staff - including directors, product managers and sales staff are on hand to answer enquiries and take bookings.

IMEX is the leading MICE fair held each year in Frankfurt, with three schemes to showcase best practice and to promote corporate social responsibility in its sector. These are gaining in prestige and each year attract a growing number of applications. The Programmes of Purpose Award for Social Responsibility "recognises meeting organisers who have put together meetings or incentives benefiting the local community - undertaking charitable acts can be inspirational to participants as well as lastingly beneficial to the community concerned". The Environmentally Responsible Meetings Award "recognises environmental awareness amongst meeting organisers, highlighting the opportunities that now exist to stage business tourism events in 'green-minded' venues, whilst also planning an agenda in which sustainability issues have been taken fully into account". The Free Wild Çard Places is one of the most innovative awards, enabling emerging destinations with MICE potential to participate and access new markets.

4.10. Internet Retailers

These are on-line retailers, in some cases complementing conventional operators and agents, but usually they are a global distribution system for mainstream products. This category also includes holiday auction sites and over-branded in-house websites used to sell distressed stock. There are very few sites that are selective and control their product according to strict quality criteria, and sometimes they act as 'matchmakers' between suppliers and operators.

The distinction between 'matchmakers' and 'sales agents' is both practical and legal. Whilst both might gain a commission from the transaction, a 'matchmaker' introduces potential clients to suppliers whilst an 'agent' sells the tourism services of a supplier directly to customers, although consumers might be under the impression that they are dealing directly with the supplier.

Internet retailers can also be divided into two categories: high volume-low margin and low volume-high margin. The large internet retailers compete on price and supply a commodity market, whilst the many small ones focus on specialist products, particular niche markets or are dedicated to a small number of suppliers, sometimes in a single destination.

The websites of vertically integrated tour operators, such as TUI, Thomas Cook and MyTravel, and those of other large tourism service providers, such as international hotel groups, airlines and car hire firms, are not considered here. This is because such websites are an extension of conventional retailing, rather than representing a specialist distribution channel.

However, unlike holidays booked through tour operators consumers will often not have the same protection provided them by the Council Directive on package travel, package holidays and package tours. Thus, whilst the larger internet retailers have developed fairly comprehensive contractual and regulatory frameworks that offer a measure of protection to consumers, the smaller ones have adopted a more precautionary approach, to protect both their customers and their own businesses. Many have therefore adopted more of a 'matchmaking' role, so that their legal agency is limited, but their ability to freely make a much wider range of specific recommendations is enhanced. Consumer confidence in the smaller retailers thus becomes a function of commercial independence and transparency.

One of the fastest growing internet retailers is the UK-based responsibletravel.com, which has grown by 250% each year since its launch in April 2001. It acts as an 'introducer' for suppliers, matching suppliers to customers and also bringing together suppliers and operators.

Every supplier is carefully screened and each product must fulfil specific criteria that include environmental, social and economic policy. This process typically takes 7-10 days. All partners must have the capacity to respond to email enquiries in English within 48 hours. Each partner pays an annual fee, which ranges from nothing for community-led enterprises to more than £5,000 for the largest tour operator, plus commission per converted enquiry, which is never more than 10%. Thus, it generates booking enquiries for its partners, who are then responsible for converting these into sales.

With a strapline inviting visitors to "Find 1000's of holidays to 100's of places not ravaged by mass tourism", the company distinguishes itself from the larger internet retailers, like lastminute.com and Expedia, both of which have huge brand recognition but which lack the capacity to deal so individually with customers. Its objective is to "market responsible tourism as a different and better product than less responsible tourism". Many of responsibletravel.com's "best sellers are wildlife trips, walking holidays ... [and] more adventurous family holidays". Given that such products are nowadays in fact very mainstream, this indicates that the online marketing of sustainable tourism is no longer a niche activity. Consumers of such products however inevitably require a lot of information which only the supplier can furnish.

A customer identifies a product through the company's website or through one of its increasingly numerous newspaper supplements, sends an enquiry to the supplier, who responds with full information and booking details. Such a service could not be offered by large retailers, if only because enabling such communication would put their commission at risk, but it is part of the unique proposition of responsibletravel.com.

Known primarily as a B2C agent, responsibletravel.com is particularly proud of some of its B2B activities: enabling tiny community tourism businesses to engage with leading international tour operators, helping numerous journalists to identify some excellent sustainable tourism products, generating significant PR opportunities and additional business for its members. It has rarely lost a member, because it offers good value for money and has created a community of suppliers and customers that value authenticity and the direct approach.

4.11. Consumer Organisations

Consumer organisations promote the rights and interests of their members, through product testing, policy lobbying and conducting information campaigns. Consumer organisations whose mandate is to protect consumer rights are increasingly showing interest in the sustainability of products as part of their overall quality, and as such are reporting quality and sustainability standards to their members. Consumer organisations' recommendations to their members are powerful marketing tools because of high member loyalty and because their assessments are perceived as independent.

In addition to general consumer organisations, there are 'membership' associations such as automobile and caravanning associations. The Alliance Internationale de Tourisme (AIT) and the Fédération Internationale de l'Automobile (FIA) have more than 42 million members in Europe, and 100 million plus members globally. They are champions of the 'mobile consumer', with the focus of their public policy agenda being sustainable mobility, road safety, consumer protection and testing, environment and tourism. These clubs promote cleaner emissions, reducing road congestion and increasing safety.

Promoting sustainable tourism has to be seen within the remits of both organisations. For automobile clubs this means they are information providers within the mandate of consumer protection. They have enormous media resources and reach with strong brands and reputations. The services these consumer organisations provide to their members include hotel guides, camping and caravanning guides, maps, holiday guide books and route planners amongst others based on the clubs' own inspections, evaluations and assessments which take some sustainable practices into account.

Camping and caravanning associations, in particular, have engaged with a range of environmental actions for their own sites, and setting criteria for other sites. In the UK the Caravan Club has an alliance with the Royal Society for the Protection of Birds as 11% of CC members are members of RSBP. AIT & FIA conduct environmental audits for camping and caravan sites, support for the new European tourist accommodation Eco-label, and the monitoring of European Bathing Water Quality.

The Consumers Union (USA) is considering sustainability certification as the criteria for including tourism suppliers in their travel directory. This is within their organisational remit of providing unbiased product testing and consumer information to protect the interests of consumers.

The Alliance Internationale de Tourisme & Federation Internationale de l'Automobile would consider a policy to increase the coverage of sustainable tourism issues in the magazines of their national member associations within Europe.

The Camping and Caravanning Club (UK) operates over 100 club sites, and is starting to operate franchised sites. With over 400,000 loyal members, the club provides one of the strongest camp site brands.

One of their most recent acquisitions in the Lake District has been renovated to the gold standard in the Cumbria for Excellence 2004 awards in the Caravan Holiday Park category, and was quoted by The Guardian newspaper as possibly the greenest camp site in the UK.

4.12. Analysis

Traditionally governments, inter-governmental organisations and non-governmental organisations have encouraged sustainable tourism by focusing mainly on the supply side of the tourism industry, or on promoting responsible citizenship through consumer education, with the aim of increasing demand. Specific policies should then be designed to support the linkage between sustainable consumers and sustainable tourism products by strengthening the opportunities offered by the various distribution tools.

The four issues used to assess each of the eight distribution channels under consideration are designed to indicate the relative value of each tool. It is generally recommended that policies should be based on the ability to promote change of tourism suppliers that is equitable, with potential for market penetration, a positive cost-benefit analysis, and normalisation or mainstreaming potential. Individual promotion and distribution channels have been analysed against these attributes.

— *Supplier equity:* High/Low - 'High' indicating that this tool/ channel is extremely accessible on fair terms to a wide range of suppliers

— *Market penetration potential:* Strong/Weak - 'Strong' indicating that this tool/channel has significant reach

— *Cost benefit analysis:* Positive/Negative - 'Positive' indicating that the receipts and other business benefits produced by this tool/ channel can reasonably be expected to outweigh any costs associated with participation

— *Normalisation potential:* Strong/Weak - 'Strong' indicating that this tool/channel has the potential to be used to promote and encourage a more sustainable development and environmental management of travel and tourism products

4.12.1. Supplier Equity

Equity, understood as the ability of companies to have the same opportunities to access knowledge, loans, distribution channels, and to promote their products, is the first attribute used to analyse these tools. Public sector intervention in the marketplace has usually been justified on the basis of promoting equal access.

Destination management companies, tourist boards and guidebooks have the highest level of equity in as far as all companies can have the same access to use these channels. Communicating and distributing through tour operators and internet retailers have varied equity because it depends on the ability to set commercial relations with them, and to accept the commissions they charge. Media, travel fairs and certification schemes have low equity, because they require capital investment usually with little guarantee of return, only few companies can be featured, or there are no schemes available.

Training at an early stage is crucial to support product and destination planning. Marketing training will help to set realistic targets, and to create more level playing fields that will make all instruments more equitable. Development plans should be realistic and market the marketable, as part of a plan for sustained and balanced growth.

4.12.2. Market Penetration Potential

Some distribution channels have the potential to make a considerable contribution towards changing the behaviour of the market they target. For all these markets, the greatest potential is to change behaviour in the adventure, ecotourism, nature tourism markets where sustainability is part of the quality of the product both experienced and expected, as the potential market is already sympathetic to the philosophies of sustainable tourism.

DMOs and tourist boards rarely reach the actual markets, although increasingly internet marketing portals are achieving where print publications failed. These are custodians of the destination brand and as such can create interest in a certain destination. Providing an internet sales portal that allows efficient bookings increases the potential for market penetration. Suppliers can achieve considerable market penetration through tour operators, with many examples in the past of over relying on few operators, that subsequently meant. suppliers losing entrepreneurial skills and self-control. However, individual suppliers need to consider working with travel guides as a mid-term investment, as there is no guarantee that they will be featured, and there is a considerable lead time between preparing information and the publication date. The media can generate short-term interest in specific destinations and provide a boost to companies starting with creative, unique concepts. But media has a short self life and cannot be relied on.

Certification has limited potential for market penetration at present because the marketing know-how as well as resources of certification programs are insufficient to reach consumers. The focus should therefore be on business to business marketing and lobbying tour operators that certified products can guarantee sustainability. While progress is being made in this respect, it is too early to say what the potential actually is. Travel fairs have very limited potential for market penetration, particularly business to consumer. Internet retailers also have a high potential for market penetration, although this depends on the type of product and market targeted, and there is often a high commission to pay for internet retailers. "Dynamic packaging" that allows consumers to pick and choose different components of a holiday from the same travel site to form a personalised package.

Companies should think about promoting to the domestic market, and the extension of current products, before trying to attract new "hard-to-reach" international tourists. Donor-funded projects in particular should be realistic about the ability to generate markets from small interventions. Many funded projects cannot be self-financed in the long run through poor understanding of market needs, simply incorporating tourism as a form of income generation for conservation projects without developing the necessary skills, or market-led product planning which sets unachievable expectations.

4.12.3. Cost-benefit Analysis

Cost-effectiveness is the third key issue reviewed here to consider the suitability of different tools. These are considered both from the point of view of government intervention as well as the investment for tourism companies.

DMOs and tourist boards are cost-effective ways for small firms to market themselves, membership costs are usually low for the service received as these organisations receive central funding to contribute to their fixed costs. Most governments undertake economic impact assessments that suggest that public sector investment in marketing functions generates a return on investment into the economy through tourism revenues in the region of 8 to 1. Policy makers are also increasingly being asked to contribute to the running of certification programs, as an extension of their duties in quality assurance. These certification programs need to move towards being self-financing. In the same way, many travel fairs require subsidies and growth is hindered by the potential benefits they can deliver, and by how many fairs one company can attend.

Distribution tools that do not require public financial support include tour operators, guidebooks, and internet retailers. Marketing to tour operators is also a cost-effective method to reach markets. There are directories of outbound operators for most key markets, and the national tourist boards of the destination country should provide the necessary market intelligence to support targeted campaigns. In the same way, marketing to internet retailers is cost-effective if the company can survive with the commissions charged, and if reasonable yield management arrangements are made. Guidebooks are a cost-effective method for unique products with a high chance of being included. But spending too long on a media campaign could be cost ineffective if the product does not have uniqueness. Finally, direct marketing can be cost-effective for specific markets and to capitalise on consumer loyalty.

4.12.4. Normalisation Potential

The last key attribute considered in analysing the suitability of different instruments is their ability to effectively be a tool to move sustainable tourism products from niche to mainstream.

DMOs and tourist boards have a great opportunity to mainstream sustainable tourism, as long as they can manage the process of giving preferential treatment to companies meeting the standards, and to encourage others to work towards them.

Normalisation or mainstreaming potential depends on the ability of these distribution channels to reach niche markets that appreciate sustainable tourism products. In this sense the number of tour operators, internet retailers, guidebooks, travel fairs, travel sections in the media and certification programs either fully or partly dedicated to sustainable tourism is growing fast.

Sustainable tourism, ecotourism, fair trade tourism claims are not regulated, and a good part of the mainstreaming potential comes down to the ability to bring in criteria that are measurable and verifiable, without increasing the cost of the product beyond the customers' willingness to pay.

References

Buhalis, D & Laws, E. (eds). 2001. *Tourism Distribution Channels-Practices, Issues and Transformations*, Continuum Publishing, London.

Carter R & Bedard, F. 2001. *E-Business for Tourism-Practical Guidelines for Tourism Destinations and Business,* WTO Business Council, Madrid.

Carter R & Richer P. 1999. *Marketing Tourism Destination Online*, WTO Business Council, Madrid.

Gupta, S & Bansal, S.P. 2001. *Tourism Towards 21st Century,* Deep and Deep. New Delhi.

Inkpen, G. (1998. *Information Technology for Travel and Tourism*, Addison Wesley Logman, Essex UK.

5

Information Supply in Tourism Management

Operators in tourism management, compared to other management sectors, are confronted with a vast field of complex aims, requiring different plans of action. The special working requirements of the services sector are a result of its business peculiarities. Problems in strategic, and frequently operational planning, are characterised by their complexity, often being intermingled, non-transparent, individualistically dynamic and requiring the achievement of multiple goals.

In order to solve complex problems, decision-makers need to have a factual knowledge of the industry and the methodology used. The wealth of knowledge is drawn from two pools; that obtained from the "storage" of already existing experiences, and by generating knowledge in the respective field. Combining these two pools creates an arena for problem solving.

5.1. Declarative Knowledge

Currently, information gains more and more importance, leading legitimately to the development of a fourth economic sector - the information sector. Information also plays a vital role in tourism for entrepreneurs and managers who spend the whole day involved in information processing. Tourism surveys of national and international market research institutes are published in ever shorter intervals and the level of itemisation of market data increases rapidly. Information collected by these means has indicated data which can be organised into the following groups:

1. Information on markets and environment,
2. Information on customer behaviour,
3. Information on competition in the industry, and
4. Internal information for executive boards.

The first three information groups are predominantly non-discretionary from a manager's point of view as the information can very rarely be directly influenced by an individual company. Information from these groups are similar in nature and scope for most sectors represented in the tourism industry. In the fourth group however, there is a larger scope for variety.

Due to high costs for primary market research many tourism managers abandon market research in general. Even the larger businesses and tourism organisations lack market research departments and employees rarely work exclusively on market research items. This results again in an inconsistent development of marketing aims and strategies, as businesses as often as not grope in the dark for their direction.

In Europe the most frequent or highly recognised of the commissioned tourism studies are either publicly financed, directly by national or local authorities, or indirectly by government agencies. This method of procuring market research, is important and often a condition for its development, as the expensive primary studies cannot be financed by the numerous small or medium-scale businesses. The resulting obligation to pass on information, created by the above mentioned research financing, has lead to a wider search - in regional tourism organisations, and other bodies representing tourism - to find means of successfully sharing and communicating information.

Traditional data resources in tourism market research are reports, records and statistics which may be presented either in printed format or are electronically driven. Computer-based information systems are currently a rarity, but usually can be found either in connection with the official statistical data of a country or a region or international institutions. The information available by this method is rarely used since it ignores the special information requirements of the end-user or is simply inaccessible due to high fees, complicated application procedures or is simply not user friendly.

Market research results are mainly available in print and they can be obtained either in bookshops, online or directly from the author. From the consumer's perspective this way of passing on secondary information has a number of disadvantages:

— Due to the complex design of market research reports the surveyed data is not up to date anymore.

— Data from different sources cannot be easily compared especially if it has been surveyed for different purposes.

— Information contained in reports is often of limited relevance for the particular problem.

— Presentation of data is either not detailed enough, not significant enough, or supplementary information is missing which prevents a faultless interpretation of results.

— Often only very specific data from a more comprehensive study is required and thus the cost-benefit-ratio becomes unattractive.

There is usually an over-abundance of available information leaving managers to cope with determining which is the best source. Often the entrepreneur has to rely on external consultants and market research specialists resulting in additional costs.

5.2. Procedural Knowledge

"The big problem with management science models is that managers practically never used them." More than 20 years ago John Little described the discrepancy between the scientific development of planning instruments, models, level of itemisation and the fact that, when available, the knowledge gathered is rarely put into practice. This is caused by the numerous, often poorly documented assumptions of model architects, which was denoted as model platonism by Hans Albert. He postulated in his article on the Decision Calculus, on-line models with the following features: robustness, ease of control, simplicity, completeness of relevant detail and suitability for communication.

The communication problem is of vital importance in the every day life of managers' daily events. It is still common practice to employ various levels of change rather than continually observe the changes in market share and volume. Many entrepreneurs do not even know terms such as market segmentation or market positioning and they do not regard them as essential. They keep on looking for measures to expand seasonal business but lack knowledge of methods that will measure their success. Corporate planning only takes place if external financing is required and supporting documents have to be submitted to the lender.

The grounds for the poor employment of methodological processes in tourism management can be divided into two groups; technological development and insufficient training. Issues related to the technological development of existing information processing and transmission systems are:

— Data required for the application of tourism models is either not up-to-date or unsuitable.
— Standard software is not able to support the relatively complex tasks in tourism management.
— Specially developed software is too expensive for single tourism businesses.

Issues related to the insufficient training of tourism managers are:

— Managers have little knowledge of existing methods or available data.
— Managers are confronted with various data sources and different results and they do not know how to cope with this situation.
— Managers do not know which data sources and models are suitable.

5.3. Transmission of Market Research Data in the Internet

Due to the vital role of tourism in many countries and regions in Europe a number of programs concerning tourism promotion have been installed. Government and private tourism organisations have been established in order to strengthen a tourism destination. Usually the aim is to increase the added value of a region. The major tasks of these bodies are:

— to provide consumers with information about the destination,
— to coordinate and implement sales promotion measures,

— tourism advertising,
— support in sales and distribution, and
— to coordinate and implement market research projects.

For most of their tasks these tourism promoting bodies provide efficient methods. The actual effect of the last item mentioned has been lost in the past due to inefficient instruments relating to the transmission and utilisation of declarative and procedural knowledge. Now with the development of cheaper hard.

In almost all industries systems are being developed in order to support investment and marketing planning. Also the tourism industry has developed decision support systems and the most important applications are: (1) systems supporting marketing decisions in national tourism organisations, (2) travel counselling systems for shipping clerks, (3) systems supporting regional planning regarding the optimal selection of locations in which to invest (4) systems providing tourism portfolio analyses, (5) simulation tools for forecasting travel behaviour in certain regions. In Austria in 1982 the Austrian Society of Applied Research in Tourism (ASART) started a project aiming at the development of a marketing information system for the national tourism organisation in Austria. The first version of the tourism marketing information system (TourMIS) consisted of a database installed in a host system of the Scientific Computer Center Vienna and an optimisation programme for the advertising budget of the Austrian National Tourist Office.

5.4. Tourism Marketing Information System

The major aim of TourMIS is an optimal information supply and decision support for the tourism industry. The first step is to provide on-line tourism survey data, as well as evaluation programmes to transform data into precious management information. Tour-MIS predominantly comprises:

1. A database containing tourism market research data
2. Various program modules converting acknowledged methods/ models into simple surfaces, and
3. Various administrative programmes which assist the maintenance of the database and track and control the information search behaviour of users.

The internet supports the transport and presentation of animated and unanimated pictures, sound and video recordings and text and numerical data and is expandable. A high performance SQL-database and a functionally designed user interface for TourMIS based on hypertext and Perl permits the development of interactive applications. The programme modules contained in the method-base are developed according to the specific requirements of tourism managers. The internet offers a number of advantages against the old PC-solution. Since changes in the database have immediate world-wide effect the speed of information transmission can be reduced to the availability of the information source. Anybody provided with access to the internet and entitled to use TourMIS may access data and information, make calculations or simulations send or receive data .

5.4.1. Conditions for the Use of the System

In the beginning TourMIS was provided with strict access control and used to be only accessible to certain users. In this respect the application did differ from traditional internet offers. However, the present concept is also not an Intranet. Unlike the Intranet which supports internal information management systems TourMIS is not owned by a certain organisation but is open to all authorised tourism organisations, societies, tourism consultants, companies, tourism training centres, pressure groups, etc. in Austria and abroad. Since 2000 this initiative has provided the Austrian tourism industry with free access to overall data and functions of TourMIS. The necessary hardware resources are situated at the Institute for Tourism and Leisure Studies at the University of Economics and Business Administration in Vienna where a major part of the necessary maintenance work is carried out.

5.4.2. TourMIS Database

In the beginning TourMIS contained data that was strongly influenced by the internal interests of its commissioner, the Austrian National Tourist Office. In this respect international tourism statistical data, empirical tourism studies and economic indicators for the most important markets of origin for the Austrian tourism industry have been collected in TourMIS. The PC-version, developed in the early nineties, contained more than 10,000 time series.

Over the years the database has continually expanded. Due to the increasing importance of overseas markets further information has been required. Unequal needs of provincial tourism organisations led to additional statistics regarding the federal provinces and Vienna, being city and federal province at the same time, acquired an exceptional position. Furfhermore data on the Austrian and international city tourism has been added. This information was collected at the branch offices of the Austrian National Tourist Office, transmitted by fax and data was entered manually into the marketing information system in order to be available to users. Later based on international co-operation the first online maintenance agreements with local tourism organisations were initiated. Besides the basic information search functions the method-base has also been continually upgraded. In this respect the system more and more meets the requirements of an efficient decision support tool. In the next paragraphs the most important data sources and the facilities for analysis and reporting are discussed.

(i) National tourism statistics Austria

One of the first data sources which was installed in TourMIS was the official tourism statistics in Austria. Data generated from the registration with accommodation suppliers is one of the fundamental supports of the official inbound tourism statistics in Austria. Accommodation statistics are divided into two different kinds of survey: the accommodation for inbound travel and the accommodation capacity.

The data on arrivals and overnights are surveyed for 50 generating countries related to 13 different accommodation types and 1,600 municipalities on a monthly basis. Thus the official travel survey offers 25 million data points per annum which can be transformed into precious information for tourism managers. From the data material important information on tourism development, trends in markets of origin and accommodation types, evaluation of the competing situation can be derived.

TourMIS presently offers official tourism statistics only at the provincial basis which nevertheless requires maintenance work of 11,700 data sets per month. The necessary data transfer from the host system of Statistik Austria (ISIS) to TourMIS takes place automatically each time after the arrival of new data segments and in accordance with various maintenance routines.

The information supply of TourMIS users takes place by means of predefined tables and reports created for the user in real time operations. Table formats conform to the data material. The design of a single table or a single report is of vital importance. The content and design of tables or reports plays an important role in the user's perception of the system's usefulness and usability. Therefore, all available TourMIS tables and reports are created in close collaboration with the tourism industry. The query results are presented in the form of tables, texts and graphics or in a data format offering the chance for further processing with another standard software product. The major advantages of TourMIS compared to the official database supply offered by Statistik Austria are:

— no particular database knowledge is required by the user,
— the data transformations and calculations implemented in the method-base of TourMIS allow for adequate problem reporting, and
— the user interface refers to a familiar technical terminology.

For example that Carinthia could defend its position regarding the three most important markets shown in the increase of market shares, despite the fact that Carinthia experienced a severe loss in bed-nights. On the other hand an apparent success regarding the increased demand of American guests has to be put into perspective since the other federal provinces outperformed Carinthia in this segment. Due to the comparative analysis and a simple and informative presentation of the statistics the data material is upgraded.

This analysis may be used for historical or current data, for each Austrian province, based either on arrivals or bednights for each of the 13 different accommodation types. Therefore there are at the end of a season 270 new tables available for interpretation. Due to the refinancing interests of data collection authorities and the lack of financial resources in the tourism industry, however, the data analysis for smaller tourism regions or report communities has been prevented in the past. This factor must be regretted since it can be assumed that the evaluation of key success factors in tourism marketing will significantly improve when they are measured in smaller regional units. Also tourism managers, especially those operating on a regional level, usually have only very little influence in the organisation of nationwide surveys. Therefore, many of the statistical series are based on administrative regions that are not always congruent with actual regional use and by tourists and subsequent flows.

5.4.2.1. Number of visitations in Austrian attractions

The collection of statistical data on leisure-time activities and especially the measurement of visitor arrivals in attractions is a rather complex project. It is rarely executed internationally on a systematic or continuous basis. The major problems lie in the delimitation of the study object and the methods of measurement. Since the early 90's the Austrian National Tourist Office has collected and distributed information on the visitation numbers in Austrian attractions.

Since 2001 this maintenance procedure is carried out online in TourMIS. Here the market research specialists at the respective provincial tourism organisations enter their information into the system. Due to the newness of the database the reporting facilities are still very limited.

5.4.2.2. Austrian guest Survey

Since 1988 alternating each third year a comprehensive visitor survey in Austria has been carried out. The Austrian Guest Survey is one of the most important sources of information in tourism market research. The Austrian Guest Survey is financed and coordinated by a consortium of authorities responsible for tourism promotion in Austria the Chamber of Commerce and the Federal Ministry for Economic Affairs and Labour. Since the Austrian Guest Survey is a primary study it presents some features which complicate the information diffusion in TourMIS compared to the above mentioned secondary data sources. The main reasons for these additional difficulties are:

(1) the much wider scope of the study,

(2) the required data analyses are more demanding, and

(3) interpretation possibilities are limited by the sample size and characteristics.

The Austrian Guest Survey has more than 200 features which are partially modified for each survey. Considering the scope of the study and that only descriptive evaluation is possible the Austrian Guest Survey offers more than 1 million findings per survey. Traditional forms of report cover just a small part of the real investigation and evaluation potential. Thus important questions managers would raise remain unanswered although theoretically the answers exist.

Data of primary analyses are available unprocessed. Regarding the Austrian Guest Survey there are 10,000 interviews per survey, all of the features being available in quantitative form. However, information processing requires the application of analytical methods ranging from calculating simple mean values to complicated data mining procedures. The necessary methodological knowledge has to be obtained from statistics experts who create costs which, in most cases, cannot be covered by the tourism industry. Contrary to a census, as found in official statistics, sample surveys do not integrate all elements of the whole picture into the study. The major aim in statistics is to draw reliable conclusions regarding to the totality from a limited number of elements.

To know whether a study result may be regarded reliable requires expert know-how. On the other hand, sometimes, statisticians have not enough technical knowledge to evaluate the fault tolerance for certain problems in the tourism industry. Thus information processing by means of electronic media becomes very interesting for primary surveys. The challenge is to combine expert know-how from two different fields: statistics and tourism. The aim is to create an arena for practitioners allowing them to access all possible evaluations concerning a data item, without considering the necessary procedures of analysis. Depending on the level of measurement of the features selected by the user the appropriate evaluation method is applied.

In addition the user may select only a certain part of the overall data set for evaluation. In order to prevent interpretation errors due to unreliability of results, those values based on a small sample are only indicated after informing the user about the problem.

The analysis takes place in real time. TourMIS provides the facilities to evaluate more than one survey, at the same time offering two alternatives: longitudinal and cross section analyses. Query support is provided by offering only variables surveyed unmodified over the overall selected period of time. The latter application increases the sample size which makes answers to detailed questions possible . This function permits for example reliable results about the share of side expenses of Italian guests in the federal province of Salzburg during a particular season.

Table 1. Automatic Selection of Analysing Methods

Measurement	*Measurement*		
	Not specified	*Nominal*	*Metric*
Metric	descriptive statistics	mean value comparison	
Nominal	frequency	cross tabulation	
Nominal multiple response question	multiple response—	multiple response – frequency cross tabulation	mean value comparison

5.4.2.3. Comparison of hotel and restaurant groups

The database supports regional planners and tourism managers in their decisions as well as managers in the hospitality industry. The results of the past 10 years of a project which has been executed by the Austrian Society of Applied Research in Tourism and commissioned by the Austrian Hotel and Restaurant Association situated within the Austrian Federal Chamber of Commerce are presented in TourMIS. In this project operating data and annual financial statements for hotels and restaurants in Austria are compared on an annual basis. In connection with the design and evaluation of continually repeated surveys a number of new approaches for the diagnosis and comparison of industry groups are developed. TourMIS presently provides the following applications:

— Industry information for more than 1,300 hotels and restaurants per year since 1991.

— Various functions supporting key ratio analyses in the hotel and restaurant industry.

— The chance for hotel and restaurant managers to participate online in the most significant hotel and restaurant panel survey in Austria.

Information about more than 50 different key ratios is provided in the form of arithmetic mean and median values for 30 distinguished industry groups. Within the industry groups additional evaluations for businesses of excellent profitability are available. For the hotel and restaurant panel database TourMIS users are provided with the following query and analysing facilities:

— Evaluation of a key ratio for all industry groups referring to a certain year.

— Comparison of all key ratios for a particular industry group.

— Development of a key ratio uncovering the main industry developments.

— Benchmarking analysis for a particular hotel or restaurant (only provided when managers are actively participating in the study).

The quality of information based on the results of the survey is strongly influenced by the number of participating businesses. Due to the chance for interaction in the internet the first results may be obtained straight after entering business data. TourMIS offers a number of plausibility controls during data entry and records data in a second, temporary database. At regular intervals experts determine which records are qualified to be stored in the general database.

5.4.2.4. International tourism statistics

Several international umbrella organisations have decided to collect tourism statistics from various countries and to observe the economic development of tourism (WTO, WTTC, OECD, Eurostat). The availability of this data is unfortunately restricted and publications are, due to complicated data collection procedures, obsolete and access to data is relatively expensive. The European Travel Commission (ETC), the umbrella organisation of national tourism organisations, and European Cities Tourism (ECT), the umbrella organisation of European city tourism organisations, have set themselves the target of representing the interests of tourism practitioners. Both organisations have taken advantage of Tour-MIS for some years now in order to collect official statistics of their members. Once a year market research experts collect bednight and arrival data of national and cities' tourism organisations broken down into the major markets of origin as well as into the number of accommodation suppliers and beds in their region.

Due to differing definitions and survey methods applied by the various countries and cities the collected data material is not readily available or comparable. Official statistics are only of limited use for the calculation of market volumes and market shares.

As with the decision 90/665/EEC of December 1990 of the European Council a milestone has been laid down regarding the development of a community methodological framework of the compilation of Community tourism statistics. Since 1997 the development of an information system for tourism statistics has been in progress. But experience with TourMIS shows that worthwhile discussions on diverse survey methods, definitions and harmonising methods depend on the number of participants. Participation is necessary in order to gain acceptance for new directives and changes.

5.5. Analysis of the User Behaviour of Tour MIS

How do we know that we have successfully implemented a system? Researchers have not really agreed on an indicator for successful implementation. One appealing approach is a cost-benefit study. In this evaluation, one totals the costs of developing a system and compares them with the benefits resulting form the system. In theory, this sounds like a good indicator of success, but in practice it is difficult to provide meaningful estimates. Obtaining the cost side of the ratio is not too much of a problem if adequate records are kept during the development of the system. Many transactions systems have resulted in increased productivity in processing paperwork without a proportional increase in cost. Operational control systems, such as those used to control inventories in large hotels and restaurants, may reduce inventory balances, saving storage and investment costs while maintaining existing service levels.

For systems that aid a decision maker, it is much more difficult to estimate the benefits. For a marketing information system, like TourMIS, use of the system is voluntary. A manager or other user receives a report but does not have to use the information on it or even read the report. In particular systems that provide on-line retrieval of information from a database can be classified as voluntary since the use of such a system is frequently at the discretion of the user. In this case the economic or personal success of its users is indirectly measured by the frequency of usage. Several authors have shown that the frequency of usage is determined by the perceived usefulness and the ease of use.

References

Phillips, P.A. and Moutinho, L. 1998. *Strategic Planning Systems in Hospitality and Tourism*. CABI: Wallingford.

Rita, P. 1993. *A Knowledge-Based System for Promotion Budget Allocation by National Tourism Organizations*. Doctoral thesis, University of Wales, College of Cardiff.

Sheldon, P. 1997. *Tourism Information Technology*. CABI: Wallingford.

Werthner, H. and Klein, S. 1999. *Information Technology and Tourism – A Challenging Relationship*. Springer: Wien-New York.

6

Investing in Ecotourism

The word "ecotourism" is generally attributed to Hector Ceballos-Lascurain, a Mexican architect, environmentalist and international ecotourism consultant, who coined the word in the July 1983. Ecotourism as an accepted and defined concept, however, with a set of principles and practices, really only started to emerge in the early 1990s, through a series of workshops and meetings, primarily driven by academics and NGOs. There is no one definition of ecotourism, but rather a generally agreed upon framework of principles. The United Nations designated 2002 as the International Year of Ecotourism (IYE) and the main document produced from that period, the Quebec Declaration on Ecotourism, lists the primary elements of ecotourism as follows:

- Ecotourism contributes actively to the conservation of natural and cultural heritage;
- includes local and indigenous communities in its planning, development and operation and contributes to their well-being;
- interprets the natural and cultural heritage of the destination for visitors and
- lends itself better to independent travellers and organised tours of small groups.

Ecotourism as the term is applied and understood today is a development concept, a social movement, a philosophy and an industry or business. In general the more social and developmental aspects of ecotourism have been emphasized over its function as a business enterprise, which is arguably one reason for the high rate of financial failure of ecotourism enterprises, and the erosion of ecotourism's ability to meet its social and environmental objectives.

Sustainable tourism is a much broader concept, and is part of the global sustainability movement that gained ground after the 1992 Rio Earth Summit on sustainable development. At one end of the spectrum, sustainable tourism seeks to make the mass tourism industry more sustainable, while at the other, it is essentially ecotourism.

6.1. Community-based Ecotourism

An emerging new trend within ecotourism is that of "community based ecotourism". It is the new buzzword that peppers the reports of donor agencies and NGOs and pervades the current research being undertaken in ecotourism. It is also a highly visible, and often contentious, aspect to international meetings.

Community based ecotourism is a "form of ecotourism where the local community has substantial control over, and involvement in, its development and management, and a major proportion of the benefits remain with the community.

This focus naturally lends itself to the agendas of the development agencies, although it is not being ignored by the private sector, and Lash identifies two models for community based ecotourism development with donor funds.

a) Conservation/NGO Model: Project money from an international biodiversity funder, e.g. GEF, is transferred either a) to an international conservation NGO who then contracts a national conservation NGO, or b) directly to a national conservation NGO.

b) Government Agency/Industry Association Model: Project money, typically in the form of the loan, originates from an international development funder e.g. the World Bank, who then partners with a national tourism organisation (NTO).

The community based approach to ecotourism leads to questions about whether or not community ownership necessarily leads to greater wealth for the community than private sector ownership, where the local community may be employees of an ecotourism business, or has some other tangible economic stake in the project. There are emergent models of tripartite partnerships between a community, the public sector and private businesses but by and large community based ecotourism projects being funded by the development agencies and international NGOs do not include a private sector partner. This has severe implications for the success of the project as the targeted communities in developing countries typically lack the resources and the skills to set-up and operate a business by themselves. Community based ecotourism projects are therefore typically characterised by outside consultants developing feasibility and market studies, weak linkages to the market, and extensive workshops and training programs. Compounding this is the observation that "small community facilities are less adept at providing consistent quality of service" and that, as Halpenny observes: donors, NGOs and the private sector alike have tendency to think of "the community" as homogenous, whereas in reality there are often very different, and competing, agendas within any one community.

Les Carlisle of CC Africa, one of Southern Africa's largest and most successful ecotourism operations, states that CC Africa has very often found that existing community structures do not actually represent the community. The existing structures may be patriarchal, traditional and conservative, and the ecotourism developer must be prepared to set up new, more inclusive and representative structures. It is, he argues, critically important to success of the venture that the right beneficiaries in the community are identified. Developing these structures and the support of the community takes time, it is a "process" rather than an "event": consultants cannot be brought in to conduct workshops with the community, then leave and be expected to have created any meaningful change or provided any realistic advice.

In a telling indictment of all that can go wrong with community based ecotourism development, Megan Epler Wood cites the case the Ju/'hoansi people of Namibia, as documented in Kalahari Family, a film series about the community and their interaction with international aid donors seeking to establish a reserve and ecotourism enterprise. The film is a "...shocking indictment of the international development workers who seek to develop a nature reserve on land without truly listening to needs and wants...after the five year project is over, and dozens of consultants have come and gone, John Marshal returns to find empty buildings and the Ju/'hoansi worse off then before the project arrived".

In cases like this, the resulting resentment from local communities at their lack of power, inability to influence decisions and lack of access to capital, can lead them to undermine the very projects that purportedly seek to improve their welfare. Agi Kiss from the World Bank underscores this problem, stating that too often donors and NGOs have sought to impose a western minded view of what land use is appropriate on a community.

She argues that if a local community wants to use the land for some use other than conservation, then no matter what payments and legal systems you have in place in order to prevent that, they will. She argues that donors and NGOs must give the community a rational interest to conserve the land: i.e. they must either match what a community earns from its current land usage, or let them use it. And in this instance, direct incentives - payments or transfers to a community - work better than indirect incentives like ecotourism. And while this may lead to communities threatening to degrade or destroy land that has biodiversity value unless they are paid not to, Kiss states that " a community is entitled to destroy its land, if that's what they want to do; it is their land".

The assumption by the countries of the North that communities in the South will sacrifice their land and environment for economic development and therefore need intervention and financial assistance to prevent this from happening is not reflective of the attitudes of many communities, however. Research has shown that that local communities who live off the land are sensitive to issues of conservation and sustainability and are resentful at the implication that they are not, and that they should therefore be kept in a state of under-development in order to salve the consciences of the North for its pattern of development.

6.2. Scale of Ecotourism

Much of the initial enthusiasm and optimism for ecotourism as the tourism of the future, bringing great social, environmental and economics benefits, has been tempered by the relatively lackluster achievements to date. Post 2001, "ecotourism development seems a risky bet for struggling communities", and there is a sense that a more diversified development strategy and more effective methodologies need to be developed. "The benefits of ecotourism for conservation and development are still very limited globally. The main challenge is to scale it up while keeping its objectives close to heart". NGOs and donors have come to favor smaller scale projects - in the case of ecolodges this would be less than 20 rooms, while the private sector typically favours larger scale projects - for ecolodges, either multiple small ecolodges in an area or larger ecolodges. Neither model is more correct than the either and the general belief that smaller facilities lead to fewer negative environmental impact is open to debate.

Eugenio Yunis of the World Tourism Organisation states that "Ecotourism companies and operations...should continue to be [small] if benefits are to remain with local communities and revert to conservation purposes. Indeed, the sustainable growth of ecotourism should be based on the replication of good practices in more and more territories rather than on aggregating existing businesses or expanding their size". Yet, it is precisely the small, fragmented and dispersed nature of ecotourism that is, to many, one of its major hurdles to becoming a true force in the market.

As described by Tony Heher, the scale of ecotourism development and investment faces a conundrum. The "lumpy" nature of infrastructure investment, together with the environmental and marketing concerns, leads to two minima that apply to the returns and two maxima to the investments which can be made in ecotourism. Ecotourism must achieve a certain minimum return in order for it to have a meaningful social impact and to justify the infrastructure cost. But its returns are capped by the level of market demand, perceived risk and the environmental and social carrying capacity of the area. This leads to the situation where ecotourism needs to be big enough to achieve the necessary returns on investment, and small enough not to become unsustainable, either environmentally or socially. It also leads to incompatible approaches by the private sector and the donor community: the private sector's approach that "maximum use needs to be made of available resources that is consistent with sustainability and market demand ...[is] in stark contrast with the traditional approach to tourism in conservation areas where the approach is more likely to be the minimum use that can be made short of total exclusion".

This problem is aggravated by differing perceptions between donors and the private sector as to what the actual environmental benefits and impacts of ecotourism development are. That ecotourism leads to conservation is still open to debate, and indeed the IFC/GEF Small and Medium Enterprise Program has just commissioned a study to assess the conservation and biodiversity footprints of ecolodges.

6.2.1. Market Demand

One final aspect of ecotourism that must be considered when evaluating the work of the donors and the private sector in developing ecotourism is how well project proposals research and assess the market demand for the product.

In the early days of the emergence of ecotourism it was generally belived that the potential market for products was growing rapidly. Time has proved that the "green marketplace" market is smaller still and more fragmented and demanding than many at first believed . The result of this gap between expectation and reality and the absence of market research about the size and characteristics of the market, has been a high rate failure of ecotourism projects – whether supported by donors or developed privately. "The management of green commerce has proven to be unwieldy for the NGO community. In the case of ecotourism, many enterprises, including some with major foundation and donor investment, failed because the green market did not respond as expected". We are going through the same process with community-based ecotourism. It is being driven by the NGO and donor community, but there is little or no data about the size and characteristics of demand for this type of product.

6.3. Assistance from Donors and Aid Agencies

The phenomenon of donor funding of development in third world countries is closely associated with the end of colonialism. As colonial powers withdrew from their territories in the 1950s and 1960s, so they "for both altruistic and selfish reasons [began] sending investment and expertise to developed countries to encourage economic growth, community development and conservation of both cultural and natural heritage". By 1980, when the World Bank closed its tourism department, "the multilateral institutions had to write-off approximately $10-$12 billion in poor tourism investments. Many of the investments were in luxury hotels and did not fit well with the institutions' mission of poverty alleviation".

Throughout the rest of the 1980s and the early 1990s, the negative image of donors' engagement with mass tourism, combined with the poor financial returns the projects had achieved, resulted in very few tourism projects being funded. With the rise of the sustainability movement in the 1990s, and the emergence of sustainable tourism models as legitimate development strategies, donors became more active in the sector again. In sustainable tourism and ecotourism, donors have a development model that is more politically correct, socially responsible and environmentally sensitive. While the Inter-American Development Bank (IADB) and some EU countries funded tourism projects throughout the 1990s, it was only towards the end of the 1990s that large donors like the World Bank started funding tourism projects again. Since 2001, donor financing has declined considerably. While the results of sustainable and ecotourism have continued to be disappointing, donors and NGOs still see it as one the better options for development.

The rapid rise of donor support for sustainable tourism has not been without its problems. Firstly, the majority of donor organisations "lack a comprehensive and at the same time specific and implementation-oriented concept for the promotion of sustainable tourism". That this is so is primarily because of the failure of most donors to categorise tourism as a separate development area.

The German development organisation, Deutsche Gesellschaft für Technische Zusammenarbeit or GTZ, for instance, had almost entirely withdrawn from all activity in tourism during the 1980s. When it realised during the 1990s that, as tourism touched on so many of the sectors in which it was engaged, it must start to deal with tourism again, this engagement was "fragmentary, uncoordinated and unprofessional" and lead to "marginal" activities that rarely yielded significant benefits.

Secondly, there is a lack of information about the nature of donor involvement in the sector. Part of the problem is that donors are still reluctant specifically to identify projects as being related to tourism development as they are typically smaller components of larger projects dealing with biodiversity conservation, rural development, employment generation etc.

Seeking to rectify this, George Washington University's International Institute of Tourism Studies has initiated a database of donor projects in the tourism sector in order to try and bring greater order and clarity to work of the development agencies. Dubbed DANTE, the Development Assistance Network for Tourism Enhancement, the head of project writes that "There is a paucity of information concerning appropriate engagement levels and policy guidance for development assistance in efforts to enhance tourism revenues for developing economies.

There are difficulties in balancing the public sector role while maintaining a competitive private sector environment; also in balancing community needs and dealing with social issues. So far the database has recorded 370 ongoing projects from over 20 donors, with a total value of $9.44 billion for the period 2001-2010. Donor engagement is therefore substantial, and is indeed the single most important source of funding for the sector as whole.

Donor and NGO engagement is currently undergoing another shift, from site and infrastructure specific interventions and investments towards projects that are more supportive and focused on developing policies and capacities. This shift is a function of both the resource intense nature and the negative history of specific interventions. The size of assistance packages is also becoming in smaller. This is more in keeping with the principles of supporting sustainable tourism and promoting the development of small and medium enterprises, but is primarily a result of financial pressures on donors.

6.3.1. Development Institutions and Assistance

There are five main sources of development funding for ecotourism projects: bilateral donors, multilateral donors and development banks, corporate philanthropy, big international NGOs (BINGOs) and international foundations.

Bilateral assistance is the transfer of funds and technical assistance from one country or organisation to another. Donors are typically the development arms of westerns countries' State Departments, e.g. the US Agency for International Development (USAID). Recipients can be either other international organisations operating in the recipient country the country's government or governmental institutions, or national non-governmental organisations (NGOs).

Multilateral assistance is the transfer of funds and technical assistance from international bodies like the World Bank and InterAmerican Development Bank to developing countries. The recipients are either governments or partner international or national NGOs. Multilateral donors are focused largely on loans, while some bilateral donors still offer grants.

Private foundations and "big international NGOs" have also become supporters of eco- and sustainable tourism. Foundations include the Ford Foundation, MacArthur Foundation, Rockefeller Foundation and some of Getty family trusts.

The most active player in sustainable tourism currently, with the largest commitment of funds to the sector, is the World Bank Group, including both the International Bank for Reconstruction and Development and the International Finance Corporation (IFC), through its Global Environment Facility (GEF) small and medium enterprise program. The United Nations Development Program (UNDP), the Inter-American Development Bank (IADB) and USAID are the next most active donors.

6.3.2. Goals of Development Agencies and NGOs

In 2002, a UNDP survey of 55 development agencies found that while private investments are driven by economic incentives, donor interventions in tourism are motivated by longer-term development objectives, including alternative local income, natural resource management, community participation, employment generation and coastal zone management.

Most development agencies link ecotourism with biodiversity conservation and poverty reduction but there were few strict criteria and evaluation procedures. Investment decisions are therefore based primarily on developmental and environmental objectives. While a more detailed discussion of the objectives, policies and projects of some donors is presented in the case studies, the range of policy and objectives are represented by the Canadian, Dutch, British and German agencies. CIDA, the Canadian International Development Agency, does not undertake tourism projects. In comparison DFID, the British Department for International Development, has published an enthusiastic paper about the possibilities of tourism to aid economic development. It has taken an active position on tourism in development policy, and has arranged conferences and meetings in order to try bring a sharper focus to its work in the sector, which is embedded within DFID's main goal, as laid out in the 1997 White Paper 'Eliminating World Poverty: A Challenge for the 21st Century', to reduce world poverty by half by 2015.

The Dutch and Germans have taken more of a middle ground. The Dutch have a strong emphasis on social mobilisation and local governance and tend to focus on the rural poor – they are working in the tourism sector primarily because recipient countries ask for these kinds of projects, rather than because there is a firm belief within Dutch development agencies that tourism is a better or more appropriate vehicle with which to pursue economic development.

The current Dutch focus is on capacity building and strengthening organisations involved in tourism. Tourism per se is not a focus area of the German development organisation, Deutsche Gesellschaft für Technische Zusammenarbeit or GTZ, but the GTZ does see it as an important element in implementing its conservation and development objectives in rural areas. The GTZ has published one of the better handbooks on how to assess and evaluate tourism projects, which lays out a comprehensive framework for assessing project proposals and advocates a model where donors support the development of infrastructure, leaving the private sector to develop actual tourism operations.

Many of the bigger multilateral agencies also have specific programs targeted at small, medium and micro enterprises (SME), with the aim of developing entrepreneurship and businesses at a very grassroots level. In this case, somewhat more financial analysis is undertaken, but the emphasis is typically still on conservation and poverty reduction. For instance the UNDP/GEF Small Grants Program channels funds to NGOs and community based organisations (CBOs) in developing countries who are engaged with grassroots initiatives to conserve and restore the environment and increase standards of living and income levels.

Similarly, the IFC/GEF Small and Medium Enterprise Program's objective is to develop a significant number of commercially viable small and medium scale enterprises producing global environmental benefits. The bank only makes a profit on loans greater than $10 million and most ecotourism projects are smaller than that.

The IFC's Environmental Projects Unit and the GEF fund, however, disregard processing costs and are able to make much smaller loans. The IFC/GEF SME program is now fully committed and the IFC is in the process of setting up a new fund, the "Environmental Business Finance Program" which will "aim to address the market failures that cause SMEs to have limited or no access to finance through the introduction of innovative financing mechanism, capacity building and replication of proven business models, technologies and approaches".

In comparison to the development agencies, the international NGO community is far more focused on conservation than development. Many of them are extremely well funded and are key players in international conservation policy and activities. Using private donations, the NGOs are less accountable to a public audience than government development agencies, which use taxpayers money, and their involvement in conservation and ecotourism has been strongly criticised.

This is perhaps an overstatement of the situation and glosses over the very real positive impacts NGOs have been able to achieve using ecotourism. But it does capture the deep sense of ire and frustration that it would be wrong to ignore, and which has profound implications for the viability and sustainability of NGOs backing and funding ecotourism development. It is also an oversimplification to assume that there is "vast amount of money" available to ecotourism – there is not. Reading through conference proceedings on ecotourism financing like that of Planeta , there are many reports from participants about how difficult it is to get money for viable projects.

Both donors and NGOs typically have substantial community development objectives in their projects. For the donors, this is partly as a result of the political pressure which the NGOs have brought to bear on them, and partly because donor money cannot be mixed with commercial business enterprises as it is hard to justify this kind of assistance to taxpayers. There is an uneasy tension between, on the one hand, responding to unreasonable demands and expectations that donors and NGOs should provide development assistance and should be in the business of ecotourism development, and on the other hand with concerns about donors and NGOs "buying-off" communities, forcing a western conservation agenda on them and denying them the ability to develop their economies like the developed countries did. One of the early initiatives to involve local communities in tourism development was in 1986 by the Annapurna Conservation Area in Nepal. "Hundreds of such projects have received support from environmental NGO's, the impacts of this global effort have been mixed and the overall result is still being debated". This has led the World Wildlife Fund International to publish guidelines for community based ecotourism, saying that "many small-scale community based initiatives have been set up which have failed owing to a lack of market assessment, organisation, quality and promotion".

These failed project have resulted in some angry and disappointed communities. A recent example was evident at the World Parks Congress which took place in Durban, South Africa in September 2003.This is an example of Epler Wood's observation of how the "the angry representatives of the disenfranchised increasingly disengage and make grandiloquent statements" which only makes a solution to the problems of community based ecotourism that much harder to find.

6.3.3. Role of Consultants

A key characteristic of donor and NGO involvement in ecotourism projects is the use of "expert consultants". Most bilateral donor agencies require that these consultants are citizens of the funding country, while the multilateral agencies and NGOs are typically more open to sourcing consultants from within the country receiving assistance or another developing country which might have consultants with more relevant backgrounds and experience. The World Bank, for instance, does not tend to bring in as many foreign consultants to do field and/or ground work as the EU, as it states that it wants to build local capacity. In contrast, the EU prefers to retain greater control of the project and so sources consultants from EU member states.

The development industry is something of a consultant's bandwagon. There is a small number of highly reputable, sought after consultants, followed by legions of others who present themselves as experts but who have very little real relevant experience and training in order to do the work. They typically have biology and environmental degrees, and very few have any hospitality, business or financial experience. These consultants have their "blueprint, formulaic solution" for ecotourism development which they then apply to every country to which they are assigned. Some describe the process as one of massaging the egos of the development officials. Certainly if consultants want to win a particular contract they need to know about the presence of the project in the proposal pipeline long before the request for proposals is issued by the funding agency.

The result of this process is that much of the work done by the "experts" is sub-standard and does not take into account local constraints and realities. At best the consultants raise unrealistic expectations and at worst they leave behind failed projects, frustration and resentment, worsening the environmental and economic situation that caused the project in the first place and making any subsequent work even harder to implement successfully. However the idea was a political hot potato that no-one wanted to pick up, as this would compromise the ability of the donor agencies to maintain their own procurement policies, which some have described as "subsidised employment".

REFERNCES

Bar kin, D. 2002. *Eco tourism for sustainable regional development*. Current Issues in Tourism. pp. 5(3–4):245–253.

Vivanco, L. 2002. *Ecotourism, Paradise lost - A Thai case study*. The Ecologist. pp. 32(2):28–30.

Isaacs, J.C. 2000. *The limited potential of ecotourism to contribute to wildlife conservation*. The Ecologist. pp. 28(1):61–69.

7

Accounting Systems for Tourism

Within the globalised economic and business environment, the assessment of accounting systems has become a crucial process for researchers. Accounting throughout history industry has undergone a drastic change. As a branch of economics, accounting provides information about a firm and its transactions to facilitate resource allocation decisions by users of that information. Via an extended literature review, researchers have attempted to approach theoretically accounting's catalytic contribution to the tourism business environment. However, a review of the hospitality literature revealed a paucity of academic research to assess the connection between accounting for tourism and its applications within the last five years.

Accounting interest and approaches have expanded in recent years. Accounting history is worth studying since it puts contemporary accounting into perspective and may easily give us an account of all the information collected in the past which could provide solutions to the problems of the present. It is worth teaching as part of the overall cultural formation of future accountants, in particular to stress that "presently acceptable practices of accounting have not been immutable over the decades and centuries of environmental change". The key role of accounting is to provide information for economic decision making in support of the current political paradigm of economic growth and development. Solomons describes accounting as being like a telephone – a neutral medium that promotes the exchange of information between the enterprise and the user; and while it is not an actor in the exchange, it is important that accounting measures be representationally faithful.

Miller and Napier argue that like any social phenomenon, accounting presents a "historically and geographically localised result", but that does not imply that accounting should be viewed in isolation at a particular point of space or time. Just as international accounting aims to situate local accounting practices of today within a comparative framework across space, so country-based histories of accounting attempt the same process across time. However, its expansion can assist in generating "a focus on examining and explaining cross-national differences in accounting development".

Accounting history literature witnessed a vast growth during the recent years. This growth has manifested itself not just in the number of publications but in the topics examined, research approaches adopted, and range of theoretical perspectives applied to the study of accounting through its history. Accounting concepts, techniques and institutions have been diffused through both space and time. Based on an admittedly limited population of English language papers appearing from 1996 to 1999 in the specialist accounting history journals, Carnegie and Potter concluded that their analysis indicates "the existence of a relatively insular international accounting history research community dominated by a small number of institutions and authors". Carnegie and Potter contended that accounting history authors seldom engage in cross-border collaborative research and display a limited tendency to venture beyond core themes and the modern period. Furthermore, Edwards broader review of the accounting history literature identified concerns about areas of fading interest, publication media and the dissemination of research findings.

7.1. Theoretical Background

Tourism industry is of great importance for the world economy today. It is one of the largest single employers and in many countries it is the largest services exporting sector, making an outstanding contribution to the balance of payments. Tourism industry has many of the characteristics of a competitive market:

— there are few barriers to enter

— it is a truly global market with few unnatural barriers to trade;

— there is a large number of firms and

— prices are set on the basis of market expectations.

A lot of researchers have tried to define the concept of tourism. According to Monique Dacharry, tourism owes to be delimited in its historical prospect. Years later, Kaspar defines tourism as the total of relations and events that arise from the travel and the eve of individuals, when the place of stay is neither the initial and permanent residence nor the usual place of work.

Nowadays, tourism organisations are becoming truly international and the issues they face equally universal. In "the age of service competition" that is depicted by international hospitality and tourism, the customer reigns supreme. Such is the power of customers that the term "service management" is increasingly used to emphasize management imperatives in this age of service competition and market forces. Therefore, to sustain competitiveness hospitality and tourism providers must continue to meet if not exceed customer expectations that are themselves dynamic. Enrichment of the tourism industry with national characteristics is vital for a healthy development of tourism. Tourism has outperformed most other sectors and contributed significantly to the economic and employment growth. Generally speaking travel and tourism encompassing transport, accommodation, catering, recreation and services for travellers – is the economic engine for developed and developing economies worldwide.

7.2. Applications of Accounting Systems

Consideration will also be made of the literature that reviews the impact of accounting systems for tourism, directly. It should be noted that there is little objective research on this specific impact. At first, Harris and Brown presented an overview of development in accounting management with particular emphasis on the contribution of applied work for the tourism industry. In this context Mia and Patiarb stressed the use of management accounting system in hotels. More recently, Mongiello and Harris described the design of managerial accounting systems in multinational hotel companies. Moreover, Anderson and Guilding emphasized the potential of competitor-focused practice to hotel business. Finally Burgess emphasized the major importance of outsourcing accounting functions, particularly in the hotel sector.

There are many proponents who now define the industry as competing on global terms. Tse and West provide persuasive reasoning when they indicate that a firm competes on global terms when its competitive position in one country is significantly influenced by its position in other countries.

Internationalisation has become a key research theme in the study of the hospitality industry and its constituents.

Like its domestic counterpart, the international hotel industry competes via the placement of its units in significant and appropriate locations.

Recall that accounting entails several broad processes:

— Measurement is the process of identifying and quantifying economic activities. These measurements provide insights into the profitability of a firm's operations and the strength of its financial position.

— Disclosure is the process by which accounting measurements communicated to their intended users.

— Auditing is the process by which specialised accounting professionals attest to the reliability of the measurement and communication process.

In this context, accounting plays a vital role in the verification of incomings and expenditure per field of operation in the hotel business. By the term 'fields of operation' of a hotel we mean those sections of the hotel in which the production procedure of the tourist goods and services occur with the purpose of achieving profit. The main fields of utilisation within a modern hotel unit are:

— the bedrooms

— the bar

— the buffet

— the restaurant

A lot of researchers argue that all these fields of operation are the most essential centres of earnings and cost and accounting plays a vital role in them. The risk of losing capitals and also credit risk appear to be the determining factors from its viability. Within the framework of limiting the risk of correct constitution of financial affairs, the following actions are in effect:

— Controls of the procedures, whereby a check is held to ensure whether the investments are always in accordance with the approved investment policy.

— Controls of the evaluations, whereby the cost of the investments with the running values is mainly compared as well as a check of the "deposits" and the "loans".

— Controls of the availabilities, the bank deposits and loans, during which their frequent update and the confirmation of other ones is necessary.

Furthermore, accounting systems contribute to the provision of information for performance measurement. From the above mentioned, it is clear that accounting enables the hotel management to examine whether the right strategy of financial management is followed. Furthermore an appropriate accounting system is able to satisfy hotel managers' information needs aiming to support management decision-making. Unfortunately, hotel companies do not fully utilise accounting information to assess the value of merger and acquisition, which is increasing to improve international competitiveness. This neglect of accounting information in merger and acquisitions leads to inappropriate evaluation of its value in markets.

References

Harrington, D., Lenehan, T., 1998, "*Managing Quality in Tourism; Theory and Practice*", Oak Tree Press, Dublin.

Harris P., J. & Brown Jackie Brander, 1998, Research and development in hospitality accounting and financial management, *Hospitality management*, 17, pp. 161-181.

Ingram Hadyn, 1995, "Hospitality and tourism: international industries experiencing common problems", *International Journal of Contemporary Hospitality Management,* University Press Limited, 0959-6119 7(7), pp. 44-54.

Jayawardena, C., 1993, "Harmonising the tourist needs and country's expectations from tourism industry", *Tourism, Hoteliering and Hospitality Education*, pp. 28-31.

8

Disasters in Tourism Industry

Nowadays, tourism is an important economic sector in many countries. Between 2004 and 2020, the World Tourism Organisation (WTO) forecasts that international travel will increase from 760 million trips per annum to 1.5 billion trips. If domestic trips are included, the 2020 total will be 15 billion trips per annum. Globally, tourism is a $625 billion industry, the single largest non-government economic sector in the world. Europe registers a falling growth rate from about 4 to 3 percent; the regions with a dynamic growth rate are all related with Asia. The globalisation of the tourism industry has led to a rapid expansion of tourism businesses on an international scale in order to expand their market share and profitability. However, these processes have also opened businesses up to a wider set of "global risks" involved in running businesses at such a scale, as globalisation is often seen as complex and chaotic.

Tourism is often described as a fragile industry in that demand for travel is highly susceptible to numerous shocks, such as wars, outbreaks of deadly contagious diseases, incidents of terrorism, economic fluctuations, currency instability, energy crises, and so on. Many scholars have noted an increasing number of disasters and crises, which affect the tourism industry, ranging from natural to human influenced incidents. In recent years the global tourism industry has experienced many serious crises and disasters including terrorist attacks, political instability, economic recession, bio security threats and natural disasters. Contemporary crises do not recognise or respect national borders and do not confine themselves to a particular policy area .

Tourism is therefore highly susceptible to external factors and pressures in the wider operating environment. However, tourism is also an important economic sector for many countries and many destinations are dependent upon tourism for their growth and survival. This puts increasing pressure on managers and planners concerned with tourism to consider the impact of crises and disasters on the industry and develop strategies to deal with the impacts to protect tourism business and society in general.

Faulkner argued that there is a lack of research on crisis or disaster phenomena in the tourism industry, on the impacts of such events on both the industry and specific organisations, and the responses of the tourism industry to such incidents. Since then – 2001 – the literature has expanded upon these issues. No matter how far the existing literature has gone, there is a constant need to understand better such incidents and examine strategies that can be used to stop or limit their impacts on a growing and important industry sector.

8.1. Crises and Disasters

The term "crisis" is widely used in several scientific contexts. It originates from the Greek word "krisis", which means judgement, choice or decision. The use of the term, however, varies depending on the context in which it is being used and the researcher's discipline. In the organisational literature, crisis is defined as follows: a low-probability, high-impact event that threatens the viability of the organisation and is characterised by ambiguity of cause, effect, and means of resolution, as well as by a belief that decisions must be made swiftly. Seymour and Moore suggest that crisis can threaten reputation, lives and the survival of an organisation. Faulkner argues that crises or disasters can be described as 'sudden challenges which might test the organisation's ability to cope'. All the existing definitions and approaches converge to that crisis is an unpleasant and difficult situation that has to be managed as effectively as possible.

Crises are now occurring more frequently, possibly as a result of greater pressures on business and industry from global market demands, and they may have a much more severe impact. Elsubbaugh et al. suggest that crisis is an inevitable part of business today and cannot be separated from regular business activity.

As far as tourism is concerned, Laws and Prideaux argue that the term crisis in tourism industry usually refers to an event that leads to a shock resulting in the sudden emergence of an adverse situation. McKercher & Hui point out that, crises are inevitable, 'episodic events that disrupt the tourism and hospitality industry on a regular basis' and Coles adds 'when not in crisis, destinations are in an extended programme of practically pre-event-limbo, almost waiting for the important trigger event to take place'.

Parsons gave a very interesting view that can be used for the classification of tourism crises. He suggested three types of crises depending on their gestation period:

a) Immediate crises, where little or no warning exists therefore organisations are unable to research the problem or prepare a plan before the crisis hits,

b) Emerging crises, these are slower in developing and maybe able to be stopped or limited by organisational action, and

c) Sustained crises: that may last for weeks, months or even years.

Similar to Parson's classification is the one of Seymour and Moore, who have suggested that crises are of two types:the "cobra" type, which strikes suddenly and the "python" type which occurs gradually.

Karagiannis et al. suggest an alternative aspect to classify the crises that affect tourism industry, using the factor of human involvement in the crises cases. Similar is the classification of Sausmarez, who argues that crises are traditionally classified as either natural or man-made. But which are the types of crises that although happen locally, affect the global tourism industry? Beirman focuses in five main reasons that result in a destination crisis:

— international war or conflict and prolonged manifestations of internal conflict,

— a specific act or acts of terrorism, especially those directed at or affecting tourists,

— a major criminal act or crime wave, especially when tourists are targeted,

— a natural disaster, such as an earthquake, storm or volcano, causing damage to urban areas or the natural environment and consequently impacting on the tourism infrastructure,

— health concerns related to epidemics and diseases; these may be diseases which impact on humans directly or diseases affecting animals, which limit access to tourist attractions.

Lepp and Gibson through their literature review pick out four major risk factors: terrorism, war and political instability, health concerns and crime. At the recent International Society of Hospitality Consultants (ISHC) Annual Conference held in San Diego, California, ISHC Members participated in a series of roundtable discussions to identify the ISHC Top Ten Global Issues and Challenges in the Hospitality Industry for 2006.

Combining these issues together with the categories of disasters and crises that have been presented above, we consider that the main kinds of crises which occur on local level and can be magnified in a considerable area, sometimes affecting the global tourism industry, are terrorist attacks, natural disasters, political instability and war, and epidemics – diseases.

Table 1: Cast of features of "happen locally – affect globally" tourism crises

Type of crisis	*Gestation Period*	*Cobra-Python*	*Human Involvement*	*Man Made - Natural*
Terrorism	Immediate	Cobra	Direct	Man made
Natural Disasters	Immediate	Cobra	Indirect & No Involvement	Man Made &Natural
Political instability and War	Sustained	Python	Direct	Man made
Epidemics - diseases	Emerging	Python	No Involvement	Natural

8.2. Terrorism

The new millennium has been defined by several crises since the terrorist attacks in New York City and Washington D.C. on Sept. 11, 2001. These acts of terror shocked the world and marked the beginning of a gloomy sentiment in the tourism industry. Several terrorist inflicted tourism crises followed including Bali bombings on October 12, 2002, Madrid train bombings on March 11, 2004, frequent armed unrest in Southern Thailand since January 2004, London terrorist acts in July 2005, hotel bombings in Sharm-el-Sheik Egypt in July 2005, the second round of Bali bombings on October 2, 2005 and the most recent hotel bombings in Amman Jordan in November 2005. These terror acts have obvious negative impact on tourism.

Tourists are often the specific targets of terrorist organisations. Tourism is viewed to represent capitalism and conspicuous consumption and an attack on tourists signifies ideological opposition to these western values. In other areas of the world, where tourism is a state sponsored industry, an attack on tourists can symbolise an attack on the government.

Usually, the problems that terrorism crises cause regarding the tourism sector, which can be magnified and affect a considerable area or the globe in all, can be summarised as following:

— Challenge of tourists' safety attitudes and beliefs. Although terrorist attacks occur in a single place they affect, most of the times, the tourism industry worldwide, as they challenge travellers' and tourists' security beliefs. When people travel, they do not want to be exposed to personal hazards, so safety is a paramount concern of most travellers. Not surprisingly, terrorist incidents and other threats to personal safety reduce people's propensity to travel. The attacks on the World Trade Centre clearly demonstrate the potential risk which terrorism poses for the tourism industry.

— Impacts on several travel and tourist procedures. Terrorist incidents usually lead the responsible authorities to adopt several measures in order to provide a higher security level for civilians and tourist as well. These measures, which can be temporary or permanent, result in changes in several procedures regarding for example mass transportation facilities or places that attract great numbers of visitors. Nowadays, it is much more difficult for a foreigner citizen to obtain a passport visa for visiting United States, after the 9/11 attacks.

The attacks in New York WTC on 11th September 2001, is the most representative example of terrorism impacts on tourism industry. Although the incident occurred at a particular area, it affected the world's life and economy, included tourism industry. Of course the case of 11th September cannot be viewed as a purely local crisis, but it is a clear supportive case of the interdependence and the globalisation of travel and tourism industry. Some of the impacts of the terrorist attacks of September 11, 2001, on tourism sector, coming from the literature, are the following:

— Heightened fear of travelling following the attacks led to a number of cancellations and a drop in new bookings. Reservations worldwide fell by an estimated 12 to 15 per cent in October 2001 compared with the previous year.

— The drop in tourism traffic has also been asymmetrical, with some of the countries that depend most heavily on the industry experiencing the largest number of cancellations.

— A number of sectors were hit hard. As far as EU tourism is concerned, manifest fear of travel primarily affected the high-spending tourists from America, Japan and the Middle East who concentrate on specific destinations.

8.3. Natural Disasters

Several authors have emphasized the vulnerability of tourist destinations, and thus tourists, to disasters and some have suggested that, in these situations, tourists might be more exposed to danger than anyone else. Murphy and Bayley suggest that the exposure of tourism to natural disasters is linked with the attractiveness of many high-risk exotic locations, where events such as hurricanes, avalanches and volcanic activity are common.

Natural disasters appear to have become more frequent in recent years. The implications are profound, especially since many affected areas are heavily reliant on tourism for economic vitality.

Usually, the problems that the natural disasters cause regarding the tourism sector, which can affect a considerable area, can be summarised as following:

— Increase of tourists' concerns about security and safety. Natural disasters can affect the attitudes and the beliefs of citizens around the world about the broader area where the catastrophe took place. Alternatively, some people may opt to change their travel plans and visit destinations where they are exposed to less personal risk. The successful management of the disaster and its consequences minimises the negative effects on people beliefs regarding the affected area. Oppositely, the unsuccessful management enforces the negative attitudes towards the area hit by the disasters from the safety point of view. These issues of course would be better to be further researched.

— Destruction of infrastructure and facilities. The destruction of infrastructure and facilities that are strongly related to the tourism industry, such as transportation facilities, motorways, hospitality facilities, inflicts tourism activities in the wider area, as the destroyed area can serve as an intermediate terminal for several other destinations around. This means that businesses that are involved with tourist activities have to modify their patterns in order to adapt them to the new reality.

The December 2004 tsunami catastrophe in Indonesia is an indicative paradigm. The immediate economic impact was direct, with negative effects on consumption and business activity in the regions and sectors affected. But, the influence of the tsunami reaches beyond the borders of the area affected. Some of the main impacts of the tsunami catastrophe for the tourism industry are the following:

— Many tourists tend to perceive the whole of Southeast and South Asia as a risky destination.

— The tsunami has caused a redistribution of outbound tourists and stimulated a rapid increase in some other outbound and domestic destinations.

— The decrease of the arrivals was important for the affected area. Although this decrease hit the area's tourism industry, it is obvious that there were also negative consequences on several businesses involved with tourism.

8.4. Political Instability and War

Political instability describes a situation "in which conditions and mechanisms of governance and rule are challenged as to their political legitimacy by elements operating from outside of the normal operations of the political system". At first glance, political instability and terrorism may appear unrelated. Closer examination, however, brings into focus certain situations, which demonstrate otherwise. War and political instability can also affect neighboring countries not directly involved in any conflict. As a result of the conflict in Tiananmen Square in China, approximately 11,500 tourists canceled visits to Beijing in 1989. The Persian Gulf War in 1990 caused such a massive redirection of tourists away from the Middle East that hotels in Israel were used to house Russian immigrants instead of tourists.

8.5. Epidemics and Diseases

Health issues associated with international and domestic tourism attract the interest of researchers from a wide range of social science and medical disciplines. Such researchers are recognising that there is an interface between health and tourism and this is an integral part of the "tourist experience" which affects overall satisfaction levels for tourists and can ultimately affect their quality of life. Since tourism quality and visitor satisfaction are intrinsically linked to the experience which is derived from a holiday, trip or visit, it is widely acknowledged that adverse effects on the health of tourists may significantly tarnish the resulting experience of a holiday or destination. Having in mind that nowadays, there are a lot of people traveling world wide, it is easy for a local epidemic to be transferred abroad. Carter found in a study of healthcare as a perceived risk factor that entire continents could be generalised as perilous or safe. The SARS epidemic, which started from a Chinese province, is a representative example of an epidemic with a negatively profound impact on tourism around the world. Some important impacts of SARS were the following:

— International tourism arrivals fell 1.2% to 694 million in 2003, according to World Tourism Organisation (WTO) figures.

— Air travel to areas affected by the advisories decreased dramatically during the epidemic, although the impact of advisories compared with other sources of information to travelers, such as news media, is difficult to assess.

— In a survey conducted by the Society for Human Resource Management in the USA, based on 423 human resource professionals, 20 percent reported cuts in employee travel as a result of SARS.

— In East Asia, tourist arrivals dropped by 41% between April 1st and April 21st compared to the same period in 2002, with the following Asian destinations suffering in particular—China, Hong Kong, Vietnam and Singapore.

— The FIFA women's world cup, originally scheduled for China, was moved to the United States. On March 30, 2003, the international ice hockey federation cancelled the 2003 IIHF women's world championship tournament, which was to take place in Beijing.

8.6. Crisis Preparedness

As it has been shown from the previous cases, the globalisation of the tourism industry and the fact that the world is also becoming more interdependent and connected, have led to a new reality for tourism industry, where crises that occur in one single place of the world can affect the tourism around the broader area or worldwide. However, the negative consequences of these incidents can be moderated if the stakeholders involved in tourism industry get prepared for confronting such incidents. So, the need for crisis preparedness is obvious. Kovoor – Misra defines crisis preparation as an ongoing process of developing organisational capabilities to prevent, contain and recover from crises, and to learn from experience. Pearson identifies the obvious: there is no way to ensure that an organisation will escape crises. The only way for an organisation to minimise crisis damage is either to avert crisis if possible or to manage it effectively. This can be achieved by being as best prepared as possible. Crisis preparation should be of high concern for every business involved in tourism industry.

References

Beirman, D., 2003, *Restoring Tourism Destination in Crisis: A Strategic Management Approach,* Allen & Unwin, Crows Nest, Australia.

Douglas, M., 1994, *Risk and Blame: Essays in Cultural Theory*, London: Routledge.

Drabek, T. E., 1995, "Disaster Responses within the Tourist Industry". *International Journal of Mass Emergencies and Disasters*, 13(1), 7–23.

Elsubbaugh, S., R.Fildesn and M.B.Rosenn, 2004, "Preparation for Crisis Management:A Proposed Model and Empirical Evidence", *Journal of Contingencies and Crisis Management*, 12(3),112-127.

Faulkner, B., 2001, "Towards a framework for tourism disaster management", *Tourism Management*, 22, 135–147.

9

Role of ICT in Tourism Business

Tourism has a significant economic impact at an international, domestic and regional level. This impact is underlined by statistical evidence demonstrating the significance of tourism in terms of GDP, employment and economic development. The tourism industry can be seen as one of the first business sectors where business functions are almost exclusively using information and communications technologies (ICT). Information Technology (IT) and ICT has played an important role in the development of tourism. Computerised reservations Systems (CRS) were among the first applications of IT worldwide. Werthner & Klein suggest tourism is a hybrid industry since even though it is dominated by the provision of information, essentially it is about a physical product.

ICT facilitates this integration and enables customisation of tourism products to suit the needs of individuals. Due to changes in consumer behaviour of the tourist the market is becoming more segmented with each potential consumer belonging to a number of market segments simultaneously. Tourist operators need to be aware of these changes and be equipped to respond, or better still, take a proactive approach. The challenge for the tourism operator is the provision of accurate, localised data, increasingly via IT, whilst maintaining a relationship with the tourist. Rather than being just transaction based longer term relationships need to be fostered and IT can play a role in this relationship building.

The Australian tourist industry is characterised, as is the case in most other economies, by two tiers. Tier 1 players dominate, for example, the hotel sector. They are few in number, being global players well versed in strategy, management practices and information management systems which tends to be centralised. SMTEs are characterised by lower levels of resources generally, including financial resources as well as technical expertise and tend to focus on operational issues rather than taking a strategic view. In Australia, they also tend to be located in regional and rural areas.

9.1. Traditional Technologies

Inter-organisational systems (IOS) represent one use of IT and allow the transfer of information across organisation boundaries. In the past electronic data interchange (EDI) and electronic funds transfer (EFT) have been the technologies to enter into IOS. The standards required for EDI and the high set up costs have tended to act as a barrier for Small and Medium Enterprises (SMEs) to enter into IOS. The first step to achieve this goal of a one-stop service is via global distribution systems (GDS), a form of IOS. GDS evolved from computer reservation systems and enable the aggregation of information from airlines which enables travel agents and tourists to 'make reservations and order other services in a single marketplace'. Examples of GDS are Sabre, Galileo, Amadeus and Worldspan.

There is increasing debate concerning the long term viability of the large GDSs. The systems themselves are dated, based on 1960s architecture and code, never intended for use with the Internet and as proprietary legacy systems are difficult to interface with existing modern computer and network architectures.

Chains of hotels (tier 1 players) generally have in place integration of the Property Management System (PMS) with the corporate Central Reservation System (CRS) and GDS. CRS integration allows for individual properties to benefit from the extensive reach of the chains marketing network and to allow for cross selling amongst properties within the chain. This interoperability of systems is an example of collaboration around IT especially the CRS which has been the most commonly used Wide Area Network (WAN) application in hotels. This extends insofar as some independent hotels link to a GDS such as Sabre.

Interoperable systems already exist in chains, but do not exist amongst independent hotels. Independents appear to resort to subscription to affiliate reservation networks that allow non-chain properties to participate as overflow facilities rather than network amongst themselves. In this way "independents to maintain their individuality and distinctive methodology, while still benefiting from the economies of scale that an affiliation with a larger group of likeminded properties can offer".

9.2. Internet and Tourism

The Internet is especially relevant to tourism since it enables knowledge about the consumer or tourist to be gathered, as well as vice versa. This gives 'rise both to global visibility of destinations and a global merging of market segments'. The use of web-based tourist information systems has grown significantly. In 1996, 3.1 million consumers used these systems and this jumped to 33.8 million consumers in 1998. It was predicted that by 2008, 30% of the whole tourism business will be Internet based.

Travel revenues on the Internet have consistently ranked highly in comparison with other goods and services. The reasons cited for this prominence relate to the richness and currency of information provided online and the breadth of the audience as well as the intensity of competition and the emergence of new players with countless web sites supported by efficient transaction support. Clayton and Criscuolo argue that technology behind the modern information society, particularly by way of the Internet, has bought about four key changes for the way in which business is conducted. These changes, which apply equally to the tourism sector, are:

1. the ability to turn ideas into marketable innovation for a wide range of customers, with reduced buyer search costs and costs of access to markets;
2. increased speed to market and access to new product offerings via the Internet;
3. changed processes and the sharing of information within and between organisations; and
4. a shift in the balance of power between suppliers and customers due to the increased availability of information.

The issues raised above point to the benefits emanating from IT, especially the Internet.

The first two factors have been discussed elsewhere. It is the third and fourth that will be considered here. The third point outlined above essentially makes 'vertical disintegration' of the value chain easier as the integration of electronic processes within and between firms is easier to achieve. This integration can take many forms, to its full extent collaborative commerce and mean that 'it may no longer be necessary for a firm to own a process in order to control it'. This is associated with various forms of collaboration or business networks that may emerge.

The fourth point demonstrates the extra choice available to the buyer – therefore shifting the 'balance of power' to them since they can research their purchase and compare the offerings of competitors. The tourist has more choice when buying travel products also because of the options provided by on-line travel agents and direct marketing by airlines. Increasingly tourists are becoming more computer savvy and are expecting to be able to experience the destination 'virtually'. Other changes in the way they consumers behave – preferring to take shorter holidays with decisions made more spontaneously – have the effect of placing more pressure on tourist operators who need to be more flexible in their offerings and in the way they relate to the market.

9.2.1. Benefits of the Internet

Benefits from IT, particularly the Internet for tourism, are substantial. These benefits are no longer dependent on proprietary information systems as has been the past experience, since the Internet is a commonly available technology. Dogac, et al, considers the Internet provides many advantages to players in the tourism industry. Some of these benefits are:

- enhanced level of collaboration between tourism operators, for example, between travel agencies and service providers;
- prearrangements with respective suppliers no longer necessary;
- web service discovery will identify alternatives, enabling holiday packages to be constructed;
- greater negotiation of service to be purchased and customisation of services/activities; and

— generally greater levels of interoperability with internal and external applications.

Whether these benefits have come to pass remains to be seen. Their realisation requires a new approach to be adopted by operators in the industry, particularly for SMTEs. The question is whether they recognise these potential spin-offs and are able to take advantage of them. They all point to the need for greater levels of IT adoption to be more flexible and responsive to the market, or collaboration with other players to achieve a 'one-stop' planning and booking experience desired by the tourist.

As the above diagram indicates, many businesses or tourism operators are loosely connected over the internet so as to endeavour to serve the tourist's needs, providing the seamless integration of information necessary to plan and book a travel experience. Potentially the Internet overcomes the barriers SMTEs especially have experienced re accessing GDS and CRM, yet it is considered more progress is needed in this regard. Gonzalez et al., suggests a coming together of or cooperation amongst small players is required to generate 'coherent heterogeneity' – differentiation amongst the players in the midst of providing an integrated tourist offering.

9.2.2. Issues raised by the Internet

The internet has resulted in a proliferation of many ineffective html document based web sites with small and medium tourist enterprises (SMTEs) possessing inadequate skills and insufficient resources to conduct web site effectively. A Yahoo search reveals in excess of 250,000 tourist oriented websites. This exponential growth in the number of tourist related web sites means a 'lack of notoriety in a saturated market'.

It is not clear that individual SMTEs are able to use this business intelligence, or recognise its value. If so, information may be lost and not acted upon. A sharing of information, either in a centralised or in a more collaborative manner would assist in the use this 'asset' of information and knowledge.

The internet is a commonly available technology, however awareness of its functionality and resources and expertise to take advantage of this functionality is required. It is observed that many

SMTEs either are not aware of this or do not possess or have ready access to resources need to make the most of the opportunities potentially available.

For these benefits and others to be achieved however, and so full exploitation of web services, 'it is necessary to introduce semantics to web services'. The semantic web which is an extension of the World Wide Web, is designed to bring structure and meaning to the vast array of information available on the World Wide Web. In bringing this structure, the web creates knowledge which is readily accessible by both humans and machines. The structure imposed by semantic webs is achieved through the imposition of an ontology to give meaning to information.

9.2.3. Intermediaries

Collaboration around the Internet is a way for tourist operators, such as hotels, to deal with excess capacity and increase occupancy rates quickly. This already occurs within many chains and is evident in the participation in intermediaries or distressed websites such as needitnow.com, Travelocity.com; whatif.com and others. Three reasons have been identified for this change in the distribution of hotel rooms:

— a lack of understanding of hoteliers of how the Internet and online distribution works;

— hospitality lags other tourism sectors in adopting the Internet as a distribution medium. Hotels were unprepared to deal with boom in online bargain hunting and bookings;

— exploitation by intermediaries of the situation following 9/11 as hoteliers looking to increase revenues via increased occupancy relied on intermediaries to promote their product.

Starkov estimates that by 2010 around 18-18% of revenues for hotels will come from hotel bookings made on the Internet, compared to the current 8 – 10% of revenues. The active role of these intermediaries may be viewed as a positive development for the industry. Online bookings are more cost effective, tend to attract more affluent customers and reduce reliance on more expensive distribution channels. However a closer analysis of the impact of this reveals a loss of control by tourist operators and a tradeoff between occupancy rates at the expense of yield and the associated RevPAR.Yield represents the return to the business resulting from its operations. RevPAR represents the revenue achieved per available room. The aim of a hotelier is to maximise yield and RevPAR. It is clear that selling rooms via distressed websites at a cheaper rate increases occupancy but has a negative impact on the other indices. The long term impact is brand erosion in terms of quality following downward pressure on room rates.

Starkov suggests that by 2005 around 54% of hotel online bookings will be direct sales reflecting a greater role of online intermediaries in the reservation process. Hoteliers, 'have difficulty maintaining market share and finding the right formula to deal with online discounters and intermediaries' Starkov, demonstrating a lack of internet strategy and ineffective e-Distribution approaches. Hotels need to transfer their direct sales expertise to the web environment. Realisation of the need to develop a direct web distribution strategy is critical as hoteliers seek to deal successfully with online intermediaries. Distressed web sites have a role to play in distribution, however should not be the only web distribution channel.

9.2.4. IT and Collaboration

Increasingly business network behaviour is becoming more prominent in research and is of interest to the tourism industry. A sharing of information, either in a centralised or more collaborative way, would assist in maximisation of the value of information and knowledge. This collaboration is made possible by the spawning of online technologies, IT being a critical driver of integration and co-operation. This integration though requires internal integration of processes and systems as well as externally with other organisations and this has acted to impede co-operation in the past.

9.3. IT Developments in the Tourism Sector

9.3.1. Internet Forums

An Internet forum is 'an online facility that provides local businesses with an internet portal using the locale, or an industry particular to the locale, as the unique selling point, or common brand'. This acts as an anchor providing more of a profile to entice visitors to the web site that represents the location or destination.

Galloway, Mochrie & Deakins have examined how the development of internet-based virtual business forums assists tourist operators in rural areas.

Reasons cited for a lower uptake of the Internet in more remote reasons are several and are discussed in a number of papers. Yet the Internet offers the potential to overcome the disadvantages that remote locations raise. Impediments to SMTE adoption of e-commerce need to be revisited and addressed to encourage the use of IT and to seek to reduce the impact of the digital divide.

By developing a strategic approach that adopts a clear identity focusing on the destination and its features encapsulated in an integrated website, the forum concept has significant merit with respect to regional tourist destinations.

9.3.2. Internet as a Facilitator of Collaboration

In their study Palmer & McCole examine independent businesses with unique resource locators (URLs) located in one region. They then followed links out of those sites to identify the extent to which such sites were linked. They concluded there was a lack of cooperative initiatives between tourist operators in the region of interest.

9.3.3. MEDINA Project

Cultural tourism is a good example of the way in which online technologies have been influential as its emergence has been fostered by the Internet. Cultural tourism focuses on the presentation of an areas cultural heritage, ranging from environmental attractions through historical, artistic, archaeological and folkloric components. A specific example of this form of tourism is the MEDINA project started in 2002, due for completion in 2005, which established a cultural web portal for fourteen Mediterranean countries . Access to the portal by a tourist is achieved through mobile devices and allows the tourist to make informed decisions concerning cultural sights. Mobile devices are increasingly being used by tourists as electronic personal tour guides.

9.4. Challenges and Opportunities

The revolution in ICTs has profound implications for economic and social development. It has pervaded every aspect of human life whether it is health, education, economics, governance, entertainment etc. Dissemination, propagation and accessibility of these technologies are viewed to be integral to a country's development strategy. The most important benefit associated with the access to the new technologies is the increase in the supply of information. Information is shared and disseminated to larger audience. Secondly it reduces the cost of production. Knowledge is produced, transmitted, accessed and shared at the minimum cost. With the reduction in the transactional costs, there is also a reduction in the degree of inefficiencies and uncertainty. Thirdly it has overcome the constraints of distance and geography. ICTs have cut across the geographic boundaries of the nation states. Fourthly it has led to more transparency. Networking and information sharing definitely leads to demands for greater openness and transparency. Whether you want to know the status of the central banks' foreign exchange agency or the cost prize of potatoes in the local market, ICTs empowers the individual with the information access, which is transparent. Efforts are under way to integrate ICTs to all sectors and developmental activity.

9.4.1. ICT and Economic Growth

Development of Information and Communication Technologies (ICT) has transformed the contemporary business environment. It has led to new information economy which is digital in nature. ICT is a broad terminology referring to multiple communication technologies which range from simple and complex namely Cell Phone applications Digital Cameras, Internet, Wireless VOIP,GPS, GIS, Convergence Digital radio, These technologies are creating a new global market place, which is more competitive. With e-commerce and e business the market has more opportunities and possibilities than ever before.

E- commerce is expected to benefit economic development in several ways:

1. Through allowing local business access to global markets
2. By providing new opportunities to export a wider range of goods and services
3. By improving the internal efficiency with in the firms.

First, e-commerce allows business to reach a global audience. In Africa, for example, the tourism and handicrafts industries are realising their ability to deliver their product information directly to consumers. Tourist lodges, hotels, and governments across the continent now maintain sophisticated websites advertising their unique features, handling booking order, and promoting specials to interested consumers. Secondly opportunities created by e-commerce and its predecessor technologies is that ICTs can create digital market places to manage supply chains and automate transaction, increasing efficiency and opening previously closed markets to firms in developing countries. Thirdly, e-commerce is improving the culture of business.

Thus ICTs are the backbone of the capital accumulation. They are connected with new business opportunities, increased trade and investment although they are risks involved sometimes. It suggests a positive relationship between ICT development and economic growth. Indeed an often cited achievements of Indian economy during the last decade has been the emergence of an ICT sector which has shown remarkably vibrancy in terms of output and export growth. However, the contribution of ICT to an economy can be viewed at two different levels. While the former refers to the contribution in output, employment, export earning etc on account of the production of ICT related goods and services, the later refers to ICT induced development through enhanced productivity, competitiveness, growth and human welfare on account of the diffusion of this technology to the different sectors of the economy and society.

9.4.2. Nexus between ICT and Tourism

Tourism is currently one of the fastest gowning industries across the world. It is primarily a service industry as it does not produce goods but renders services to various classes of people. It is an combination of various interrelated industries and trade like food industry, transport industry etc. It is an complicated business because it involves multiple socio-economic activities like attracting people to a destination, transporting them, housing, feeding and entertaining etc. In the process it brings about tremendous infrastructural improvements and helps in the development of the region. Perhaps tourism is one such rare industry, which earns foreign exchange without exporting national wealth. Tourism, like other economic activities flourishes best when it fits into the context of general economic policies and programmes designed to lead to the optimum growth of the economy of a country as a whole.

Tourism industry is currently an extremely sensitive hybrid industry and incorporates distinct features of information society. Although the core product in the industry is physical service, which are produced and consumed in the physical world, it is dominated and achieved though information services. The perfect integration of information and physical services is the challenge for the contemporary tourism industry across the globe. Hence it is largely a information product.

One has to travel to the place of consumption to test the product or services and which cannot be done in advance for a trial. Since, tourism services are consumed the very time they are produced, it is largely based social interaction between the supplier and the consumer. The quality of the service or product is mainly defined by the interaction. To be more elaborate, consumer has access to only an abstract model of the product at the time of decision-making and contractual agreement. Such gaps can be overcome by the information about the product, which is available in advance to the consumer. The mechanism leads to the establishment of specific product distribution and long information and value adding chains.

Contemporary information society has made Toursim a highly information-intensive industry as ICT has a potential impact on tourism business. The role of ICT in tourism industry cannot be underestimated and it is crucial driving force in the current information driven society. It has provided new tools and enabled new distribution channels, thus creating a new business environment. On the other hand consumers are also using online to obtain information and plan their trip and travel. Information is the key element in the tourism industry. ICT pervades almost all aspects of tourism and related industry. For instance, we depend upon it right from the scratch while identifying and developing tourisms site and destinations itself. The use of Geospatial Information Technologies in the recent years across the globe for varied purposes is popularly known and Tourism industry has not been an exception in availing its advantages. It can be used by tourist professionals to define the boundaries of the proposed tourist site as well its surrounding areas and the communities living in it. Such technologies are also useful for site management and monitoring. The role of ICT tools in the industry for marketing, operation, and management of customer is widely known. Marketing techniques can be more innovative through ICT tools. The table below reveals the potential use of ICT tools in the industry.

Recent studies on ICT and tourism has revealed the transition in the industry as a result of ICT impact and have explored its possibility and potential. Poon analyses some of the major challenges facing tourism industry and outlines the nexus between tourism and ICT. He traces the rapid shift-taking place between 'traditional tourism sector' and 'new tourism industry'. Technology has a strategic role in reshaping the value chain in the industry and in the process, consumers are gradually adapting to the new values, lifestyles and new tourism products, which has re-engineered by the new technologies. Although some of the technologies described are now obsolete, the implicit message is relevant and gives an overall review of the changing face of the tourism industry. Some of the world's largest GDS namely Sabre, Galileo, Amadeus and Worldspsan are examined. Besides analysing the telecommunication technologies in the industry, the hospitality sector, entertainment sector, transport sector, management sector and other intermediaries have been diligently explored.

Werthner provides a more detailed and logical understating of the industry's structure by focusing on the concepts, definitions, consumer behavior, economic aspect, market transactions, etc. Information Technology information management, intelligent applications and system integration etc are examined carefully. Additional information on business strategy exploring the relationship between ICT, strategy and organisation is also articulated. Buhalis also stressed on strategic management in his book providing a comprehensive overview of both operational and strategic management. The distribution strategies and approaches from a destination point of view is explored and discusses the possible future research in tourism distribution channels.

Connor's work serves as a textbook on electronic distribution with its logical explanation and case studies. GDS, CRS and DMS are analysed with example of cases from across the western world. The growing phenomenon of travel distribution through Internet and its impact on distribution channels structure and functionality is explored with rigor. Carter & Bedard and Carter & Richer have focused on the operators in the tourism industry. Developments of the e commerce and DMO and their changing value chains are analysed intelligently and clearly so that importance of internet presence for consumers, intermediaries, travel media and other players in the industry is noted and understood through their works. Marcussen attempts to provide an overview of innovative developments in distribution of travel and tourism services in Europe. It documents the wealth of statistical data on travel and related transactions in the European tourism industry. However, most of the experiences are based on the western developed world, which could possibly a limitation while trying to understand the nexus of ICT and Tourism in an Indian context. They have used the existing theoretical framework on ICT and e-tourism developments in other parts of the world namely Europe and America to examine their impact of ICT application in the tourism industry contemporary China. There have been tremendous developments at the destinations levels in the recent years. Studies like have revealed that Internet and strategic implementation of IT is now critical for companies to survive in the global economy. However, not many efforts are made to study e-tourism developments in India and other developing countries.

9.5. Transition in the Industry

Technological progress in the recent decades has made tourisms enterprise across the globe more innovative than even before. The three important innovations, which have redefined the organisational structure of world truism industry, are the following.

1. Development of the Computer Reservation System (CRS)
2. Development of the Global Distribution System (GDS)

3. The Internet.

GDS refers to the network connection integrating the automated booking systems of different organisations which enables the user to access it through the intermediation of a travel agency. The supply of services is presently concentrated with four global suppliers owned by airline companies namely Sabre, Amadeus, Galileo International and Worldspan. The functioning of these companies depend upon a network of agreements with local partners which ensures access to travel agencies all over the world. Important features include:

1. Network which is based on proprietary system accessible only to professional users
2. High cost of implementation and maintenance.
3. Involvement of multinational players
4. Invisible in the market and unknown to the final users as they are not commercial brands.

However its non-visibility does pose constraints, as it cannot be the successfully exploited by the end user's market. GDS technology has also broadened the gap between large and medium or small suppliers of tourist services as the former are more benefited.

The advantages and evolution of CRS and Internet are well known. Internet strategy has provided all players in the industry an easy access to the end user. Exploitation of opportunities through Internet depends upon marketing strategy, communication strategy, pricing strategy etc. Direct communication with the clients, which is facilitated by the Internet, has made the industry more effective and efficient.

The overall structure of the industry has been transformed ever since Internet has been the essential communication tool for the industry. Several new developments can be noted.

1. Direct selling to the customer has increased
2. Increase in new intermediaries such as Internet portals specialised in selling tourism products.
3. Customers have access to the distribution channels traditionally used by tour operators through Internet.

4. Companies can regularly alter products and services based on the needs and expectations of clients through regular interaction through Internet.
5. Increase in the transparency and the efficient relationship between customer and management.
6. Change in the consumer behavior. Consumers are now asking better services. They are more specific with regard to content and the details of the arrangement. They are more cost conscious and often tend to make comparisons between two products.

However, the increase in the distribution channels is been an serious challenge for the industry. It demands critical cooperation across different sectors with in tourism industry. While tourism destination management organisations develop internet portals to distribute information and products, transportation companies offer services for transport. Industry needs professionals who are technically trained to deal with ICT tools, systems and information sources. Tourism professionals also need profound knowledge in areas of marketing, finance, management, statistics, distribution trend etc since it also involves rigorous revenue management.

Successful navigation is possible only if professionals have the skill to identify efficient combination of distribution channels and opportunities for cross promotion and cross selling. While such skills get sharpened during work, education on tourism and related areas can be a platform for training the professionals. The role of ICT is crucial both in theory, practice and praxis. There has been a paradigm shift in the management of contemporary organisations related to tourism industry as a result of the more established relationships between business and technology. Information and communication tools are indispensable to the tourism industry as the ICT system is being rapidly diffused throughout the industry allowing none of the players to break free from its impacts.

9.6. LIMITATIONS AND FUTURE POSSIBILITIES

There is a need for a well-structured Information System or Intelligent System technologies in tourism industry to facilitate the access of tourist information by the users. The current ICT system has certain limitations. For instance, accessing information through Internet and www is an intelligent mean of getting the information, but many a times, the information is highly fragmented. One shall arrive at it only after intelligent navigation, which is time consuming and may mislead in the process. Search engines for tourism should be developed. Facilities to browse according to the topic portals can be made.

Wireless is likely to be the next major event in the history of technology. Its application in tourism industry is also likely to increase in future. Mobile services shall continue to be an important channel of information and tourism services distribution for both providers and consumers. Future mobiles might decrease in size, weight ad prize and likely to increase in power, storage, connectivity, position and capabilities. Electronic personal guide might be in frequent usage. Besides SMS WAP standard for accessing the Internet with wireless devices like mobile phones should be increased. GNSS which gives the position, and GPRS enabled mobiles which can handle larger amounts of data than the GSM network shall be useful in tourism industry.

W-LAN and Blue tooth, which gives wireless access at short distance about few meters, can be useful too. It is also essential that usability studies and research is conducted to examine the ICT integration in tourism and its impact. Usability is the measure to the quality of a user's experience while using the ICT tools. It could be a product of a system, website, a software application, mobile technology, or nay related technology. It is important to note the technology and application to work together with respect to bandwidth, user interface, position etc. All applications, technology and services should be user-friendly which can be used both by the veterans as well as the new-bees effectively. It should have utility value and simple to comprehend. Customer relations management can be improved by strategies which sustains the old customers interest besides attracting new prospective clients. Planning of the trip should be inclusive such that booking should take care of travel, lodge, local tours etc. It should take care of the trip from the beginning till the end. Pre trip session, during trip session and post trip sessions should be properly laid out and implemented. Arrangement should be made for 'Live Chat' so that all queries of the customer is answered at any time.

Reviews by the customer, feed backs and surveys should be in progress to know the gaps if any. SMS can also be used for logistic updates.

9.6.1. E – Tourism

It is important to examine the characteristics and dynamics of the industry in the developing countries. While the opportunities are many, challenges are nevertheless increasing especially for the developing countries. It is crucial for the developing countries to design efficient destination managements systems to compete with international tourism market with equal footing. Often, it is found that developing countries are unable to adopt ICT despite the competitive advantage of such application.

ICT has enabled to create business linkages across regions, cultures and different business sectors. However, many parts of the world do not have access to these technologies. This is especially true in the least developed countries (LCD). Inequality arising out of such issues is referred to as Digital Divide. It is a reflection of economic and social inequity between two regions, counties or two groups etc. Hence it becomes all the more important for the developing countries who are sufferers of digital divide to integrate themselves into the new Information society and participate in it effectively. The strategies for national and regional e-tourism should be developed in the developing countries with adequate research keeping in mind the broad framework of ICT strategies for development. Practices of e-tourism strategies in various countries differ and exchange of ideas might help developing countries to adopt new strategies.

If the digital divide is overcome, then many developing economies can distribute their products and increase their customer base and have both trading partnerships. E-tourism shall enable tourism stakeholders across the globe to access the information. It might increase the sales and generate more revenue into local economy. Imbalance between competing destinations in global markets can also to some extent be addressed through tourism. Developing countries should be more aggressive in understanding the implications of ICT developments in tourism industry. It is believed that now edevelopment strategies should be an integral part of all policy planning. It also includes policy planning related to tourism industry.

While stressing on e-development initiatives on tourism industry, Paul Ridoutt recommends some policy implications. She feels that e-tourism strategies should be integrated with broader framework of national ICT policies. Contributions and involvement of public authorities is essential in providing infrastructure and human capacity, which encourages the ICT usage.

ICT's use should be supported and promoted by SME's and consumers especially from remote areas. Low cost access to ICT solutions can be made available. Regular meetings and interactions should be facilitated between different destinations to share information, knowledge and define ICT strategies and implementation. She urges that it is important for developing countries to develop and promote sustainable tourism. Unless the respective national government understands these opportunities and challenges and attempts to address them by adopting strategic policies, tourism industry might fail to take advantage of etourism and its products. Developing countries especially should develop an ICT environment, which involves multiple factors like access, infrastructure, education, capacity building, legal framework etc. for a promotion of ICT enabled tourism industry.

9.6.1.1. E-Tourism Facilitates Regional and Tourism

Extensive and intensive Rural Tourism can be promoted through ICT application. Rural tourism can be main economic activity and can be crucial for agribusiness and rural development. It gives an opportunity for the farmers to profit from tourism directly besides generating new market for the agrarian products in the region.

Rural e-tourism is largely individual oriented and may or mat not have a mass appeal unlike the industrial tourism. Budget constraints are bound to exist as small farmers may lack resources for advertise and promote their products. Rural e-tourism might bring many ancient historical monuments, galleries, museums, theatres and sites into mainstream tourism. It is essential to build a userfriendly model for rural tourism, keeping in mind the ICT tools, cultural policy, state and local region.

Information from the local communities can be also protest and preserve cultural heritage. The use of ICT in tourism can have significant impact on the management and development of heritage sites. However intervention of the state and cultural policies is essential to make ICT application meaningful. Another obstacle to the development of local cultural heritage through ICT tools is the fact that it is the subject of initiatives targeted on the local population. While the major players in the tourism industry have adopted ICT tools for sales and promotion, cultural sector are yet to comprehend the potential of ICT applications for preserving cultural heritage. They are yet to discover that heritage preservation is possible through e-tourism. Sustainable tourism can be the tool for preservation and development of natural and cultural heritage.

A common ICT based heritage tourism development strategy can be evolved using the points of convergence between cultural sector and tourism industry. Such a strategy common to the culture and tourism sectors on a regional level could be an appropriate solution to overcome major challenges associated with ICT based heritage tourism development.

The dynamics of Information exchange among the tourism industry players has drastically changed in the recent years. The industry is now more complicated as there has been considerable changes in the distribution and sales. Distribution cooperation is expanding. While transport companies now provide opportunity to book accommodation, destination management organisations are developing internet portal to distribute information.

It is essential for the tourism professional to understand the Tourism Value Net. They also need to know the main players in the industry. Statistical database should be developed and research should be undertaken. Educational institutions should have access to such knowledge. Educational institute should promote ICT based courses.

The industry is generating excessive information and indeed information is the strategic and important resources for the industry. ICT tools are providing new means for analysing the information for the industry. Emphasis should be upon converting this valuable information to knowledge system. There should be gradual transition from data system to profound knowledge system for the benefit of future generations.

9.7. E-Business Applications in Hospitality Industry

The application of the Internet in the business world has become a major trend in practice and generated a hot stream of research in the recent literature. The Internet, as a collection of interconnected computer networks, provides free exchanging of information. Over 400 millions of computers on more than 400,000 networks worldwide today are communicating with each other. As such, the Internet has been becoming a powerful channel for business marketing and communication, and for new business opportunities - as it is often called as "*e-business*" or "*e-commerce*" today. This new *virtual* marketplace allows small companies competing with business giants by *just* having a better web presentation of their products/services. Under the same wave, online customers can enjoy a wider choice of products or services, more competitive prices, and being able to buy their favorite items/services from the sellers located thousands miles away.

E-commerce has been defined as "the buying and selling of products and services by *businesses and consumers over the Internet*". The Internet and ecommerce give consumers an opportunity - through the easy on-line information gathering and convenient online shopping - to be better prepared to purchase the right product at the right time. New entrepreneurs and traditional small to medium sized businesses are the pioneers exploring on the forefront of ecommerce.According to a published survey, more than 90% of new entrepreneurs and starting businesses are using the Internet. Numerous studies have been reported about the Internet applications in business – including the application in the service operations, such as: the health care industry banks and financial institutions and the hospitality & tourism industry. Those Internet applications have attracted a great amount of attention from industrial practitioners and academic researchers, due to the fact that the information exchanging and sharing is a key part of those business operations, where the use of Internet will provide an advantage in the related information flow. Given the competition from powerful traditional businesses, a successful e-business can only occur if this business can satisfy its consumers' needs better than those traditional business approaches and provide consumers with at least one of the following advantages: (a) lower price, (b) wider selection, (c) better choices, (d) superior services, and (e) more convenient.

One key issue for the e-business application in service operations is about the possibility of online delivery of the services customers ordered - as not all types of services can be delivered online, such as haircut. Specifically, the services requiring customer participation are difficult to be purchased and delivered online. In this regard, the online booking of hotel/motel rooms, airline tickets, advanced car rental, or a total travel package has become one of a few good example services - which can be inquired, checked, and ordered easily while conveniently communicated and delivered online with the Internet. In fact, the use of internet information delivery and on-line document printing has provided the backbone for the current stream of e-commerce. In the current performance criteria for service operations, fast service delivery and prompt and reliable service have been identified as two key competitive priorities for the future Web-based service delivery operations, while time-based competition through better customer service has been reemerging as a major tool of delivering high-quality services to customers through a total operation cycle – including planning, design, processing, marketing, and distribution.

The hospitality industry has followed the trend of Internet application in recent years, and sometimes even gaining its own name of Internet application - called "*e-traveling*" referring to all travel related business transactions now completing through Internet applications. Some key issues addressed in the recent literature about the e-traveling include: customer acceptance and satisfaction, services rendered, value added for both the travel businesses and consumers, privacy concerns, profitability, operational risks, and competition from traditionally non-traveling firms.

9.7.1. E-Booking

It has been reported that the online booking in the hospitality industry is increasing at a very rapid speed recently, especially at the lower rate end, as illustrated in Table 1 below. As seen from Table 1, online hotel room bookings has been increased by six times just during last four years from $1.1 billions in 1999 to $6.3 billions in 2002. As a result, its percentage as of total annual bookings is increased over 400% - from about 2% in 1999 to 9% in 2002.

Table 1: Recent Annual Online Hotel/Motel Bookings

Year	*1999*	*2000*	*2001*	*2002*	*2003*	*2004*	*2005*
Annual Bookings (in Billions)	$1.1	$2.8	$4.2	$6.3	$9.9	$11.8	$15.8
As % of Total Annual Bookings	2%	4%	6%	9%	13%	16%	20%

More significantly, the groups who are now going online bookings are those of business travelers and above-the-average vacationers – who are traveling more frequently than the average publics. Targeting great deals while still in control of their search process, those online bookers claim that more than often they are able to book a hotel room at much lower rate online comparing traditional phone reservation systems or old styled travel agents.

The hotel industry is certainly full aware of this trend and fully willing to contribute its share in this effort. In fact, the industry has realised that during those early forays into cyberspace, the industry didn't view e-booking strategically and handed over too much control of inventory and pricing to those third party online travel agencies, and now the industry is in the unenviable position of trying to take back the reins after early shopping patterns have been established.

First, now every hotel/motel chain has developed its own website in which bargain hunters can book their hotel rooms online – other than though an Internet travel agency. By 2002, over 51% of the total annual online bookings of $6.3 billions were earned through hotels' own websites. Another attempt by the industry is to change its early agreements with those online travel agencies – from old "merchant model" where hotels making rooms available to online travel agencies at wholesale rates and the agencies marking up those rates by 15% to 30% before peddling them to the public at fixed prices for fixed periods of time to a new "sharing model" where the hotels will have more control of their rooms via online booking by providing a higher priority to their own websites over the websites of those third-party travel agencies. Thirdly, other than allowing those online travel agencies to profit for an average 20% from original wholesale prices, some hotel chains now offer a more competitive price on their own websites to directly compete with those online travel agencies. For example, Six

Continents PLC chain and Starwood Hotels & Resorts Worldwide Inc. both started to promote their special online packages since May 2002 – which are guaranteeing the best price deal available on all online websites. The slogan of their programs is "If a customer is able to get a better rate for the same room on another website within 24-hour of booking, the company will not only match that price, but beat it by extra 10%." Both companies reported increased online bookings on their own online systems. This combined discount room site provides negotiated cut-rate deals at more than 10,000 properties and nearly 100 hotel brands. The claimed advantages to online room hunters include: a better deal in room rates, a direct link to all airlines' websites, reservations are made directly into hotels' systems to eliminate any potential snafus, and a fast payments to hotels where rooms are booked online. And finally, the hotel/motel industry has realised the importance of flexibility and thus developed new programs to provide hotels with more flexible room offerings and pricing schedules on an available-as-needed-basis.

While the e-booking of airline tickets has reached about 26% of total annual sales in 2002, the online hotel room booking is just account for half of that proportion – 13% to total annual hotel room bookings. As every two out of three hotel rooms are currently booked through traditional telephone reservation systems, the industry has predicted more quick increase in online room bookings during next few years – as the Internet technology becomes more popular and the access to the Internet becomes more easy and convenient to the public. Both hotel chains and existing online travel agencies have seen those potentials and prepared for the coming competition.

Table 2: Breakdown of Annual Hotel/Motel Room Bookings

Year	*Online Travel Agency*	*Tradition Travel Agency*	*Hotel Chain Own Website*	*Hotel Telephone Reservation*	*Individual Walk-In Customers*
2001	3%	21%	3%	63%	10%
2002	5%	20%	5%	60%	10%
2005	9%	18%	11%	53%	9%

The competition among all online travel agencies has been intensified during the past years. As the end of 2002, current major players in the e-booking business include:

There certainly are some challenges and issues in the application of Internet technology in the hospitality industry. One major obstacle addressed most in the practice is the security concern. Customers are certainly concerned of giving their personal financial information online, and many oldfashioned customers somehow afraid to pay an invoice through Internet. Another issue challenged to the online booking is the quality of delivered service - including both delivery speed and delivery reliability. It has been predicted that in the travel industry to be successful in long-term, the operations of an online booking business must compete in a more creative way comparing to those traditional business counterparts. That is, the strategic positioning decision of an online booking business must establish its own unique competitive advantages over its traditional business competitors as well as its online business counterparts.

9.7.1. 1. E-Booking: Case Study of Macon, Georgia

Tourism is the second largest industry in Georgia – behind only to agriculture industry. In 2002, tourism expenditures in the state is reached to $23.9 billions – with 42 millions visitors who traveled to Georgia as their primary destination – a 2% increase over year 2001. Among those visitors, 81% were traveled by vehicle, and 63% had destination of overnight trips in Georgia were leisure travelers.

Hospitality has grown into big business in the Macon area in the past several years. As the size of the city increases, the bigger the challenge is to manage the tourism and the hospitality industry within the area.

The application of Internet in the hospitality industry such as e-booking has made tourism and traveling easy to the public and provided a new business opportunity to the local hospitality industry. As the tourism industry faced enormous change in the aftermath of the September 11th attacks, the shift was to smaller and more secure areas. "Major metropolitan areas have trailed off in both business and leisure segments." This thought pattern and central locality make Macon, Georgia becoming a prime attraction for state tourism.

The city of Macon is located at the center position of the state of Georgia, and ideally between Savannah and Atlanta on the interstate highway system. The city is one of several middle-sized cities in the state - with a total population of approximately 150,000, and about 80 miles south of Atlanta – the capital of the state. The city has a small town spirit feeling while provides enough entertainment to keep one busy.

There are seven recreational centers in Macon. These centers offer summer activities, workshops, classes and sports. Programs for senior citizens, physically challenged and mentally disabled citizens are also available. There are also over 75 public parks that are maintained in the city.

Two public tennis courts featuring 36 courts and three private clubs offering 26 courts to its members. If one enjoys a different kind of physical activity, there are over 50 shopping centers offering virtually any product or service to suit your needs. The Colonial Mall Macon has over 170 stores and is the only mall in the State with 6 anchor stores.

This case study is an attempt to examine the current stage of the Internet application in the local hospitality industry, especially about the hotel/motel room online booking and reservations. There are 50 hotels/motels in Macon area, representing a total of 4,500 rooms. The average annual occupancy rates of recent three years are listed in Table 3, according to a report by Macon Convention & Visitors Bureau.

Table 3: Annual Occupancy Rates in Macon Area Hotels/Motels

	2001	*2002*	*2003*
Average Annual Occupancy Rate	54.8%	55.5%	58.5%
Annual Percentage Increase	0.2%	1.3%	5.4%

In cooperation with the Greater Macon Chamber of Commerce, a questionnaire survey among the hotels/motels that are a member of the Macon Chamber of Commerce was conducted to collect the related data, especially about the online hotel/motel room booking and reservation information. Half of those hotels/motels are registered with online travel agencies such as Hotel.com and Priceline.com – two major Internet based traveling service businesses - which are allowed to book rooms at certain discount rates from these hotels/motels. For a better control and management, 60% hotels/motels surveyed indicated that they have a monitoring system in place for the online bookings. Thus the feedback information from its monitoring system can provide a basis for further analysis to identify any potential trends or patterns in the online bookings – upon which an improved promotional effort can be lunched thereafter in a more effective way. Finally, the information about the current shares of online bookings for each hotel/motel revealed that one hotel has an exceptional high percentage (80%) of online bookings for its rooms – because this motel is not a part of any national hotel chains and its management placed all its rooms at a discount prices to those Internet based travel agencies.

This is an ongoing research project. The above survey showed that 18% of the hotels/motels had no room booking tracking system to monitor their reservations. As such, an instrument of information sheet is recommended from this research project for those hotels/motels to be placed at the reservation desk. When a customer checks in a simple question is the most efficient way to monitor the reservations. The clerk then records a tally on the log. Once the log is complete and the night audit begins, a summary is placed in a monthly excel spreadsheet that will allow management to monitor not only the number of reservations but also monitor the way in which the reservations were made. It has been proposed to those hotels/motels that currently track their online reservations that after the above monitoring instruments are implemented for certain periods of time, they should then collect all the information available from those records. Upon which several statistical techniques would be applied to identify any meaningful trends and patterns in the online booking such as if additional marketing efforts could increase the total number of online bookings and what kind of effort would be more effective.

9.7.1. 2. Caste Study og Travelocity.com

Travelocity.com is one of the leading travel agents who provides online bookings for more than 700 airlines, 50,000 hotels and over 50 car rental companies, as well as more than 6500 vacation packages, tour and cruise trips and a large database of destination and interest information . The company started during the hot stream of dot.com e-business era in 1996 and located its global headquarters in Fort Worth, Texas. Travelocity targets two primary markets: (1) offering travelers assistance with every aspect of their trip in terms of air, hotel, car, cruise ship over the Internet, and (2) aiding the hospitality industry by selling tickets, renting cars, or making reservations online for the traveling business.

From the beginning, the company developed its own business model – which can be characterised with the following ten long-term strategic objectives: (1) Market Leader, (2) National Brand, (3) Robust Member Database, (4) Key Alliances, (5) Powerful Shopping System, (6) Trusted and Reliable Customer Care, (7) Diversified Revenue Mix, (8) Strong Ad Sales, (9) Broad M-Commerce Alliances, and (10) Global Reach. This business model has helped the company to gain a quite success in the extremely competitive Internet-based travel business.

Travelocity has been a leader in the online travel agency business - among top three of market share holders in 2002 and currently the sixth largest travel agency in the world, competing with travel agencies around the globe. In order to compete effectively, the company developed its own business strategies. First, to establishing certain partnerships within the industry for more flexibility and cooperation, as in 2001, *Travelocity* entered into formal partnerships with its past competitors:

Priceline and *Hotel Reservations Network* to help in offering its customers more options. Secondly, realising that the market for those traditional travel agency will continue to decline, the company moved one step ahead of most of its competitors by having affiliate members: travel agencies who use Travelocity to book vacations and trips for their old customers. Next, to form powerful alliances with major airlines and web providers - *Travelocity* now has exclusivity deals with *America Online*, *Netscape*, *CompuServe*, *iwon*, and *digitalcity*. In addition, the company also has alliances and agreements with many airlines, hotels, car rental companies, and cruise lines to offer the best deals for their customers. In addition, as the whole online travel booking business is based upon the Internet technology, the company has pushed for the development of new Internet technology and attempted to use the technology as competitive resource for its advantage. Finally, along with the increasing popularity of international traveling, the company wasted no time from very beginning to expand its operations beyond the U.S. boundary. Then global expansion started in 1998 when <*Travelocity.co.uk*> was launched in London. By April 1999 <*Travelocity.com.ca*> opened in Toronto, and in October 2001 <*Travelocity.co.en Francais*> was launched in French. In fact, its performance and the ability of Travelocity to handle its 30 million-member database had lead its official website earning many special awards including: *Best Commerce Website Webby Award* in 2001 and being selected as one of <PC Magazine's> *Top 100 Web Sites.*

From the perspective of operations management, the service provided by *Travelocity* is still in the growth stage - being only a few years in existence, there is still a large untapped market to the Internet-based travel booking business. While its current service line offers all types of travel assistance and booking including: air, hotel, cruise, train, and car rental, the company certainly can go beyond in a near future- such as online bookings for concerts, sport events, and other entertainments. As mentioned earlier, *Travelocity* is a leader and pacesetter in the industry when it comes to new developments. Foe example, its official website provides a personalisation for their users. The website not only welcomes its customer by name, it has this customer's *"Fare Watcher"* section where one can see the prices on flights one has listed to keep an eye on. But don't worry about missing out on a good sale, when the price drops below a mark set by the customer, the customer will be e-mailed with the price and airlines offering the sale. Other noticeable new services provided by the company include: fast, immediate pricing of travel, multiple options of travel, customisation to individual needs and individual travel history, updates by e-newsletters, and the ability to plan every aspect of a trip in one sitting and on one website. Since 1996, *Travelocity* started its online booking services for airlines and car rentals, thereafter expanded its online booking services to hotel/motel rooms, cruise, train. The benefits to expand its operations are obvious, not only to maintain its leadership position in the marketplace, but also to diversify its revenues.

The company's official website is continuously upgraded with new available Internetbased technology. While the headquarter of the company is located in Fort Worth, Texas, to better serve its customers, the company also has branch offices in San Francisco and New York, and several regional customer service centers in San Antonio (Texas), Plains (PA), Clintwood (VA), Ottawa (ONT), Stansted, UK, and Munich, Germany. In fact, having its customer service centers across global locations allows *Travelocity* to focus on the quality of customer service. For an e-business organisation, good customer service is an apparent top priority in the online travel booking industry and if a company can offer assistance in customer's native language 24 hours a day and seven days a week - customer satisfaction will be enhanced. In terms of quality management, there are standard "*dimensions of service quality*" that are important to the online travel booking industry, including fast delivery of services, competitive price, understandability of online booking websites, customer service, and customisation of customer needs. As discussed in earlier section, *Travelocity* has been the industry leader in most of those quality dimensions.

References

Buhalis, D & Laws, E. (eds). 2001. *Tourism Distribution Channels-Practices, Issues and Transformations*, Continuum Publishing, London.

Buhalis, D. 2003. *e tourism –Information Technology for strategic tourism management*, Prentice Hall, Harlow, UK.

Carter R & Richer P. 1999. *Marketing Tourism Destination Online*, WTO Business Council, Madrid.

Gupta, S & Bansal, S.P. 2001. *Tourism Towards 21st Century,* Deep and Deep. New Delhi.

Inkpen, G. 1998. *Information Technology for Travel and Tourism*, Addison Wesley Logman, Essex UK .

Marcussen, C. 1999. *Internet Distribution of European Travel and Tourism Services*, Research Centre of Bornholm, Denmark.

Werthner, H & Klein, S 1999, 'ICT and the changing landscape of global tourism Distribution', *Electronic Markets*, vol. 9, no. 4, p. 256.

World Tourism Organisation 1999, *Marketing tourism destinations online: Strategies for the information age*, Madrid.

10

Communication and Sustainable Tourism

Tourism is one of the world's largest economic sectors and one that continues to expand very rapidly. Done well, tourism development can be a powerful tool for economic growth, poverty reduction, and for the conservation of natural and cultural resources. Wise planning and management of tourism development is key to keeping it a force for good.

Tourism is truly cross-sectoral, involving a wide range of issues that can include the following:

— trade and investment policy
— employment and labour laws
— enterprise development
— public-private partnerships
— community and urban planning
— infrastructure development
— conservation of cultural heritage, protected areas and biodiversity
— management of natural resources
— safety and security
— education and workforce development.

There are vast numbers of stakeholders, with their different and sometimes opposing interests and agendas. The multiple stakeholders at both national and local levels must be able to access the information they need to understand their long-term interests, articulate their opinions, identify proposals, and network effectively with one another.

Tourism development choices must balance between national and local needs, public and private sector, host communities, civil society, tourists, and mass media. Sustainable tourism development thus represents a very complex task.

Communication has a huge role in supporting sustainable tourism development and managing its multiple dimensions. Communication can create and facilitate a system that allows stakeholders to exchange opinions and arrive at consensual solutions. Effective use of communication tools can also link products to markets, and can contribute to visitors' safe and positive experiences. Communication processes can build awareness of this responsibility and persuade stakeholders that sustainable practices ultimately benefit their long-term interests.

A comprehensive communication strategy, which should identify how information, awareness creation, advocacy, network building, conflict mitigation, and communication platforms will be supported, is essential for any successful sustainable tourism development activity.

An e-conference addressing the role of communication in sustainable tourism development took place between May 29 and June 9, 2006. The World Bank, the US Agency for International Development (USAID) and the UN World Tourism Organisation (UNWTO) envisioned the forum as a means to bring together development practitioners, tourism professionals, decision-makers, academicians and communication specialists representing various national institutions, private sector and media organisations, NGOs, international institutions, and donors active in the field of communication and sustainable tourism to discuss the role that communication can play in designing and implementing sustainable tourism strategies and projects at national and local levels, and to consolidate knowledge on development communication in sustainable tourism programs. Discussions focused on the following topics:

- The role that communication can play in designing and implementing sustainable tourism strategies and projects at national and local levels;
- The importance of sharing experiences, information and perspectives;

— Identification of lessons learned and most effective practices; and
— The exchange of knowledge on development communication in sustainable tourism programs.

The e-conference was part of the preparation for the World Congress on Communication for Development (WCCD). It consisted of the following five concurrent sessions, moderated by the persons listed below. The e-conference benefited from the active contribution of more than 700 registered participants from all six continents.

10.1. Role of Communication in Planning Sustainable Tourism Policies

The fact that the tourism sector is multisectoral, and can be very fragmented, was a recurring theme in the discussions. The wide range of stakeholders at both local and national levels having a role in the formulation and implementation of sustainable tourism policies and strategies includes:

— Public authorities in the fields of economy, environment, tourism, transportation, education, culture, etc.
— Tourism businesses and their associations at the national and local levels
— Local communities;
— NGOs and civil society groups;
— Academic and research institutions; and
— Media organisations.

Participants agreed that policy and strategy development must be a process where all stakeholders are able to freely express their viewpoints and have their interests taken into account. National and local policies must be coordinated, consensual and responsive to the needs of different stakeholders. Undertaking ample consultations is key to the successful formulation and implementation of tourism policies. In addition, the many different interest groups often hold disparate viewpoints that must be coalesced into a common vision.

10.1.1. Multi-level Stakeholder Involvement

<table>
<tr><th>Local/National</th><th>International</th></tr>
<tr><td>Public authorities</td><td>International / regional organisations</td></tr>
<tr><td>Media organisations</td><td>Donors</td></tr>
<tr><td colspan="2">Tourism businesses and their associations</td></tr>
<tr><td colspan="2">NGos and civil society groups</td></tr>
<tr><td colspan="2">Academic and research institutions</td></tr>
</table>

Participants stressed that effective communication is therefore essential for policy-making and implementation. They agreed that both conventional communication methods and the application of new technologies are key to developing sustainable tourism policies. The need for governments to create and maintain websites with regularly updated information was stressed, as was the notion that websites should not serve just for tourism promotion purposes, but also to disseminate information on tourism policies and plans.

10.1.2. Use of Public Events to Promote Tourism in Tanzania

Development and institutional processes leading to the design of national and local level tourism policies can benefit from public events supported by political leaders, national and international media, and regional and international organisations. An example was provided from Tanzania, where MIGA, an agency of the World Bank, promoted a tourism investment conference with the Ministry of Tourism. President Mkapa made the opening speech, and also met with individual investors. The Africa Travel Association (ATA) was instrumental in securing interviews on the conference with BBC, which were broadcast live, and ATA published several articles in their magazine. The local newspapers provided event coverage.

10.1.3. Success of Zambia Tourism Newspetter

In addition to international and national institutions, smaller organisations and individual initiatives can also disseminate information and promote cooperation to encourage sustainable tourism practices. Other e-conference participants pointed out that multiple international development and donor organisations often carry out overlapping policy-development and institutional strengthening activities in the same country or area and that improved communication is essential in order to coordinate donor activities, minimise duplication and maximise synergies.

10.1.4. Internet as a Tool for Consultation

With growing numbers of users and improving access worldwide, the Internet is an increasingly important tool for stakeholder consultation and information transfer. In Australia, the Tourism White Paper Implementation Plan 2004 was launched by the Minister for Small Business and Tourism, and refined through on-line consultation with key tourism industry stakeholders, Australian Government departments and state and territory government. The list of organisations that participated in the consultation and their input was made public on the website of the Department of Industry, Tourism and Resources, together with an advanced strategy draft that incorporated the different views.

The Internet is also a key tool for information-sharing and exchange of experiences on tourism policies. DestiNet, a new initiative of the European Environment Agency was cited as a good example. The information resource and communications platform contains selected, quality assessed information on the ways in which tourism is being made more sustainable. It acts as a single European-level gateway to environmental sustainability for the tourism sector, allowing users to:

— Understand and report on sector impacts on the environment;

— Learn how to improve tourism sector sustainability; and

— Coordinate information exchange between tourism stakeholders.

10.1.5. Advocacy

Many developing countries are looking to tourism development to solve their economic problems. For many of them, their natural and cultural heritage represents one of their few economic resources. Natural and cultural heritage are, however, not renewable and tourism must be addressed in a sustainable way to prevent irreversible degradation to the resources that draw tourists to a country. Unfortunately, developing countries frequently experience some difficulty in planning and promoting sustainable tourism policies. Politicians are often guided by the necessity to achieve rapid and visible results during their tenure. Choices about tourism development policies and strategies are too often dictated by the necessity to satisfy immediate needs: sustaining balance of payments, creating new jobs to reduce unemployment, etc. However, tourism development projects producing immediate benefits may turn out to be negative in the long term if they threaten natural and cultural heritage.

An extended dialogue developed under the discussion topic "Advocacy for sustainable tourism policies," focusing on the role of education and awareness-raising activities. Various messages stressed the need to integrate sustainable tourism policy issues in school curricula in different types of education programs related to tourism management and planning, including vocational and technical schools as well as universities. It was also suggested that sustainability issues need to be incorporated into a general education curriculum in order to ensure that future generations of tourists are sensitive to environmental and social concerns when engaging in touristic activities.

It was subsequently noted that, while education in schools and academic institution is critical, awareness raising activities about sustainable policy issues should also target public officials and business persons. Suggested communication tools for awareness-raising among stakeholders include seminars and workshops, internships/ mentor relationships with leaders of successful programs in other communities, and Web forums to share lessons learned from other experiences.

NGOs can have a key role in awareness-raising activities targeting public authorities. In Bulgaria, the Foundation for Local Government Reform, an NGO specialising in supporting local governments, used specific tools such as newsletters, workshops, training, and grant schemes to educate mayors and their administrations and the municipal councils about the benefits of sustainable tourism.

10.1.6. Training and Knowledge Management

Some participants stressed "tourism knowledge management" as a key factor to be considered in all countries, suggesting that universities and schools of tourism and professional studies should be involved in collective actions.

Tourism portals, however, fail to provide regularly updated calendars of events with descriptions of courses and instructors. Also, participants should be able to rate their instructors and some sort of public evaluation should occur after six to twelve months.

10.2. Communication and Local Tourism Development

One of the key principles of sustainable tourism is that the local population is placed at the centre of tourism development interventions in terms of participation in the decision-making process and benefit sharing. It is at the community level where tourism impacts are mostly keenly felt, conservation challenges must be met and culture is most affected. Several econference participants therefore stressed the importance of community involvement and active participation in sustainable tourism development as one key to success. Among the principal challenges that participants mentioned related to community involvement:

— Frequent changes in local government
— Lack of government support
— Conflicting interests between groups
— Lack of funds
— Late attempts to involve local communities
— Lack of commercial skills at the local level
— Too many different actors often engaged in well-intentioned but underfunded projects that are not coordinated with other efforts
— Failure to consider the whole tourism system of a country or region and not taking into account demand for tourism products
— Communication gap between communities and the private sector.

Communication tools mentioned as effective ways to involve local communities in tourism development included training; participatory workshops; community, group and individual meetings; local radio; school newsletters; and local events.

Another issue that frequently surfaced in discussion was the need to consider tourism as a business, and community members as business people. Community-based tourism projects should therefore be focused on market demand. This implies a need for professionalism in the tasks required to start a business such as: a business feasibility study, business administration, hospitality, marketing strategy, development of IT marketing tools, market analysis, etc.

Communities generally need support to carry out successful tourism development initiatives. Technical experts however, must simply provide expertise, experience and advice, and act as facilitators to help local communities make informed decisions and build their own strategy. This means supporting consultative processes within a community to allow the different segments of the population to express their opinions. Signing a contract between the community and the consulting organisation can be one way to enhance the sense of ownership within a community.

Community workshops are an important way to identify problems and concerns, and to determine available options before decisions are made and actions taken. Workshops can also be used to introduce communities to new topics such as marketing techniques, or to design project proposals which will be used to seek out funding.

The Internet was often mentioned as an important tool to put local tourism micro-enterprises into direct contact with the global market of travellers. Some participants stressed that it is essential to gain the trust of local communities prior to any productive interaction with them. Others pointed out the need to avoid making communities dependent on development workers. Finally, participants stressed the obvious, but often neglected, necessity for consultants and other outside entities to consider culture, beliefs and traditions in tourism planning, and to avoid preconceptions while listening and facilitating participatory processes.

10.2.1. Communities and the Private Sector

Many participants described a communication gap between the private sector and local communities, feeling that the private sector is not prepared to communicate with communities because it requires more time and patience than most business people are willing to invest. These different perceptions, different assumptions and different priorities, as well as mistrust and a lack of willingness to collaborate, can generate misunderstandings between the private sector and local communities. Another issue raised in the e-conference was that communities are often not considered to be a component of the private sector. However, the moment they enter into the tourism business they become part of the private sector and need to adopt a business-related point of view.

Methods of overcoming barriers mentioned by e-conference participants included awareness-raising activities and dialogue between businessmen and communities to aid in understanding different points of views, opinions and interests. As one of the e-conference participants remarked, "Who should be responsible for supporting the local communities in undertaking a profitable tourism business? It is a question to consider in each situation."

10.2.2. Investment and Marketing

If government or public donors are not supporting a community tourism initiative, communities need to find creative ways to access financing. Sponsorship might be one option for community tourism. An example was given of the BC Aboriginal Tourism Association in which sponsors have their corporate name affiliated with the Association and see value in the exposure they receive from financing specific activities.

In the case of Great Bear Rainforest in British Columbia, combining large scale nature conservation within First Nation traditional territory has been key to forging a link between private sector funds and communities. One element of these historic land use agreements has been the creation of the "Coast Opportunities Funds," a conservation-financing program developed through a remarkable collaborative process involving First Nations, environmentalists, philanthropists, and government representatives. Establishing this program required a decade of negotiation, again highlighting the length of time some processes need.

One of the biggest issues facing all community tourism projects in remote locations is marketing – creating awareness and stimulating interest in widely dispersed geographic market areas. In May 2006, the Lonely Planet travel publishers produced "Code Green – Experiences of a Lifetime".

One example of a private/public sustainable tourism partnership is now underway in Clarendon Parish, Jamaica. "Clarendon Express" is a partnership between a wide variety of stakeholders from the private sector, the Jamaican government, environmental NGOs, a protected area, local hotels, the Chamber of Commerce, and others. Jamalco is collaborating with national and international partners to convert an industrial train route into a tourism train that links the sea to the mountains with diverse visitor opportunities along the way.

10.2.3. False Expectations

It is necessary for local communities to realise that sustainable tourism development is not a panacea, and that hard work is required to receive any benefit. The community must approach tourism as any other business that involves risks. They need sufficient information and capacity to assess and mitigate these risks. They also need to realise that they are service providers who are in a long chain of interdependent tourism-related businesses and they need to be familiar with the other actors. Capacity building training and equity in tourism benefits can also build the trust of communities and reduce false expectations.

10.2.4. Inappropriate Tourist Behaviour

Many e-conference participants felt that the best way to inform tourists about appropriate behaviour in host countries is to reach them prior to travel via guidebooks. Many books already incorporate a chapter on responsible travel. Other channels that are important vehicles for carrying information to a wide range of tourists include travel agencies, Internet sites and magazines. However, travel magazines and travel narration too often present destinations just as tourism products, forgetting that people with other cultures and sensibilities live there.

10.3. Tourism and CSR

The notion of CSR is not new, but its adoption and integration into the tourism industry is in very early stages, voluntary and largely spearheaded by the ecotourism movement. However, the adoption and endorsement of the basic principles of sustainable tourism that address the new paradigm of triple bottom line assessment has steadily grown over the last decade – although it is undeniable that the major focus has been on environmental protection and conservation rather than addressing social issues such as labour standards.

The thrust of CSR in the mainstream (mass) tourism industry is accused of being largely environmental, the skeptics say, simply because environmental management systems help reduce costs or are perceived as a potential selling point. Philanthropy by major tourism players also is another element of CSR that has been adopted to varying degrees, becoming more accepted and even expected, although largely as ad hoc gestures of goodwill. However, CSR in the tourism industry is not simply about potential environmental savings, certification programs or philanthropy – it is increasingly being considered by enlightened corporations and individuals as the only way to ensure long term sustainability, and often leads to better businesses with increased profitability. There are many in the business community who see CSR not as a "luxury" that is indulged in when and where resources allow – but as a fundamental tool to doing business well, and hence one that needs to be built into strategies to ensure risk management and reputational enhancement. The e-conference participants' contributions certainly clarified the need for increased communication about and for CSR in tourism. A regulatory framework is needed not only to facilitate "seamless" communication but also to create common grounds and a common understanding of some of the sustainability issues and the potential of CSR to enhance business viability and longevity.

— help tourism businesses and consumers understand and adopt relevant environmental and social sustainability standards and systems;
— help tourism businesses that are adopting appropriate CSR principles and relevant standards in being rewarded by increased business; and

— create better links among large tourism operators, local communities, and small and medium enterprises to develop win-win partnerships.

10.3.1. Lack of Internationally Recognised Definition of CSR

A large part of the e-conference discussion concentrated on different perceptions and definitions of sustainable tourism and corporate social responsibility. Despite a multitude of definitions by several international and national institutions, tourism enterprises, non-governmental organisations (NGOs) and individuals, there is no coherent and internationally recognised definition framework according to which CSR activities can be structured or scrutinised. The lack of an internationally recognised definition of CSR leads to a range of obstacles for communication on CSR between stakeholders. Many companies misunderstand sustainable management or CSR as simply "philanthropy", "charitable giving", or "humanitarian aid," etc., rather than using sustainable management to improve their local business context. On the other hand, there were also a number of participants who argued against one univocal standard or definitive "definition" for CSR. Given the diversity of cultures, differently sized operations.

10.3.2. Stakeholder Identification

Participants highlighted that, to their knowledge, there isn't one preferred, or leading organisation that is necessarily the only or even the most successful model to communicate about and help with mainstreaming CSR principles and practices. Therefore all possible stakeholders need to be identified and held to account for spreading the principles of sustainable development. Aside from the industry, consumers and NGOs, these include:

— Certification and standards-setting organisations

— Governmental organisations

— Intermediaries.

The government was most often identified by the participants as the stakeholder responsible for creating the appropriate framework environment to encourage and ensure successful and transparent communication on CSR. Appreciating the current structures of the tourism business and its sales structure, two additional stakeholders were identified as important intermediaries and ambassadors for sustainable development and CSR:

— Sales staff

— Media.

A study on marketing certified products recently completed by The International Ecotourism Society (TIES) concluded that "green" tourism certification programs can get the "biggest bang for the buck" by marketing to intermediaries such as tour operators, guide books and the media, rather than directly to consumers. These intermediaries can, in turn, market directly to consumers. With time, as certification programs grow in size and spread to more countries and as more tour operators use and promote certified products, consumer awareness and demand is likely to grow. While critics of certification often cite the current lack of consumer demand as a reason why it will not work, TIES would argue that, based on lessons learned from other industries, consumer demand takes a long time to grow and is best built through certification programs targeting and convincing intermediaries such as tour operators/wholesalers. The identification of charismatic leaders who would be able to win the minds of small entrepreneurs was suggested as a possible strategy. A potential threat would be that communication would be then limited to individually perceived and defined issues rather than incorporating the real needs of all stakeholders.

10.3.3. Certification and Standards

Certification and standards were identified by the participants as the current most effective option for actively supporting and guiding CSR processes on the individual company level. In the (self-proclaimed) sustainable tourism industry, the development of standards and voluntary certification that provide some form of "guarantee" of sustainability standards is common, but widespread adoption and use of these standards is unfortunately still rare. Consumer surveys are confusing, for although they often proclaim a general willingness to pay a premium for products that demonstrate a commitment to sustainable tourism practices, only a small percentage of consumers appear to seek these products or understand much about what appropriate environmental, social or cultural standards *are*. "Green" tourism certification standards certainly measure and seek to mitigate the negative environmental, social, and cultural impacts of tourism businesses. Certifying tour operators and hotels facilitates mainstreaming of CSR and sustainable management practices in the tourism industry and serves not only as a relatively easy way for consumers to identify "responsible" and "ethical" product, but communicates CSR and other important issues both B2B and to other stakeholders. Certification programs and their standards can serve to effectively communicate an in-depth review or insight through their criteria into the large range of issues that affect sustainable tourism development.

10.3.2. CSR Tools and Measures

With regards to communication within the tourism industry, e-conference participants highlighted various different issues that should be addressed to support the incorporation of CSR principles and tools among tourism businesses Suggestions included:

- Obtain a clear understanding of the capacity gaps;
- Ensure that CSR tools and examples are adapted to take into account the knowledge, capacity and the culture of the countries to which CSR modules are transferred adopting "adaptive management" practices;
- Create a clear and univocal understanding of what CSR means
- Maximise the participation of local communities in defining what CSR means at the local level to go beyond a simple ecolabel. Community-based organisations and NGOs at the local level are seen as very "good intermediaries" to promote a local interpretation of general CSR frameworks; and
- Joint and cooperative work on CSR in tourism through networks like the Tour Operator Initiative (TOI), who are contributing to a vital exchange on CSR practices between the large tourism players.

Participants appeared to feel that the industry had not yet fully embraced CSR as there was a lack of understanding on what it was and how it might help their business. There was certainly a perception that there was a lack of common understanding about the "business case" of CSR in the tourism industry. The willingness to pay more for responsible and ethical operators by a growing number of customers is not yet evident in the mass tourism sector, despite surveys that declare a growing percentage of customers demand more responsible products and are willing to pay more for a certain "feelgood factor". It was felt that this "special" customer was largely confined to niche market segments, which are smaller in size, more transparent and easier to be recognised as such at the individual consumer level.

With regards to communication from tourism enterprises to their consumers, two key points were expressed by the participants:

— Demand from consumers for CSR and sustainable tourism was seen as an essential communication tool to steer companies towards more responsible practices. Socially responsible purchasing and ethical purchases were concepts proposing that the mind-shift towards more sustainable products has to take place on both the producers' and consumers' end.

— There was mention of the need to ensure end users' participation in the formulation of the tools. This will ensure the 'buy-in' of target audiences from the outset.

References

Kadison, H., Weismann, J.E., Modahl. M., Lieu, K.C. and Levin, L 1998, *On-line Retail Strategies*, Forrester Report 1/1, http://www.forester.com, April 1998.

Leatherman, JC. 2000, *Internet-based commerce: Implications for rural communities*, U.S. Economic Development Administration, viewed 15 April 2005.

Palmer, A & McCole, P. 2000, 'The role of electronic commerce in creating virtual tourism destination marketing organisations', *International Journal of Contemporary Hospitality Management*, vol. 12, no. 3, pp. 198-204.

Porter, M.E., 2001, *Strategy and the Internet*, Harvard Business School Publishing Corp, Mass, USA.

Sheldon, PJ. 1998, *Tourism information technology*, CABI Publishing, New York.

11

Tourism: Socioeconomic Impacts

This chapter considers some of the social aspects of tourism in order to measure and understand the socio-economic impacts. The main macro-level indicator is employment created by the tourism economy for subregions and selected nations in Asia and the Pacific. The discussions cover the gender aspects of employment patterns in the tourism industry.

There are various definitions of social development, and most of them converge around the concepts of improving the well-being of a country's citizens, promoting higher standards of living, increasing employment and creating conditions of economic and social progress.

11.1. Tourism and Employment

Tourism contributes significantly, both directly and indirectly, to the creation of employment. In 2006, the tourism economy provided jobs for about 140 million people in the selected subregions and countries of the Asian and Pacific region, representing an average of 8.9 per cent of total employment.

Tourism employment in North-East Asia was estimated at 87.7 million jobs, which was 10.1 per cent of the total employment in the subregion. In Oceania, the workforce in the tourism economy accounted for 14.5 per cent of total employment in the subregion, which was 1 in every 6.9 jobs. The importance of tourism becomes more significant when the workforce ratios in selected Pacific island economies is analysed. For instance, 1 in every 3.2 persons in Fiji was employed in the tourism economy, while in Vanuatu the ratio was 1 in every 2.4 jobs in 2006. By comparison, 1 in every 1.7 persons in Maldives was employed in the tourism economy.

Comparisons among countries in other subregions show that the share of tourism economy employment as part of total employment in 2006 varied from 5.4 per cent in India to more than 10 per cent in Cambodia, the Philippines and Thailand. Patterns of employment growth in the tourism industry and tourism economy for a number of Asian and Pacific countries indicate significant fluctuations within many countries over time as well as strong declines in employment for some countries in particular years. In many cases, such as Australia in 2005; Azerbaijan in 1995; Cambodia in 2000, 2004 and 2005; China in 2000 and 2004; Hong Kong, China in 2000 and 2004; Lao PDR in 1995 and 2000; Malaysia in 2000 and 2004; Maldives in 2004 and 2006; Myanmar in 1995 and 2004; Nepal in 1995; Pakistan in 2005; Solomon Islands in 2004; Thailand in 2000 and 2004; Turkey in 2000; and Vanuatu in 2000 and 2006, strong employment growth occurred simultaneously in both the tourism industry and tourism economy.

In view of such fluctuations and wide variations within countries and among countries, there is a compelling need to study and analyse further whether steep declines mean jobs are lost or whether there is temporary unemployment followed by rehiring. Detailed study would have to account for unique situations and factors affecting particular countries or subregions, although analysis of a longer time series could account for large increases or declines over the short term, thus giving a more complete overall picture. This could contribute to improved planning and policy making for job creation and human resource management as part of tourism development. Patterns of employment growth and decline in the tourism industry and tourism economy have direct implications on the social benefits and opportunities expected from tourism development.

When growth of the tourism industry is sustained, it is more likely to be a significant provider of employment in countries of the Asian and Pacific region. It is then possible to improve the social situation of people, often through Government policies and programmes. In addition, revenue generated from tourism has enabled Governments to allocate financial resources for improving education and health conditions. The infant mortality rate declined from 121 per

1,000 in 1977 to 35 per 1,000 in 2004. Over the same period, the average life expectancy at birth increased from 47 years to 67 years.

The quantitative and qualitative dimensions of issues related to gender balance in employment in the tourism industry require more analysis on both, especially if tourism is expected to give women more and better employment opportunities and improve their well-being. There is a general lack of available quantitative data that disaggregates tourism employment, wage levels, types of jobs, etc. by gender.

At the level of general impression, employment of women in the hospitality sector, the term used by ILO, was higher than in many other industries, in part reflecting the high percentage of low skilled jobs in hotels and restaurants such as waitresses, chambermaids and so on. As a broad generalisation, the ratio between male and female employees in the Asian and Pacific region was fairly equally split. Among respondents to the ILO survey, there was no indication that recruitment of women was more difficult than recruitment of men. In Thailand, it was reported that the majority of people working in the tourism industry were 21 to 30 years old, and there was a relatively even split between men and women. 22 However, it was mentioned that in China there were legal regulations protecting female workers.

The ILO reported that the hospitality sector in Singapore attracted a relatively high proportion of female workers. In 2000, there was an almost even ratio of females to males working in the hotels and restaurants sector. This is compared with a 39:61 gender ratio for the Singaporean workforce as a whole. It was noted that there was a higher proportion of younger and older workers, particularly women, in the hotels and restaurants sector compared with all sectors generally.

According to the ILO study, the South Pacific Tourism Organisation (SPTO) stated that most small and medium enterprises (SMEs) in the Pacific island countries are run as family operations. In that context, tourism offers opportunities to both male and female entrepreneurs, especially in the case of ecotourism, when businesses are established within their natural and cultural framework. In some cases, SPTO noted that wives are operating and children are working in small family operations.

More up-to-date, systematic statistics and general descriptions of gender patterns in national tourism industries throughout Asia and the Pacific can help strengthen the analysis about the social impact of tourism from a gender perspective. This can help to improve the image of career opportunities for women and men in the tourism industry. Based on such understanding and analysis, it would then be possible to decide whether protective, corrective or inclusionary policies and regulations might be needed.

11.2. Approaches to Assess the Socioeconomic Impacts

Socio-economic impact of tourism can be assessed at the macro-level and the micro-level. Various techniques, such as TSA, social accounting matrix, project level approaches, and value chain analysis, are reviewed. The discussion also covers the assessment of linkages, leakages and multiplier effects. The overall aim of the discussion is to emphasize the importance of the knowledge base to clearly show the socio-economic importance of tourism.

A full assessment of the socio-economic impacts of tourism requires that the linkages between tourism and socio-economic development need to be clearly identified. Having established the linkages, policymakers are then in a better position to consider specific interventions that can raise standards of living and reduce poverty.

11.2.1. Macro-level approaches

Aggregate approaches include tourism satellite accounts (TSAs), input-output tables, social accounting matrices and computable general equilibrium models, as well as econometric, correlation and regression analysis. The World Travel & Tourism Council (WTTC) is the leading organisation, which produces annual data and time series data on tourism's contribution to GDP, employment, exports, imports, taxes, among others. Since 1998, the Council has developed tourism satellite accounts for 176 countries. At present, 33 are members or associate members of ESCAP.

In addition, India and the Philippines have produced their own tourism satellite accounts. Thailand has begun its tourism satellite account project and has reached the stage of approximating preliminary tables. Once constructed, TSAs can help to answer questions about the direct and indirect impacts of tourism on GDP and employment; the strength of linkages between tourism and other sectors of the economy; the multipliers and the leakages.

In India, it was found that adjustment factors had to be applied since some expenditure, particularly for transport services, was considerably underestimated. Overall, it was reported that the direct contribution of tourism accounted for 2.78 per cent of GDP and when the indirect effects were added, the tourism share was 5.83 per cent of GDP. The results for the total tourism output multiplier suggested that the combined direct and indirect impact was 2.1 times the actual spending by tourists. The tourism industry accounted for 4.59 per cent of employment and the tourism economy accounted for 8.27 per cent of total employment in India, which was estimated to be 38.6 million jobs. Adjustment factors were applied to account for same-day tourism, which was a large and growing segment of India's tourism industry. After making adjustments, it was found that the direct contribution increased from 2.78 per cent to 3.78 per cent and the tourism economy contribution went from 5.83 per cent to 6.83 per cent. The contribution to employment also went up from 8.27 per cent to 9.27 per cent. In 1997, the Government of the Philippines created the Inter-Agency Committee on the Development of a Satellite Account on Tourism and applied the TSA framework to data covering 1994 and 1998. The Philippine TSA consisted of ten tables, which included: two types of tourism value added; tourism GDP; tourism employment; tourism gross fixed capital formation; tourism collective consumption and tourism demand.

In the Philippines, the TSA framework showed that between 1994 and 1998 total tourism demand grew at an annual average of 11 per cent. Visitor consumption expenditures accounted for more than 60 per cent of total tourism demand and grew at about 20 per cent a year. Domestic tourism consumption expanded at an annual rate 33 per cent and inbound tourism grew at 13 per cent. Government consumption expenditures had an average annual growth rate of 23 per cent and its share of total tourism consumption was 22 per cent in 1994 and 26 per cent in 1998. The value added of tourism industries was 12 per cent of GDP in 1994 and per cent 1998. This is in contrast to the general pattern where women accounted for a larger share of total employment generated in the economy. However, among all employed women, the proportion in tourism was 24 per cent in 1994 and 25 per cent in 1998. In comparison, among all employed men, 17 per cent worked in tourism in 1994 and 20 per cent in 1998.28 In Viet Nam, data was gathered in 1999 in order to prepare a social accounting matrix (SAM) as an economy-wide simulation model. The aim was to develop SAM multipliers to show which components of the tourism sector have the greatest impact on the overall domestic economy, which have the strongest linkages with other sectors and how much household income is induced for a given expansion in various sectors of the economy. Issues about the impact of tourism on poverty could be addressed by including data from the Vietnam Living Standards Survey which provided information valid to the regional and provincial level. Among 13 sectors with total SAM multipliers ranging from 2.24 to 9.48, the tourism multiplier was 5.16. The range of multipliers for linkages with other sectors was 0.63 to 4.11, with tourism having a multiplier of 2.07.

11.2.2. Project-level Approaches

Among the project-level approaches used to assess the impact of tourism are traditional cost-benefit analyses, including their extensions to social impact analysis and environmental impact analysis, livelihood analysis, accountancy-based lodging and enterprise assessments, local economic mapping, tourism value chain analyses and ex-post documentation of specific case studies.

Some preliminary information provided by ESCAP-member countries shows how various project- level approaches could be applied more extensively and systematically to assess the socio-economic impacts of tourism. For example, in Indonesia there was a joint venture project between the local government and Patra Pala Foundation with support from the Japan International Cooperation Agency (JICA) to provide alternative income for villagers living in the area surrounding the Borobudur World Heritage site. The project was designed to provide agro-forestry activities, develop community-based ecotourism, improve local awareness of resource management, set up a training centre for villagers and establish a community forum for networking and monitoring. More significantly, the wider benefits have extended to the Borobudur World Heritage site since the villagers understand that environmental resource management strengthens the zone surrounding the site.

Another example is in Nepal where the Ministry of Culture, Tourism and Civil Aviation initiated the Tourism for Rural Poverty Alleviation Programme (TRPAP) from 2001 to 2005. The immediate objectives were to demonstrate sustainable tourism development models, review and improve policy formulation and strategic planning, adapt institutional mechanisms, including decentralisation, in order to achieve sustainable tourism development that would be pro-poor, pro-environment, pro-rural communities and pro-women. Six districts and 48 villages were involved in this pilot programme, which was supported by UNDP and the development agencies of the United Kingdom and the Netherlands. According to one report, regular monitoring and evaluation to assess the benefits was difficult at the field level due to lack of communication, limits on transportation and on-going armed conflict in some districts. Monitoring activities from the rural community level to the central level in order to sustain the pilot rural tourism models required a different evaluation strategy.

An evaluation tool known as the "Development Wheel" was designed for communities to self-monitor their progress through discussions about changes in the community structure, development of enterprises and natural and cultural resources. The "Development Wheel" is one of several evaluation tools that is part of an evaluation methodology known as the Appreciative Participatory Planning and Action (APPA). The APPA methodology focuses on having local people identify plans and activities that are positive, successful and strong so they can serve as a means to empower communities.

11.2.3. Value Chain Analysis

One technique that has become increasingly popular in the current era of globalisation is value chain analysis (VCA). This type of analysis enables policymakers to consider each element of a tourist's experience to see how the product or service is produced, distributed and sold—that is, the value added by each element. This can help to identify where to make interventions that will increase linkages with the local economy and create more opportunities for local people to gain the benefits from tourism. Key aspects included in any form of local assessment are local employment, the earnings of sole traders, micro-enterprises and SMEs, ownership by the poor of tourism-related enterprises, the significance of tourism income at the household and community level and linkages with other sectors.

The study estimated the expenditure per tourist, including their expenditure on accommodation, restaurant food, drinks, crafts, transport and guides. For each enterprise chain an assessment was made of which owners and workers would benefit if the value chain were developed further.

VCA can help to generate recommendations for interventions designed to increase the socio-economic impact of tourism. The methodology of VCA requires that the analysis starts with careful definitions concerning the income levels and types of jobs used to categorise people as poor, among other variables used to define poverty. The way in which data are collected and the scope of its coverage, even at the local level, must be carefully planned and implemented as well. It should be noted that VCA identifies existing value chains that can be developed further. Gap analysis can be used to identify those income-earning opportunities that have not yet been developed locally. With these conditions in mind, VCA can provide policy makers with information to help set priorities when considering the socio-economic impact of programmes and projects at the micro level.

11.2.4. Assessing Linkages, Leakages and Multiplier Effects

As the global tourism industry has grown and spread to more developing country destinations, crucial issues about assessing the impact of tourism at the national level concern how benefits are created and how they are distributed in the host developing country.

In order to see if the initial tourism expenditure has significant effects throughout the economy due to a process of spending and re-spending, the concept of multiplier effect is used as a measurement of economic impact. The multiplier effect refers to the cumulative impact of a unit of tourism expenditure as that expenditure is re-spent in the local economy. The multiplier effect arises because induced increases from tourist spending affects consumer spending which occurs due to the increased incomes and because of the feedback into increased business revenues, jobs, and income.

In socioeconomic terms, linkages refer to the connections between the tourism industry and local suppliers of goods and services through both the formal and informal economy. Leakages refer to payments or financial flows made outside the economy of the destination country. For companies in various sectors of the tourism industry, linkages are seen in business terms as the supply chain. Linkages can stimulate increased economic activity and have a positive effect on balance of payments as local products replace imported ones. The positive impact of linkages also relates to the capabilities and competitiveness of domestic firms. In addition this could improve efficiencies in productivity, managerial capabilities and market penetration.

Other forms of linkages that create benefits at the local level include: employment in larger enterprises of the formal sector; development of traders or micro and small and medium enterprises, especially in the informal sector; distribution of tax revenues and collective income to communities; and infrastructure improvements such as roads, potable water, telecommunications and other services such as health, waste management, and banking. Local ownership of land or businesses is another linkage mechanism that helps to avoid marginalising local people, especially if it results in more local expenditure or reinvestment.

Linkages can involve complementary products, which are those that do not directly compete with the goods and services sold by the established industry at a tourist destination. Tourists can be encouraged to purchase complementary products in the local economy in order to create more linkages. Goods such as handicrafts, art and local food and beverages or services such as guiding, massage, dance and music add to the tourism experience and provide opportunities for local producers to create linkages with the tourism industry. It could also be the case that analysis of complementary products is one way to measure the informal sector of the tourism economy at the local level.

Local authorities can facilitate linkages at the local level in ways that create opportunities for the informal sector as well as micro, small and medium-sized enterprises to sell to tourists and locals alike. One example is the creation of street markets such as in Luang Prabang, Lao People's Democratic Republic. The night market in Luang Prabang enhances tourism's links to the local economy.

One review observed that leakages in the tourism industry occur when revenue arising from tourism-related economic activities in a destination country is not available for (re-)investment or consumption of goods and services within that country. Financial resources "leak away" from the destination country to another country, particularly when the tourism company is based abroad and when tourismrelated goods and services are being imported to the destination country, thus limiting the economic benefits of tourism development. However, the extent of leakages depends on a number of factors such as economic size, industrial structure, among others. Updated analysis can support or refute the argument about whether the more established a country becomes as a tourism destination, the greater the proportion of revenue which will leak away. In the absence of reliable data, however, it is possible to have only general impressions about the amounts and share of tourism revenue that leaks from tourist destinations in developing countries. The complexities of the industry must be taken into account as well. That is, some leakage occurs where tourists spend money at the destination for imported goods and services; other leakages are external payments that never make it to the destination country, such as travel agent commissions, tour operator profits and financial transactions of foreign airlines.

Most information about leakages is in the form of general estimates and approximate shares, which makes it difficult to analyse the impact or take related policy action. Tourism businesses and governmental tourism organisations can be encouraged to buy supplies from people in the host country, recruit labour locally, use locally-owned accommodation and work more with informal tourism enterprises.

Analysis of the multiplier effect leads to the understanding that the true impact of tourism is not simply the actual expenditure by visitors since there are indirect and induced effects that can be measured. Input-output (I-O) modelling has usually been used to derive multipliers, although this approach consumes time and resources and has significant limitations. The multiplier effect provides one way to take account of the interrelationships between the tourism industry and different sectors within an economy. However, there has been little recent work or research to update the reports about tourism multipliers that were done in the 1990s.

11.2.5. Strengthening the Knowledge Base

A variety of techniques using data at the macro level can clearly show policymakers the importance of tourism for national economic development. The time-series data available from TSA can show some of the complex interrelationships and patterns involving the tourism economy and the tourism industry. When these patterns are assessed, their relationship to important social indicators can be the subject of in-depth research and analysis.

Thus far, development of TSAs has focused mainly on production of the accounts. There is still a need for more analysis and assessment derived from TSAs in order to contribute to the processes of policy-making and decision-making. The Seventh International Forum on Tourism Statistics held in June 2004 encouraged researchers to report and evaluate TSA with examples of usability and analysis. A search on the Internet using the words "poverty reduction tourism", for example, yields a vast amount of information on the subject.

At the sub-national and local level, value chain and supply chain analysis as in the case of Lao People's Democratic Republic have given insights into who benefits from tourism activities. In particular, such analysis can provide detailed information to policymakers about the role of the formal and informal sectors, income groups and gender distribution in the supply of tourism products and services. A briefing was made recently to assess the key lessons from using tourism value chain analysis in six developing countries, including Lao People's Democratic Republic, Sri Lanka and Viet Nam.

11.3. Tourism and Transportation Infrastructure

As part of the growing impact of globalisation in Asia and the Pacific, international tourism is dependent on efficient, reliable and cost-effective transport infrastructure and services to support continued growth and development. At the same time, transport policies and infrastructure development influence the quality, capacity, extensiveness and efficiency of transport, which contributes to the competitiveness of national tourism industries. Tourism will benefit from the work being done by countries and areas of the region at the national and regional level to provide a framework for internationally agreed routes and infrastructure standards.

The various forms of transportation and related infrastructure play a vital role in economic growth by providing fast, reliable connections between population centres for business, tourism, ordinary citizens and government. An infrastructure policy environment that includes consideration of tourism development would have to address:

(1) constraints to sector development;

(2) which infrastructure sectors to prioritise;

(3) how to strengthen international and/or cross border linkages; and

(4) the complexity of relations between tourism development.

11.4. Economic Impact of the Tourism

Tourism is considered according to its contribution in the form of receipts; share of gross domestic product (GDP) and exports; and growth rate patterns for the tourism industry, tourism economy, government expenditures and capital investment.

The economic impact of the tourism industry is usually assessed at the macroeconomic level and can be measured in several different ways. The most general measurement focuses on tourism receipts and the contribution of tourism to a country's GDP.

The United Nations Statistics Division and the World Tourism Organisation (now UNWTO) developed the tourism satellite account in 2001 as one of the most systematic measurement of the economic impact and contribution of tourism at the national level. According to the World Travel & Tourism Council (WTTC), the TSA is based on a demand-side concept of economic activity, because the tourism industry does not produce or supply a homogeneous product or service like many traditional industries. Instead, the travel and tourism industry is defined by a diverse collection of products and services that are delivered to visitors. It is important for policy-makers at national and local levels to see that this diversity has many complex links to all parts of the economy. This is what makes the economic impact of tourism so significant for development.

There are two basic aggregates of demand: (1) travel and tourism consumption and (2) total demand. Satellite accounting produces two different and complementary aggregates of travel and tourism supply when input/output modelling is used separately with these two aggregates. The first aggregate is the travel and tourism industry, which captures the explicitly-defined production-side industry contribution for comparison with all other industries. The second aggregate is the travel and tourism economy, which captures the broader economywide impact of travel and tourism—both direct and indirect.

The largest travel and tourism economy contributions to GDP have been in the island states of Fiji, Tonga and Vanuatu. Many small island economies are highly dependent on tourism for export earnings as well. In 2006, the tourism economy contributed 43.5 per cent of total export earnings of Fiji and one third of GDP.

The tourism economy provided a contribution of 13.7 per cent to China's GDP in 2006. Countries in the Greater Mekong Subregion are also benefiting from the tourism industry thereby taking full advantage of the potential of their natural and cultural tourism resources. In 2006, tourism in Cambodia and the Lao People's Democratic Republic accounted respectively for 22.3 and 21.4 per cent of their total export earnings and contributed 19.6 and 9.3 per cent respectively of their GDP.

In other countries, the contribution of tourism to GDP and total exports averaged between 7.0 and 10.0 per cent, mainly because their economies are more diversified. However, in light of the continuing growth expected for the region's tourism industry in the foreseeable future, it can be assumed that the share of tourism in the region's economy will become more significant.

Additional data from WTTC provides a time-series description for a number of macroeconomic variables that show the economic impact of tourism.

The two dimensions are:

(1) the tourism industry, which shows the direct impact and

(2) the tourism economy, which includes the wider direct and indirect impact of tourism activities.

There is clearly a wide variety of results among the 33 countries and areas of Asia and the Pacific, as well as fluctuations over time for each country. However, when there is strong annual growth for the tourism industry, there is strong growth in the wider tourism economy for at least nine countries.

Some distinctive patterns for island developing countries in cases where there have been strong annual declines in the contribution of both the tourism industry and the tourism economy to GDP. This appears to underscore the dependency of some countries' economies on tourism, although in subsequent years some recovery in the growth rates was possible.

Following up is data on the growth rate variable for various years along two dimensions:

(1) government expenditures (GOV) and

(2) capital investment in the travel and tourism industry.

The descriptive statistics show a wide range of results among and within the 33 Asian and Pacific countries and areas over time.

The 1997 economic crisis in South-East Asia had a strong impact on government expenditure on tourism as well as a significant impact on capital investment. However, strong growth quickly followed such declines in growth; although subsequent declines lead to questions about sustainable support and investment in the tourist industry. The South Asian growth pattern for government expenditure showed some fluctuation in the 1990s, but the pattern since 2001 has been a fairly steady increase in the growth rate.

Capital investment in North-East Asia had declined from 1995 to slightly negative growth up to 1999 and then began a trend of strong positive growth until about 2004. For the subregion of Oceania, government expenditure showed wide fluctuation over the period from 1995 to 2005, but this never declined into negative growth. The growth rate for capital expenditures on tourism in Oceania showed the greatest fluctuations of all subregions during the period from 1999 to 2005.

The data and patterns suggest that the relationship between government spending and capital investment to develop the tourism industry is complicated and in need of more detailed study. Once again, statistical analysis can give an improved understanding about relationships involving government expenditures, private investment and growth of the tourism industry, among others, in order that tourism policies and plans of the government and business decisions of the private sector complement each other.

Several important issues need to be taken into account when considering the economic impact of tourism development. For example, policy-makers need to know whether growth or decline in government expenditure leads or lags more general growth in the tourism industry or tourism economy. It is equally important to know if capital investment leads or lags behind general patterns of growth or decline in the tourism industry or tourism economy.

Policy-makers and planners can make use of a wealth of data and information when tourism satellite accounts are fully implemented. As noted by WTTC, the tourism satellite account can help governments understand: (1) the economic dynamics of tourism beyond the traditional scope of tourism expenditure research and travel service sector production when it is narrowly defined; (2) the relationship between tourism and the durables sector of the economy; (3) the relationship between tourism and government spending to help establish a clear linkage between tourism results and government support for tourism; (4) the balance of payments arising from the comprehensive flow of tourism goods and services necessary to make tourism possible and the possible discovery of hidden trade surpluses or deficits; and (5) the relationship between tourism and capital investment to assist in long-term planning for infrastructure, resort development, promotion, and so forth.

11.5. Tourism and Millennium Development Goals

The Millennium Development Goals (MDGs) represent a global partnership aimed at responding to the world's main development challenges, including poverty reduction, opportunities for education, better maternal health, gender equality, and reducing child mortality, AIDS and other diseases. The MDGs are an agreed set of goals to be achieved by 2015 based on all actors working together at global, regional and national levels. Strategies based on working with a wide range of partners can help create coalitions for change that support the MDGs at all levels; benchmark progress; and help countries build the institutional capacity, policies and programmes needed to achieve the MDGs.

However, greater attention has been given to the argument that tourism could be more effectively harnessed to address poverty reduction in ways that are more direct. Although the focus is usually on economic benefits, there can also be social, environmental and cultural benefits. Poverty can be reduced when tourism provides employment and diversified livelihood opportunities, which provides additional income. This can contribute to reducing the vulnerability by increasing the range of economic opportunities available to individuals and households living in conditions of poverty. Tourism can also contribute through direct taxation and by generating taxable economic growth since taxes can then be used to alleviate poverty through education, health and infrastructure development. When considering targeted interventions aimed at achieving specific MDGs, then actions to make tourism contribute to poverty alleviation at local and community levels needs to be considered.

Targeted interventions to address the issues raised in the Millennium Development Goals require that the linkages between tourism and poverty be identified.

The creation of income and employment in the tourism industry and the tourism economy would contribute to reducing the proportion of people living on less than a dollar a day . Similarly, the provision of infrastructure facilities and services for tourists can be designed to benefit local communities at the same time. Such facilities can contribute to the achievement of Goals 4, 5, 6 and 7. In the area of gender equality and the empowerment of women tourism is recognised as a sector that employs a high proportion of women.

The MDG agenda and the role of tourism in poverty alleviation converges with recent efforts based on the concept of pro-poor tourism. Pro-poor tourism is an approach to tourism development and management that results in increased net benefits for poor people by enhancing linkages between tourism businesses and poor people. Its strategies focus on the local or community level and aim at increasing tourism's contribution to poverty reduction and enabling poor people to participate more effectively in tourism development. Among the many different types of poor people to be considered are: staff, neighbouring communities, land-holders, producers of food, fuel and other suppliers, operators of micro-enterprises, informal businesses, craft-makers, other users of tourism infrastructure and resources, and so forth.

Types of pro-poor tourism strategies include economic benefits, livelihood benefits and increasing local participation by building mechanisms for consultation. Such strategies often begin by policies, processes and actions designed to reduce negative impacts on poor people. An instructive example of taking action based on the MDGs and the Tenth Plan of the Government of India is a four-year project entitled "Endogenous Tourism for Rural Livelihoods" being funded by UNDP. The project incorporates strategies designed to work with a wide range of partners to create coalitions for change in support of achieving the MDGs at the local level and build institutional capacity based on a new model known as endogenous tourism, which is linked to the concept of rural tourism. Urban-centric industrialisation along with the stress of urban lifestyles has led to "counter-urbanisation" thinking. That is, theories of demographic transition due to migration based on past patterns presumed a series of three major population movements as determined by industrialisation, economic development and urbanisation.

Demographers have recently recognised a fourth movement, especially in developed countries: urban to rural, or counter-urbanisation. It is generally presumed that developing countries such as India are going through a delayed transition in migration patterns, where urbanisation has contributed to falling income levels and fewer job opportunities in rural areas, thus contributing to ongoing rural to urban migration.

The Indian government aims to identify and strengthen local resources and empower communities in rural areas through management of endogenous tourism with a view to influencing the patterns of migration.

In 2004, UNDP began concrete planning on an Endogenous Tourism Project for Rural Livelihoods in India, involving communities throughout the country. The project is structured in terms of India's cultural heritage and indigenous traditions, with common facility centres set up for crafts people with local showcases for art and craft wares, along with the history and traditions of each area. Rural tourism in India is in line with increased levels of awareness, growing interest in heritage and culture, improved accessibility and environmental consciousness.

This new style of tourism in village settings would allow international and domestic tourists visitors to experience a unique lifestyle as well as sustain livelihoods in villages. It has been noted that results from such strategies could mean that low numbers of people are employed and they might be concentrated in certain types of jobs. However, the spread of earnings, collective income and other livelihood benefits throughout a community can make pro-poor tourism significant to local poverty reduction. It is not always possible to say what contribution this makes to national poverty reduction efforts, since that depends on the scale of tourism within the economy and the degree of pro-poor change within the sector. However, final evaluation of multi-site projects such as India's "Endogenous Tourism for Rural Livelihoods" suggests the possibility of learning and then scaling up such a project for wider coverage. Consideration of the linkages between tourism and the MDGs clearly illustrates the potential of tourism to have a greater socio-economic impact. Governments and other stakeholders face the challenge of translating the potential into actual achievements. One effort to assess the effectiveness of tourism projects was a World Bank study that examinined the role of tourism in the World Bank's development strategy and its lending activities in order to estimate the impacts on the sustainable development of Bank actions. While tourism has not played an important role in the Bank's development strategy in the recent past, there are some signs that it is being seen as more important.

Others that have tried to mitigate the negative impacts of tourism, such as the spread of diseases such as HIV/AIDS. In terms of strategic and policy advice, the Bank has supported projects that were environmentally and socially sustainable and that helped reduce poverty. The assessment looked at projects that focus on economic development through infrastructure provision. Among the 1,500 or so projects that were appraised, 32 had tourism as a central or significant feature. Only eight of the 32 provided any real quantification of the benefits of tourism. Smaller projects with investment in improving facilities and providing technical assistance were more effective and yielded higher returns. Projects involving cultural site development and promotion were also effective in yielding large benefits.

In terms of environmental impacts, the projects generally followed good practice and ensured that negative environmental impacts were avoided or mitigated. Social impacts were studied in less detail, according to the study.

References

Lepp, A., and H. Gibson, "Tourist Roles, Perceived Risk and International Tourism", *Annals of Tourism Research*,30(3),606–624

Conservation International. 2003: "Tourism and Biodiversity: Mapping Tourism's Global Footprint". http://www.conservation.org

Department for International Development (DFID). 1999. *Changing the nature of tourism: developing an agenda for action*. DFID. London, UK.

Johnson, Stanley P. 1994. *The Earth Summit: The United Nations Conference on Environment and Development*. Boston: Graham and Trotman.

Sitarz, Daniel, ed. 1993. *Agenda 21: The Earth Summit Strategy to Save Our Planet*. Boulder, CO: Earth Press.

World Tourism Organization, 1998, *"Tourism: 2020 Vision", Madrid: WTO.*

World Tourism Organization, 2005, *"Tourism Highlights"*, 2005 Edition.

12

Business of Medical Tourism

Medical tourism can be broadly defined as provision of 'cost effective' private medical care in collaboration with the tourism industry for patients needing surgical and other forms of specialised treatment. This process is being facilitated by the corporate sector involved in medical care as well as the tourism industry - both private and public. Medical tourism refers to traveling to other countries to obtain medical, dental, and surgical treatment. At the same time they could also tour, and fully experience the attractions of the countries they visit. Exorbitant costs of healthcare in industrialised nations, ease and affordability of international travel, favorable currency exchange rates in the global economy, rapidly improving technology and standards of care in many countries of the world, and most importantly proven safety of healthcare in select foreign nations have all led to the rise of medical tourism.

More and more people are traveling abroad as an affordable, enjoyable, and safe alternative to having treatment in their home countries. Medical tourists are generally residents of the industrialised nations of the world and primarily come from The United States, Canada, Great Britain, Western Europe, Australia, and The Middle East. But more and more, people from many other countries of the world are seeking out places where they can combine vacationing and obtaining their medical care at an affordable cost. Non resident Indians form a big group of medical tourists to India. Currently medical tourists are traveling in large numbers abroad where the quality of healthcare is equal to anywhere else in the world and yet the cost is significantly lower. These regions also offer numerous options for touring, sight-seeing, shopping, exploring, and yes, even lounging on sun drenched beaches. Although India, the East Indies, and South America are currently the most popular choices for medical tourists, the industry is growing so rapidly that more and more countries and medical centers around the world are beginning to tailor services aimed specifically at medical tourists, and the expectation is that the options for where medical tourists can choose to travel will continue to increase at a rapid pace. The ranges of treatment the medical tourists obtain vary widely. They start from simple comprehensive medical check up to elective procedures such as rhinoplasty, liposuction, breast augmentation, orthodontics, and LASIK. Often they do visit for larger and life-saving procedures such as joint replacements, bone marrow transplants, and cardiac bypass surgery etc. Medical tourists can now obtain essentially any type of medical or surgical procedure abroad in a safe and effective manner for a fraction of the cost that they would face in their home countries.

The average cost of private heart surgery in the United States is $50,000. That same operation with comparable rates of success and complications costs only $10,000 in the finest and most state-of-the-art hospital in Bombay. A bone marrow transplant that costs $250,000 in the U.S. costs only $25,000 in India. For the same price as a week long vacation for two in Hawaii, a couple can travel to India's south coast to include airfare, boarding & lodging, personal tour guide/concierge, and have LASIK corrective surgery for two. Large price disparities such as these exist across the board for numerous medical and surgical procedures. And because of favorable currency exchange rates for medical tourists, the costs associated with accommodations, food, shopping, and sight-seeing are similarly very favorable.

The countries where medical tourism is being actively promoted include Greece, South Africa, Jordan, India, Malaysia, Philippines and Singapore. India is a recent entrant into medical tourism. According to a study by McKinsey and the Confederation of Indian Industry, medical tourism in India could become a $1 billion business by 2012. The report predicts that: "By 2012, if medical tourism were to reach 25 per cent of revenues of private up-market players, up to Rs 10,000 crore will be added to the revenues of these players". The Indian government predicts that India's $17-billion-a-year health-care industry could grow 13 per cent in each of the next six years, boosted by medical tourism, which industry watchers say is growing at 30 per cent annually.

Most citizens of developing nations cannot afford to pay for services offered in these hospitals, while nationals of the United States of America and/or Western Europe find the Third World prices for medical services quite affordable. While this affordability makes medical tourism attractive to its prospective patients, risks such as lack of protection in cases of malpractice, possible lack of adequate pre-operational assessment and/or follow-up can also accompany it.Before discussing advantages and probable drawbacks of medical tourism, it is useful to explain the origins of medical tourism and trace its development throughout time. Even though medical tourism has become a "hot" issue in recent years, according to the Derek Morgan, "it is not a new phenomenon as such".

Since the early nineteenth century, when there were no restrictions on travel in Europe, people went to neighboring countries in order to improve their health. At first, mere traveling was considered to be a good therapy for mental and physical health. Later, mostly wealthy people began traveling to the Swiss lakes, the Alps and special tuberculosis sanatoriums, where professional and often specialised medical care was offered.

In the twenty first century, however, medical tourism expanded to a much larger scale. Thailand, followed by India, Puerto-Rico, Argentina, Cuba and others quickly became the most popular destinations for medical tourists. Complicated surgeries and dental works, kidney dialysis, organ transplantation and sex changes, topped the list of the most popular procedures. It was estimated that in 2002, six hundred thousand medical tourists came to Banghok and Phuket medical centers in Thailand, while approximately one hundred and fifty thousand foreign patients visited India during that time.

By 2012, medical tourism is projected to increase in India to more than half a million patients, while generating an astonishing $2.1 billion dollars in revenue. This projection is largely based on the assumption that six hundred thousand Baby Boomers from the United States, Europe and Australia will age and seek medical care by that time. Additionally, many countries began advertising these low cost-world class treatments and treating this tourism as a profitable business. For instance, India's "government has signaled its intention to promote medical tourism" and in the Philippines "medical tourism was included in last year Investment Priorities Plan". Undoubtedly, medical tourism has greatly developed overtime and it is likely to further expand more as people find it more and more advantageous.

One major reason why medical tourism is so attractive to many people is that it offers medical treatments to people at a comparatively low cost. To begin, there are "an estimated 43 million people without health insurance and 120 million without dental coverage" in the United States. If these people require urgent medical attention and do not have medical coverage, they must pay for a medical procedure either in cash or take out a loan. For many, this kind of expenditure might be unachievable. According to the CBC News, a cardiac surgery in the United States and the United Kingdom on average costs from $30,000 to $50,000, while root canal costs approximately $3,500. For many uninsured people prices this high can easily create financial difficulties. Medical tourism, on the other hand, offers a solution.

In India's top hospitals, for example, the above-mentioned procedures can cost anywhere from $4000 to $9000 and $200 to $400, respectively. Mike Adams points out that "offshore medical procedures can be performed for as little as one-tenth the cost of what would normally be charged here in the United States". These countries sustain low costs by having less paperwork processed and less strict liability policies.

Medical doctors spend a large percentage of their income on insurance coverage in a case of lawsuits, further increasing healthcare costs. Another major appeal of medical tourism is that people can get medical treatments abroad in less time than in their home countries. In developed countries the public health-care system is so overburdened that it can take years to get needed care.

In Britain and Canada the waiting period for a hip replacement can be a year or more, while in Bangkok or Bangalore, a patient can be in the operating room the morning after getting off a plane". For those patients who experience severe pains that limit their everyday lives, traveling to a foreign country for immediate medical care is often a solution to the problem.

In general, medical tourism offers many North Americans and Europeans an alternative that often proves more beneficial than visiting their own doctors. Furthermore, medical tourism is popular and generally accepted among people because it provides them with medical help accompanied by a five-star treatment and exclusive vacations. Thailand, one of the emerging popular spots for medical tourism, is known as a "luxurious place" in regard to its services. India's most acknowledged hospital, Apollo, "greets its patients" upon their arrival to the country, and afterwards, these patients "stay in private rooms with one-on-one nursing care".

Medical tourism, therefore, has advantages over medical care at home, since in the United States patients are frequently left waiting for a considerable amount of time until, for instance, a nurse becomes available and/or arrives. In addition, foreign patients do not have to worry about language barriers since "they're cared for by more than 500 doctors, most with international training" and knowledge of English and/or other languages. As a final "treat," people get to enjoy exotic vacations that frequently are included into packages along with their medical treatments. To make an intelligent decision about whether one should travel to another country for medical care, each person must be aware of possible drawbacks associated with medical tourism.

First, even successful procedures require a number of follow-ups. A person who returns home after medical treatment in a foreign country must be aware that "complications, side-effects and post-operative care are then the responsibility of the medical care system in the patient's home country". As a result, new expenses may surface. In addition, foreign liability laws are not as protective as those in the North America or Europe. Most countries that offer medical tourism have weak "malpractice laws, so the patient has little recourse to local courts or medical boards if something goes wrong". Besides, some hospitals require their patients to "sign paperwork that says [the patient] agree[s] not to sue under certain conditions".

As a result, a maltreated patient may be left with serious complications, while the foreign hospital will go unpunished. On the other hand, each hospital is aware that attracting new patients from developed countries depends on the hospital's reputation. Consequently, it is in the hospital's and doctors' best interests to provide people with the best possible care and services. Finally, there are treatments offered in developing countries that are not FDA-approved. When choosing a treatment for any condition, patients must be aware of possible risks that are involved in undergoing an unapproved procedure.

Though, once again, there is a certain benefit that people gain from such procedures. As featured in the CBS news, Stephanie Sedlmayr needed a hip replacement. Since she did not have insurance, she decided to travel to India. Instead of undergoing a regular hip replacement, she chose surgery that is called hip resurfacing. The practice is not FDA-approved in the United States, but is frequently performed in India. It is less radical and patients seem to recover faster. When asked about her experience, she responded that it was "combining surgery with paradise".

Medical tourism is, undoubtedly, a trend that is still in its infancy, but it has an enormous potential for growth and development. In the last ten years many countries saw an increase in the numbers of foreign patients. In comparison, ten years ago the number of people traveling for medical procedures abroad was not significant enough to even be recorded. The twenty first century, however, saw a rapid increase in this trend. Moreover, it is projected that medical tourism will soon become a billion dollar industry for the Third World countries with more and more people joining the ranks of medical tourists every day. Many people do not hesitate to take advantage of cheaper costs of medical procedures and short waiting lines combined with luxuries of having a private room with a separate bathroom, a private nurse and the most advanced technology.

12.1. Globalisation and Medical Tourism

Globalisation has caused many countries to re-evaluate their economical strengths and weaknesses, as well as reassess what products or services in which nations can benefit. One such product and service that has emerged over the past decade is medical tourism. Medical tourism involves the practice of citizens exercising their personal healthcare choices in less restrictive areas. It is the traveling by candidate service recipients from one institution, jurisdiction or country where treatment is not available to another institution, jurisdiction or country where they can obtain the kind of medical procedures and innovative treatments they desire. Despite the less restrictive policies that encourage this business, these services often can also be offered as a lower-cost and more-timely option.

Because of the nature of this practice and its policies, this phenomenon has only occurred in certain, specific areas around the world. These regions and nations have attractive policies in place and have implemented unique marketing strategies that encourage the medical tourism business. This industry has demonstrated significant impact on these nations's economic health. Unfortunately, other nations, like the United States, have not been as successful in attracting the medical tourism business. Therefore, the issue is to more thoroughly understand, through the analysis of other country's experiences, policies and marketing strategies, why the United States should take advantage of the opportunity to further participate in this emerging industry.

The policy behind medical tourism has two distinct functions. In the case of those countries benefiting from medical tourism, standing policy allows for the nation to promote this business to consumers who are willing to travel and have the ability to pay. In essence, policy allows consumers new and different options for their healthcare needs. Medical tourism policy offers consumers choices. Secondly, this policy can also be enacted to protect the nation and its consumers. In the healthcare field, ensuring necessary and quality service is of the utmost importance. Therefore, policy, in the medical tourism sense, protects the rights of its participants while also giving consumers more opportunity and choices in their healthcare.

While medical tourism focuses on fulfilling healthcare choices, traveling to a different country or state is also necessary. This is the basic premise behind medical tourism. Thus, by traveling to another geographical area, it is promoting tourism to location. Tourism is being used as a means for providing capital for development and preservation of these geographical areas.

Medical tourism has had significant economic impacts on particular geographical regions and nations. The goal of this industry is to provide economic stimulus to the geographical areas, often developing nations. The objective of this business is to increase jobs, income, and quality of life of the participating nations of medical tourism. This business also promotes infrastructure development to support the industry.

Since this is an emerging, competitive industry, countries seek education, advanced skills and training to benefit from this profitable business. Therefore, medical tourism, and the policies around it, has encouraged participants to receive continued education and training. Additionally, this business also requires the use of advanced technology, and this, in turn, encourages participating countries to gain more exposure to these various technologies.

While there are several specialty markets of medical tourism that are very controversial, specifically reproductive and suicide tourism, countries are reconsidering and/or analysing their standing policies. There are consumers who take advantage of these opportunities, as well as opposition from non-market groups who have forced possible policy reform. Thus, these nations must continue to analyse and revise their policies in order to protect the practice of medical tourism and its consumers.

While there is no main policy issue, policy, or less restrictive policy, is the backbone of this industry. Most often, consumers are willing to travel to receive medical procedures in a geographical location that maintains policies that are less prohibitive than their current location's policies. There are other factors, too, that encourage medical tourism, like time and money. However, if policy is not in place to encourage this business, regions or countries would not be able to participate and benefit from this industry. Additionally, because of their particular standing policies, nations are better able to market themselves to new consumers globally.

The concept of medical tourism is primarily to encourage travel by consumers globally. Therefore, most countries enact a policy framework that is attractive to worldwide consumers on the basis that if they are willing to travel and pay the necessary fee, consumers are able to receive the healthcare practice they desire.

Medical tourism does not require a consumer to have to cross national borders. Often, medical tourism is evident from state to state or jurisdiction to jurisdiction. In this case, policy encourages consumers to travel from one area to another area where policy is more attractive or less restrictive. This type of medical tourism that markets this practice is more often seen in the specialty market of reproductive tourism.

Although countries do not tend to formulate policies based on regional expectations, there are certain geographical areas that do benefit more from the medical tourism industry. Southeast Asia has marketed itself as the primary geographical area to cater to medical tourism consumers. Since this has become a competitive business, countries in this geographical area continue to analyse and reform their policies to encourage this practice and rise above their competitors. Additionally, as this industry continues to emerge, this similar phenomenon is becoming more apparent in the European Union as well.

Policy is often shaped by numerous actors. The government plays are large role in outlining medical tourism policy in its nation. However there are other actors that can affect policy. Healthcare providers, institutions, special committees, advisory boards, associations, as well as numerous other players, can all impact policy guidelines. On the tourism aspect of this industry, there are also other actors that can also influence policy. Businesses, recreational organisations, as well other associations and groups can impact policy guidelines that encourage medical tourism.

12.1.1. Legal Regulatory Framework

Although there is no documented legal regulatory framework for the medical tourism industry, there is always a legal liability concern when dealing with the healthcare industry. The healthcare industry is a much regulated business entwined with liability issues. Therefore, countries enact policies that address this concern on an individual basis. Because some countries are willing to take on more risk with healthcare liability, they have been able to emerge as leaders in this industry. Other countries, like the United States, have not been able to benefit as greatly from medical tourism because of increased legal liability and policy.

Research states that the economic profit that the medical tourism industry contributes to the nation's gross domestic product (GDP) is the measure of success. This financial revenue can be calculated by healthcare earnings, as well as the profits from tourism related activities. Besides the monetary value that is calculated, countries can measure the affects of this industry by the increase in number of tourists, as well as the number of new jobs. Together, countries are able to determine the many influences that the medical tourism industry has on its economy.

12.1.1.1. Relation of trade measure to tourism impacts

The revenue generated from the consumers traveling to the country for their healthcare needs will go towards building the nation's healthcare system and tourism infrastructure.Because medical tourism crosses many different types of business sectors, the revenue generated will also indirectly support these other sectors indirectly as well. While this practice will primarily benefit the healthcare and lodging industries, the service and recreational industries will also profit from this business. The result of the medical tourism industry is far-reaching. Not only will it benefit many different business sectors directly and indirectly, medical tourism can provide an increase in a nation's overall economic health. Revenue generation will increase the GDP. This resultant growth will encourage development of the nation's infrastructure and its people's quality of life.

Revenue generation from this business will hopefully encourage the further development of the infrastructure that is required to carry out the medical tourism product. Development of the healthcare system, as well as the travel and tourism infrastructure, will benefit the nation and its people on the whole.

12.1.1.2. Trade product identification

The medical tourism product generally provides numerous types of services. First and foremost, medical tourism is providing a consumer with the healthcare service that they need or desire. In addition, this type of business also offers the consumer the lodging services that they require to participate in this process. Often consumers will also take part in some leisure, recreational or sightseeing activities while visiting the country. Therefore, the tourism industry may also be providing a service to these consumers as well.

12.1.1.3. Trade restriction

Because the basis of this industry requires consumers to travel for their healthcare needs, trade restrictions on travel would impact its capabilities. Among the two most problematic restrictions would be on visa issuing and International Travel Bans to specific regions or countries. Thus, if the consumers are unable to travel to the desired country, the product and service cannot be sold.

12.1.1.4. Industry sector

The primary industry sector for medical tourism includes: the healthcare industry, as well as the international travel and tourism industry. The secondary industry sectors would include: service, information technology and communication industries.

12.1.1.5. Exporters and importers

In the medical tourism industry, the export is the consumer. Because the consumer comes into the country for their healthcare needs, they provide foreign currency to the economy. In the end, they leave the country with the desired medical care. It is the hope that there are no real imports and that all of the goods and services are provided domestically.

12.2. Business of Health Services

The globalisation of health services is reflected in the growing cross-border delivery of health services, through movement of personnel and consumers, and in an increasing number of joint ventures and collaborative arrangements. Using the General Agreement on Trade in Services (GATS) definitions, trade in health services occurs via four modes of supply.

Cross-border delivery includes shipment of laboratory samples, diagnosis, and clinical consultation via traditional mail channels, as well as electronic delivery of health services, such as diagnosis, second opinions, and consultations. Countries use a variety of telehealth services, including telepathology, teleradiology and telepsychiatry.

Many cross-border telemedicine initiatives have also emerged. For example, telediagnostic, surveillance and consultation services are provided by hospitals in the USA to hospitals in Central America and the Eastern Mediterranean, and Indian physicians provide telepathology services to hospitals in Bangladesh and Nepal. Telediagnosis services are also provided by hospitals in China's coastal provinces to patients in Macao Special Administrative Region of China, China and some south-east Asian countries.

Consumption abroad refers to the movement of consumers to the country providing the service for diagnosis and treatment. Under this mode, affluent patients in developing countries seek specialised high-quality treatment overseas in hospitals in industrialised countries or in neighbouring developing countries with superior health care standards. Patients from industrialised countries seek affordable, high-quality treatment or alternative medicines and treatments in developing countries.

Several developing countries export health services via consumption abroad. Cuba, for example, has made a conscious effort to attract foreign patients from Latin America, the Caribbean, Europe, and Russia to specialised hospitals which provide high-quality care at competitive prices. It has also differentiated itself by focusing on treatment of certain skin diseases which are incurable in other countries, and on the development of new procedures and drugs, such as for pigmentary retinopathy or vitiligo. In 1995-96, more than 25 000 foreign patients went to Cuba for treatment, generating an estimated US$ 25 million in sales of health services to foreigners.

India also exports health services through consumption abroad. Patients come from industrialised and developing countries for surgery and specialised services in areas such as neurology, cardiology, endocrinology, nephrology, and urology. They are attracted by India's pool of highly qualified health care professionals and by the country's ability to provide good quality, affordable treatment.

In India, a coronary bypass operation costs Rs 70 000-100 000, compared to Rs 1.5-2.0 million in Western countries. A liver transplant in India costs one-tenth of that in the USA. Specialty hospitals, such as those in the Apollo group in India, get surgery cases from the USA, foreign tourists, non-resident Indians, and foreign residents for such treatments. Each year, an estimated 50 000 patients come to India from

Bangladesh and spend over US$ 1 million per year on the treatment of specialised diseases. Several developing countries have also diversified into areas such as medical and paramedical education, health tourism, and alternative medicines and treatments. India and Thailand, for example, reserve places in medical colleges for students from other developing countries, and Cuba provides training for specialists, paramedics and students from selected countries under bilateral agreements. Cuba and Thailand have also combined health care with tourism and recreational services.

India is exploiting its niche in traditional medicines such as Unani, Ayurveda and homeopathic forms of treatment and has developed holistic health care centres, such as the Ayurvedic school in Kottakkal, Kerala, where it attracts patients from the Eastern Mediterranean, Germany, Malaysia, the United Kingdom, and the USA.

Commercial presence involves the establishment of hospitals, clinics, diagnostic and treatment centres, and nursing homes. Countries such as India, Indonesia, Nepal, Sri Lanka, and Thailand have become increasingly open to foreign direct investment. For example, approval has been given to a German company to have 90% foreign equity ownership for setting up a 200-bed hospital in Delhi. Several specialty corporate hospitals are being built in collaboration between Indian and foreign companies, including a US$ 40 million cardiac centre, set up under a consortium between Australia, Canada, and India.

Corporate hospitals in developing countries are also establishing commercial presence overseas. For example, the Apollo group of hospitals in India has established a hospital outside the country and plans to invest roughly US$ 4 billion to build 15 new hospitals in Malaysia, Nepal, and Sri Lanka. Health care companies in industrialised and some developing countries are increasingly engaging in joint ventures and alliances, resulting in several regional health care networks and chains.

For instance, the Singapore-based Parkway Group has acquired hospitals in Asia and the United Kingdom and has formed joint ventures with partners in India, Indonesia, Malaysia, Sri Lanka, and the United Kingdom to create an international chain of hospitals,

Gleneagles International. In partnership with host country investors, the Raffles Medical Group in Singapore has formed global strategic alliances with health care organisations from industrialised countries, to develop an integrated network of health care companies that offers a range of high-quality and cost-effective health services. Movement of health personnel

Health services are also traded via the movement of health personnel, including physicians, specialists, nurses, paramedics, midwives, technicians, consultants, trainers, health management personnel, and other professionals. The movement of health care professionals includes both temporary and permanent flows, each having different legal, social and economic implications for both source and host countries.

Short-term flows have mainly been driven by conscious strategies to promote health services exports, in order to earn foreign exchange and foster cooperation between governments. For instance, China and Cuba send health personnel abroad on short-term remunerated contracts to countries in Africa, under government supervision. There is also a shortterm flow of health care professionals from Ghana to Jamaica, and from India to the Eastern Mediterranean. The Eastern Mediterranean is an important host market for physicians, nurses, X-ray technicians, laboratory technicians, dental hygienists, physiotherapists, and medical rehabilitation workers from many developing countries.

Permanent migration of health professionals occurs mainly from developing to industrialised countries. It is driven by wage differentials between countries and a search for better working conditions and living standards; a search for better training possibilities; and demand-supply imbalances in the health sector between host and source countries.

A 1998 United Nations Conference on Trade and Development/ WHO study estimated that 56% of all migrating physicians flow from developing countries to industrialised countries, while only 11% migrate in the opposite direction; the imbalance was even greater for nurses. The most prominent source countries for health personnel are India, the Philippines, and South Africa, whose nurses, physicians and technicians emigrate to Australia, the Eastern Mediterranean, the

United Kingdom, and the USA. Countries have adopted different policies towards the migration of health care professionals.

To deter permanent outflows of personnel, countries such as India and South Africa have required their health care professionals to provide a period of service in their own country after graduation. Some destination markets have actively encouraged inflows of specific categories of foreign health care professionals. The USA, for example, has introduced special visa schemes and changes in immigration policy to encourage inflows of nurses and technicians from India, Jamaica, and the Philippines and inflows of specialists from Canada and the United Kingdom.

Changes in immigration policy in the USA greatly increased the emigration of nurses and physicians from developing and industrialised countries to the USA between 1990 and 1996. Between 1970 and 1993, the number of foreign medical graduates in the USA rose from 57 000 to 150 000, with India, Pakistan, and the Philippines accounting for 45% of all international medical graduates by 1993. By 1996, there were 110 000 nurses employed or residing in the USA who had been educated outside the USA: 43% of them came from the Philippines, 19% from Canada, 15% from the United Kingdom, and 9% from India.

12.2.1. Implications of Trade in Health Services

Many factors must be considered when assessing the implications of trade in health services, but ultimately the net impact of the trade depends on the specifics of a country's national health care system, the regulatory environment, and government policies. Each supply mode has associated benefits and problems. However, many of the problems would exist even in the absence of globalisation. The question is, therefore, whether globalisation of health services is likely to aggravate such problems and pose additional challenges.

Cross-border delivery of health services through telemedicine can enable health care providers to cater to remote and underserved segments of the population; help alleviate human resource constraints; enable more cost-effective surveillance of diseases; improve the quality of diagnosis and treatment; and help upgrade skills through interactive electronic means. However, these gains are possible only if the requisite infrastructure is present. Given the lack of telecommunications and power sector infrastructure in many developing countries, telemedicine may not be cost-effective.

In such cases, public sector resources for telemedicine may be better invested in improving basic health care facilities for disease prevention and cure, and in areas where there is a direct impact on the poor. The risk is that telemedicine will channel revenues away from rural and primary health care and towards specialised centres, thus concentrating technologies which cater to the affluent few in developing countries.

12.2.2. Consumption

Trade in health services via consumption abroad also has mixed implications. On the positive side, it may enable exporting countries to improve their national health systems, by generating foreign exchange and additional resources for investment in health care. It can also help in overcoming shortages of physical and human resources in the importing countries, particularly for specialised health services.

But consumption of trade abroad could also result in a dual market structure, by creating a higher-quality, expensive segment that caters to wealthy nationals and foreigners, and a much lowerquality, resource-constrained segment catering to the poor. Availability of services, including physicians and other trained personnel, as well as the availability of beds may rise in the higher-standard centres at the expense of the public sector, resulting in a crowding out of the local population.

As for consumption abroad, commercial presence in health services can generate additional resources for investment in and upgrading of health care infrastructure and technologies; generate employment; reduce underemployment of health personnel; and provide expensive and specialised medical services. The availability of private capital could reduce the total burden on government resources, helping to reallocate government expenditure towards the public health care sector. Affiliations and partnerships with reputed health service institutions in industrialised countries can also help to improve service facilities in developing countries and introduce superior management techniques and information systems.

However, the gains from reduced pressure on government resources may be offset by the huge initial public investments that may be required to attract foreign direct investment into the health sector. Furthermore, if specialty corporate hospitals are established using public funds and subsidies, this would divert resources from the public health system and could lead to a two-tiered health care system with a corporate segment and a public-sector segment, the former concentrating on high-level technology and services which do not address broader social needs.

A two-tiered systemmay also result in an internal "brain drain", as better-quality health care professionals flow from the public health care segment to the corporate segment, with its better pay and superior infrastructure. It may also cause "cream skimming", whereby those who need less but can pay more are served at the expense of the poor and more deserving. These problems have occurred in countries such as Thailand, where there has been an increased outflow of service providers from the public to the private health sector, partly in response to the emergence of jointventure private hospitals formed by local and foreign companies. This internal brain drain has aggravated the shortage of health personnel and worsened the existing inequitable distribution of health care resources within the country.

12.2.3. Movement of Health Service Providers

The implications of trade via movement of health service providers are also not clear cut. From the source country's perspective, increased mobility of health care providers can generate remittances and transfers; can help promote exchange of clinical knowledge among professionals; and help upgrade skills and standards in the country. For the host country, movement of health personnel provides an important means to meet the shortage of health care providers, improve the quality and accessibility of health care services, and contain cost pressures. In Mozambique, for instance, foreign specialists from Portugal and South Africa are used to staff large hospitals and fill public health positions. Similarly, Mauritania depends on qualified physicians and specialists from France, Morocco, and Tunisia.

If these outflows are permanent, however, there are likely to be adverse implications for equity, quality, and availability of health services in the source countries, and indeed the bulk of cross-border flows of health care professionals do take the form of permanent migration. An estimated 10 000 health professionals emigrated from South Africa between 1989 and 1997, for example, and between onethird to one-half of the health-profession graduates each year emigrates, mainly to the United Kingdom and the USA.

Similarly, it has been estimated that over 10 000 medical and biotechnology experts from Egypt have emigrated from that country and out of 1200 physicians trained in Zimbabwe during the 1990s, only 360 were practising in the country in 2001. A large number of nurses also emigrated from Zimbabwe to Australia, New Zealand, and the United Kingdom, prompted by the low wages, poor working conditions and political instability in their home country. Some 60% of Ghanaian physicians trained locally during the 1980s have also left the country, and in the Sudan an estimated 17% of physicians and dentists left the country between 1985 and 1990.

A permanent outflow of health service providers imposes significant costs on the source country. It leads to shortages of highly trained personnel, and public resources invested in their training are lost in the outflow of human capital. One study estimated that South Africa lost 67.8 billion Rand in human capital investment in the health care sector in 1997 (calculated from the training cost of R 600 000 per physician), a loss only partly offset by the remittances arising from such outflows.

Moreover, there are also income distribution and reallocation consequences, since remittances and transfers are private and do not flow directly to the public sector, unlike the direct benefits from retaining domestic health professionals. One should recognise, however, that in an increasingly globalised and interconnected world, there are increased possibilities for tapping overseas expatriate networks of technical expertise and for exchange of information and resources.

12.2.4. Trade Liberalisation

There is another general implication of trade liberalisation in health services. Neoclassical theory predicts that increased exports of health services, such as through inflows of foreign patients or outflows of health care professionals, will tend to raise the price of health services in the source country, but that the source country will be able to afford the increased costs due to income gains from increased exports. In practice, however, this has not happened.

The rise in domestic prices of health services may have a negative distributional impact on poorer sections of the population, unless the resources and income gains are redistributed to the affected sections, or are used to augment resources in the public health system. Thus, there is a need for public policy intervention to mitigate the price impact on the poorer sections of the population.

It is important to recognise, however, that many of the adverse implications of trade in health services highlighted above are due to internal factors, rather than globalisation per se. Moreover, while globalisation may aggravate some of these problems, it may also provide opportunities for correcting some of the underlying conditions that are the root causes of the health care brain drain from developing countries, such as low wages, and poor working conditions and infrastructure.

For example, the increased flows of health care professionals between countries could be helpful in retaining and attracting health professionals back to the source country, if the source country raises standards, improves infrastructure, and creates more domestic employment opportunities in the sector. Similarly, crowding out of nationals from the health care system due to consumption abroad is mainly due to inadequate human and physical resources in the health sector, and in the absence of appropriate regulations to ensure access for the needy, trade may aggravate the crowding out problem. However, if safeguards are in place to ensure such access, trade can augment the resources available for investment and alleviate the pressure on the health care sector by expanding facilities for all.

12.2.5. Issues and Policy Priorities

The preceding discussion highlights several important and interrelated issues and suggests priority areas for action. Chief among the priorities are to: address the brain drain; upgrade and invest in the health care sector; and promote linkages between the public and private health care segments.

There is both an internal and external brain drain in the health sector and to tackle this problem, whether by retaining health professionals or by attracting emigrants to return to their home country, the root causes have to be addressed. For this, bilateral, regional, and multilateral cooperation is required. One approach would be for source and host countries to negotiate short-term bilateral agreements on cross-border flows of health care professionals in line with their domestic supplyand-demand conditions. Such agreements could include special visa schemes and recruitment programmes, and they would yield benefits by upgrading skills and by increasing exposure and foreign exchange earnings, while reducing permanent outflows.

Multilateral cooperation on immigration, labour-market policies, professional standards, mutual recognition, and licensing norms is required in the context of GATS discussions on the movement of health personnel, and in multilateral forums, such as the Organisation for Economic Co-operation and Development and WHO. Similar discussions are also required in regional agreements, such as North American Free Trade Agreement, Mercosur, and the European Union, where there are provisions for cross-border labour mobility.

To stem the brain drain, countries could introduce negative incentives via migration taxes, for example, by requiring emigrating professionals to reimburse the government for training costs and by requiring a mandatory period of service in the source country. Positive incentives could also be considered, such as income-tax exemptions, measures to improve working conditions and facilities, and increased opportunities for professional development. Expatriate health professionals could also be induced to contribute to their home country's health sector under official ''return of talent'' programmes; through contractual and visiting appointments; through collaborative research and training arrangements; by establishing ''brain gain'' networks, through online communication and exchange with local health care professionals; and through foreign direct investment by the expatriate community.

12.2.5.1. Increasing investment

A root cause of many of the problems mentioned above is that investment in the health sector of many developing countries is neither sufficient nor efficiently deployed. If the availability and quality of human and physical resources in this sector are to be improved, expenditures on health care need to be increased and allocated efficiently, in line with local needs and priorities. Other measures include: reducing the high cost of land in urban areas; providing land at subsidised rates in urban areas for setting up medical facilities; providing financial assistance, such as soft loans for hospital construction and equipment; rationalising the costs of specialised facilities by having institutions share the burden; and revamping management procedures, to increase efficiency and reduce the cost of health care services.

Revenue generated from trade in health services could also be partly used to develop the domestic health care sector. Taxes collected from foreign-owned commercial hospitals, for example, could be reinvested in the public health system. However, countries need to assess their needs in specific segments of the health profession and invest accordingly in training and facilities.

12.2.5.2. Linking public and private health care services

There is a need to establish linkages between the public and private health care systems, since this could help augment the financial capacity of the public health sector, improve the overall availability and quality of services for the public at large, and reduce the disparity in standards and working conditions between the two segments. Linkage could be established through professional exchanges; cooperation in training; use of facilities; telemedicine; sharing of information and research; and by providing complementary or specialised treatments. Another means of forming linkages would be to crosssubsidise the public and private health care sectors, by transferring tax revenues from the latter or by providing beds free or at subsidised rates in high-quality corporate hospitals. Such provisions, however, would need to be monitored. Mechanisms could also be introduced to channel resources from the export of specialised and niche services to the public health system, and to promote linkages between these niche areas and basic health care delivery. To encourage the provision of health care services in rural, peripheral, and underserved areas, incentives should be given to the private sector to support independent practitioners via funds and other amenities.

In addition, the experience of various countries suggests that it is important to adopt conscious strategies for promoting trade in health services. The strategies should aim to: exploit a country's comparative advantage in niche areas, such as traditional and alternative medicines; exploit natural resource endowments; tap regional, cultural, and other opportunities; and integrate policies in the health sector with those in related areas, such as telecommunications, insurance, and education. International and regional cooperation will also be required to address emerging issues in health services trade, including issues such as crossborder payments and insurance systems, malpractice liability, privacy in the context of telemedicine, and consumption abroad.

12.2.6. Demand for Hospital Accreditation Overseas

In this age of globalisation, patients are shopping for affordable healthcare world-wide, giving rise to the phenomenon known as medical tourism. Patients who have no health insurance, or arc wait-listed for procedures in their own countries under government plans, travel to developing countries to get a cardiac bypass or a hip replacement at a fraction of what it would cost them in their home countries.

As an added bonus, the medical tourist gets to recuperate in style at a spa or resort as part of the vacation-cum-treatment package.In order to attract medical tourists, investors in developing countries have built five-star hospitals staffed with expatriate doctors who are either board certified in the United States or are specialists with advanced degrees from the United Kingdom.Increasingly, such hospitals also seek accreditation because they see accreditation as a means of assuring medical tourists that they can get western quality healthcare at third world prices.

Most medical tourists have no medical insurance, but insured expatriate employees who staff multinational companies in developing countries also need health care. Hospitals in developing countries are also pursing these patients, with accredited hospitals entering into agreements with expatriates' health insurers to pay for covered procedures and treatments for the employees and their covered dependents.One West Virginia state legislator has even proposed that state employees be permitted to use accredited hospitals overseas for covered procedures under the state health plan and even be given a cash bonus for any savings that result.

In order to meet the growing demand for hospital accreditation overseas, the Joint Commission on Accreditation of Healthcare Organisations ("JCAHO") launched Joint Commission International ("JCI") to accredit hospitals world-wide. International accreditation standards for JCI were developed by an international task force and form the foundation for a regional or country model, selected with local input, to benchmark the quality of patient care and safety in a particular region or country. The international accreditation standards focus on core aspects of patient care, including such fundamental requirements as an admissions policy that has processes in place for access to and continuity of care, with appropriate measures in place for the discharge, referral, follow-up and transfer of patients. Such policies protect the medical tourist who has at best provided a medical history consisting of on-line health questionnaires, faxed medical records and perhaps telephone communications with the doctor's office prior to actually arriving at the hospital for treatment.

The fact that accreditation standards require the hospital to identify and evaluate the healthcare needs of the patient before admission is reassuring.After treatment, there is the question of follow-up care because the typical medical tourist goes home within a week or two after the surgical procedure or medical treatment is over. At least an accredited hospital has to have a policy in place that requires the hospital to provide all patients, and therefore all medical tourists, with a complete discharge history and recommended follow-up care that they can take home to their physicians.

If the medical tourist's decision to have a procedure done at a particular hospital is based on the doctor's reputation for performing that procedure, then the fact that the hospital is also accredited assures the patient that the hospital has licensed, educated, trained and experienced medical, nursing and other professional staff to assist that doctor. After all, surgical procedures require a team of healthcare professionals, not just a single doctor.

Medical tourists who have been warned to drink only bottled water in the country they travel to for medical treatment are naturally concerned about infection control in overseas hospitals. They will find that an accredited hospital has instituted policies requiring the use of gloves, masks, soap and disinfectants, has developed infection reduction strategies, and supports programs designed to improve patient care and safety.

Similarly, even though medical tourists often select hospitals because the hospitals are known for the type of procedures the individuals seek, the medical tourists might be better off selecting an accredited hospital because such a hospital has or can arrange to have quality laboratory and radiology services for the medical tourist. An accredited hospital will be capable of monitoring the patient according to established procedures while in surgery or when anesthesia is administered prior to and during the procedure.

Medications given to medical tourists during and after their stay in the hospital may also be safer in accredited hospitals because accreditation standards require that medications be prepared, stored and dispensed according to set norms.Many medical tourists travel with a family member or friend for physical and emotional support during their medical treatment overseas. An accredited hospital will have policies in place to support such a companion by upholding their rights to information about the patient and the medical procedure(s) being provided and by allowing such persons to participate in treatment decisions.

Just as tourists ensure that they get a good hotel when they shop for a tour package, medical tourists can ensure that they get treated at a hospital that is well-maintained, is safe for patients and that has an on-going program to improve the facility. Because medical tourists research data on-line, they can be sure that the accredited hospital they select keeps accurate records, manages data well and is headed by an organisation that is responsible and accountable.

Medical tourism is not without its problems, even when accredited overseas hospitals are involved. For example, medical tourists may be advised not to travel immediately after a procedure or to go to a spa or beach resort to convalesce after the procedure. Even if medical tourists have their procedures done at accredited hospitals, patients may face problems with follow-up care at home.

Patients may not have the money to go back for any required followups or check-ups. If the outcome is bad, a medical tourist may have no recourse to the courts of the country where the hospital is located. In fact, healthcare is cheaper in developing countries because there are no medical malpractice insurance costs to the doctor or hospital. On the other hand, as long as healthcare remains cheaper in the developing world, medical tourism will flourish until the west solves the problems of its uninsured and under-insured citizens.

12.3. Growth of Medical Tourism

The advancement in medical technologies, increased patient mobility and demand for immediate quality healthcare is arousing interest among healthcare providers globally. This is spawning the new medical tourism industry, offering clinical services to foreign patients.

Well-developed indigenous health care systems and improvements in technology have supported the growth of medical tourism among Western countries for many years. Medical tourism in Asia is however relatively new, brought on in the aftermath of the Asian Financial Crisis that led private hospitals to seek alternative revenue sources.

Thailand's Bumrungrad Hospital was among the fi rst in the region to focus on attracting foreign patients, enticing hospitals in other countries to follow suit. Governments have led the development of this industry in some countries. The Malaysian Government has successfully exerted its leadership to facilitate and encourage industry development, with the formation of National Committee for the Promotion of Health Tourism. The Hong Kong Government is starting to consider to possibility of marketing its Traditional Chinese Medicine (TCM) capabilities to the region, while concerted efforts have similarly been launched by government agencies in Singapore to market its world-class medical capabilities.

However, governments are also sensitive to their role of providing public health services for its citizens, and are mindful not to be perceived as being completely free to generate revenue from public resources sold to foreigners. In countries such as Australia, Thailand, US or the UK, the onus remains on the private sector to analyse available opportunities, spearhead sectoral development, and formulate strategies to improve their competitiveness. For this reason, governments are keen to appear politically - correct when managing the visibility of their efforts, intentions, and activities relating to public hospitals and doctors.

With the tightening of immigration rules and security checks, the US has seen a decline in the number of foreign patient visits. More patients, especially those in the Middle-East, are moving towards alternatives like the UK, France, Germany or even Australia, although patient volume is currently still limited.

Over 100,000 foreign medical tourists visit Malaysia annually, while Singapore and India are also starting to experience positive growth in patient visits as a result of their aggressive marketing initiatives to source countries like Indonesia. However, Thailand leads the Asia-Pacifi c region with about 400,000 foreign patients each year. The number of international patients that Thai hospitals see is even higher, when expatriates based in Thailand are taken into account.

Thailand is able to attract such a large volume of patients as it is itself well-reputed as a tourist haven, with a variety of existing tourist attractions for recuperating patients, a relatively low cost of living, expat-friendly locals, and a respectable quality of healthcare - especially in niche areas such as cosmetic surgery.

Healthcare providers should however consider more than absolute patient numbers when accessing their competitiveness. A small portion of affl uent patients are willing to pay more for world-class treatment, and frequently travel to "gold standard" destinations such as the US and UK. Wealthy individuals in Asia who prefer fi rst-world quality treatment within the region tend to visit Australia or Singapore. The inelastic demand among such patients represents a more lucrative revenue stream, more loyalty, and even a willingness to travel further distances.

12.3.1. Pricing Variations

Just as the perceived quality of healthcare varies across countries, so do medical fees. These are frequently a result of differences in the costs of providing such services, but moderated by the level of competition and patients' perceived value of these services.

Thailand and Malaysia take into account the prices in other countries, and offer very competitive prices on various medical treatments. As a comparison, basic operations like knee replacement in Thailand and Malaysia are signifi cantly cheaper than in countries like the US or UK. As such, many Europeans are traveling to these countries for such procedures.

Health screening packages in Malaysia costs only half of what Singapore is charging, and less than a fifth of prices in developed countries like the US or the UK. The quality of treatment was however found to be a key price determinant that healthcare providers might work with. This is a function of the higher costs involved in the improved quality of a hospital's physicians and facilities, which also directly infl ates the cost of treatment.

For example, affl uent patients are prepared to spend up to S$150,000 on heart bypass surgery in the US, with especially the more sophisticated patients reporting to be more confi dent of treatment quality. Furthermore, many foreign patients visit these countries for treatments that are not currently available in their source countries, and certainly attach a very high value to their health and wellbeing. Countries like Australia, the US, UK and Singapore, that enjoy sterling reputations as world-class healthcare destinations, can therefore afford to pass on even more than the higher costs of service provision to their patients.

12.3.2. Best Practices

It has increasingly become a given that medical tourists expect the highest possible quality of care, having traveled great distances to seek world-class doctors and hospitals. This clearly extends from the initial point of secondary referrals, through the time spent in an overseas hospital, and well into the aftercare stage. Many leading hospitals have expounded on this by branching their medical expertise into super-specialisation.

For instance, some Australian hospitals focus not only on cancer, but perhaps on specific variations of skin cancer. This also builds credibility and buy-in, when the referring doctors are trained in the post-procedural stage to provide a continuum of patient care. To support this, even nursing teams are trained to specialise as oncology nurses, while the cross-fertilisation of medical teams such as with dermatologists, radiologists and oncologists ensures that all complications are completely accounted for.

Medical quality is also supported by hardware and software investments. Hardware investments include the purchase of cutting-edge technology such as MRI or Gamma Knife machines. Software refers to the intellectual output of the hospitals as demonstrated by the latest medical research. As such, hospitals innovating on the latest treatments such as Johns Hopkins Hospital or Massachusetts General Hospital, also sometimes tend to collaborate closely with their academic counterparts in affi liated universities like The Johns Hopkins University or Harvard Medical School. This has led to a clear shift away from the pure medical practitioner model to the clinician-scientist model.

12.3.3. Non-medical Services

Healthcare providers are starting to offer non-medical services such as logistics arrangements and hospitality services, as discerning patients are increasingly demanding a total consumer experience even when seeking medical treatment. For instance, hospitals such as the London Bridge Hospital offer airport pick-up services for patient convenience. Hospital reception areas are fitted as luxuriously as five-star hotels; Bumrungrad Hospital in Thailand for instance even features a Starbucks café and McDonald's outlet. Bangkok's Piyavate Hospital may even feature spa facilities that offer a holistic wellness experience.

Western-style hospitals such as in the US, UK or Australia feature their own on-site accommodation, both for patients in the aftercare stage, as well as for their relatives. These include a variety of luxury features, across all price points. Similarly, many Asian hospitals that do not manage their own accommodations also offer link-ups with different hotels, hostels, B&Bs, etc.

A key part of training for staff taking care of international patients has been in teaching sensitivity. Apart from bedside manners, hospital staff members are also being recruited to accommodate to their religious, dietary and cultural needs. Hospitals in the US or the UK that are experienced in seeing royalty, politicians, prominent businessmen or celebrities are even trained to manage anonymity concerns, such as with the use of code names for all cases and confi dentiality agreements.

12.3.4. Marketing reforms

Patients are now learning more and more about their own illnesses, and are most familiar with their available treatment options. Patient marketing, such as with an informative website, transparent pricing schemes, or advertising placements such as within in-fl ight magazines have thus become basic information and advertising platforms.

However, healthcare providers need to be aware of the varying infl uence that other stakeholders may have. For instance, the doctor's opinion in conservative markets like Japan or Korea is seldom challenged. In contrast, a key infl uencer in the Middle-East might instead be the multinational corporations sponsoring their expatriates for overseas treatment. As such, marketing efforts across different markets could be targeted towards the patients, the referring doctors, hospitals, insurers, or corporations—depending on who the actual decision-infl uencers are.

12.3.5. Services to Foreign Patients

Medical tourism is a promising new industry in Asia, offering prospects for hospitals facing saturation in patient growth. It is with a clearer view of the addressable market potential, internal strengths and limitations, as well as the level of external competition, that healthcare providers may best move forward to realise this potential.

Healthcare providers may now consider the medical quality of their services, how non-medical services are key to encouraging patient access, and the various marketing options available to them. A final consideration towards implementing such reforms would be the partnerships that stakeholders may establish. These include partnerships with universities, referring hospitals, agents, the government, accommodation and travel service providers, and even competing hospitals. A sincere commitment to these alliances allows each stakeholder to focus on his own competencies and may even alleviate the level of competition - allowing for better long run revenues throughout the entire sector.

Hospitals that are successfully attracting foreign patients enlarge their geographical footprints with representative offi ces or agencies in other countries. For example, Cromwell Hospital in the UK has represe-ntatives in India and Pakistan, while hospitals in Singapore are also setting up offi ces such as in Indonesia or the Middle-East. These agents help establish and maintain relationships such as with local hospitals, doctors, embassies, sponsor corporations, or insurers.Participating in different events also facilitates such relationships. For instance, trade shows, exhibitions or training seminars allow healthcare providers to share their medical expertise, while longer term physician exchanges may also be organised in alliance with medical universities.

12.3.6. Health Services under GAAT

The concept of international trade in services is relatively new. Unlike the bulk of agricultural and industrial production, services have long been considered not to be tradable across borders or, more generally, over distance. The only significant exceptions have been services directly related to the exchange of goods (transport, insurance, etc.) and, more recently, to tourism. The generally low level of trade in services has been attributed to institutional, administrative and/or technical constraints, such as the existence of public monopolies (education, telephone services), strict access regulations and controls (finance, various professional services) and the need for direct physical contact between suppliers and consumers (as in health and other social services). However, in an increasing number of sectors such constraints have diminished or have even disappeared. The advent of new communication technologies, including the Internet, has helped to reduce distance-related barriers to trade. Governments have begun to reconsider their role in the provision of services, and this has presented new opportunities for private participation, both domestic and foreign.

The entry into force of the General Agreement on Trade in Services (GATS) in 1995 confirmed the global trend towards the reorganisation and restructuring of services. The Agreement was a milestone in the history of the multilateral trading system, comparable to its counterpart in merchandise trade, the General Agreement on

Tariffs and Trade (GATT), which came into effect in 1948. GATS provides a system of predictable and legally enforceable conditions for services trade, and has a potentially positive impact on investment, efficiency and growth. Notwithstanding some public misperceptions, its hallmarks are pragmatism and flexibility. Given the traditional consensus principle of the World Trade Organisation (WTO), this was the only conceivable approach to devising an Agreement involving some 140 participants, including about 70 developing and 30 least developed countries. All WTO Agreements have been signed and ratified by all Members, implying approval by their national parliaments in many cases.

Member countries have committed themselves to the progressive liberalisation of services trade, in accordance with GATS Article XIX:, regardless of the launching of any more comprehensive negotiations within the remit of WTO. A new services round was thus launched on 1 January 2000. It can be expected to promote further market liberalisation or at least to translate into legally binding obligations what has already been achieved autonomously, and thus advance or consolidate developments that have been going on for years in many countries.

The commitment to future negotiations is without precedent in GATT. Past trade discussions were initiated by large Members, usually the USA, which felt that the time was ripe to advance liberalisation, redefine rules and close perceived loopholes in the system. The launch of negotiations thus depended essentially on the existence of a leader with political vision and economic power. The fact that GATS has institutionalised this process may be attributed, at least in part, to the exigencies of a broaderbased and increasingly diversified trading system. Its membership and its coverage in terms of sectors and measures have expanded over the past decades.

As the impact of liberalising forces varies significantly among countries and sectors, so do the access commitments currently listed under GATS. While over 90% of WTO Members undertook some form of commitment on tourism services and about 70% included financial or telecommunication services in their Uruguay Round schedules, less than 40% made commitments on education and health. Education and health services have traditionally been subject to strong government involvement in many countries and this situation has changed far less rapidly than the role of governments in, for example, banking or telecommunications. From the standpoint of individual health ministries and health-related associations, the Uruguay Round might have been viewed as a threat, jeopardising basic quality and social objectives, rather than as an opportunity for reform that would improve efficiency.

Initial reservations have been compounded by a variety of other factors: uncertainties stemming from the novelty of the Agreement, widespread inexperience in concepts of services trade, and, in many countries, the absence of well-established coordination between competent sectoral ministries and agencies on the one hand and the trade negotiators in charge of GATS on the other. However, problems of information and coordination also existed in other service areas, which nevertheless drew far more commitments than health or education. It may have been social and distributional concerns that led Members not to volunteer or negotiate commitments in these two areas.However, many concerns surrounding GATS are unfounded. For example, the Agreement clearly distinguishes between external access liberalisation and governments' rights to regulate for quality purposes. It also offers an enormous degree of flexibility, allowing Members to continue pursuing basic policy objectives in liberalised sectors. Access commitments can even be made contingent on new entrants, such as hospitals and doctors, contributing directly to these objectives.

GATS allows Member countries to assume legally-binding commitments concerning their use or renunciation of trade-related measures in individual service sectors. These commitments are laid down in country schedules, one for each Member. There is wide scope to adjust schedules to domestic policy objectives and constraints. For example, GATS does not prescribe the number, level or sectoral pattern of a country's commitments and does not compel Members, even in sectors they include in schedules, to offer conditions that are more liberal than the prevailing trading conditions.

A large majority of schedules have been confined to confirming the status quo or to guaranteeing only some form of minimum trading rights below present levels. In some cases, moreover, it appears that commitments have only conceded what governments were unable to control in any event, as with the use of electronic media to interact with services suppliers established abroad, such as doctors, lawyers or architects.

The scope and content of a schedule may be taken as a first indication of a country's basic policy orientation. Confidence in marketdriven adjustment would normally translate into many relatively liberal commitments, while preference for administrative guidance or dislike of foreign influence would lead to fewer and more restrictive entries. Nevertheless, schedules need to be interpreted with care. It could be misleading, for example, to infer directly from the absence of commitments that there is an absence of trading opportunities. There may be various reasons for individual Members not to schedule sectors in which they nevertheless maintain few barriers to trade. These can include unfamiliarity with the Agreement, lack of negotiating requests, and the desire to retain negotiating leverage for future trade rounds.

Schedules of service commitments are longer and more complex than tariff schedules in the area of goods. A simple tariff schedule may consist only of two columns juxtaposing on the same line a product classification number and the corresponding tariff rate. In contrast, trading conditions for any scheduled service sector are defined in at least three columns, covering product description and two types of commitment, and four lines. This arises because of the absence of tariffs in services, making it impossible to use a single indicator to determine market entry, and because GATS involves a more comprehensive definition of trade.

The nonscheduling of a sector or a noncommitment on a particular mode do not imply that the relevant policies are beyond all GATS disciplines. Some basic obligations — first and foremost, the most-favored-nation (MFN) principle — apply regardless of such circumstances. Any form of discrimination between trading partners on grounds of nationality is prohibited. The only exemptions relate to mutual preferences between participants in economic integration agreements, such as the European Union or the North American Free Trade Agreement, and to recognition measures in the areas of licensing, certification and technical standards.Thus, while a WTO Member may prohibit all trade in a noncommitted sector or mode, it must, as a rule, operate this prohibition on an MFN basis, i.e. vis-a-vis all its trading partners. Exemptions from MFN treatment could have been sought, for a period not exceeding 10 years in principle, at the date of entry into force of the Agreement or, for new WTO Members, at the date of accession. Any later exemption would be subject to relatively onerous procedural constraints, and there have been no such cases to date.

The MFN obligation is a powerful guarantee, in particular for small and less economically developed Members, allowing them to participate automatically in any liberalisation that Members with more negotiating leverage may be able to achieve. There is thus less risk of economically weaker countries being sidelined by deals struck between larger participants. A problem for these countries is their lack of influence on the sectoral pattern and modal focus of such deals. This problem may also arise in rounds of trade negotiations. Thus it has been argued that the export interests of large OECD industries, including banks, insurance companies and telecommunications operators, provided most of the negotiating momentum that helped to bring the Uruguay Round to a successful conclusion and to shape current commitments in services. This does not imply, however, that the negotiating process was biased against smaller and weaker participants.

The existence of commitments under GATS could impinge on the ability of governments to regulate the services concerned. This reflects a profound misunderstanding. The Agreement makes a clear distinction between external liberalisation, covered essentially by Articles XVI and XVII, and internal regulation for quality and similar purposes. However, the GATS rules on regulation, laid down in Article VI, are still rudimentary. The only exception is the accountancy sector, for which Members agreed on a set of regulatory disciplines in 1998.

One of the core elements is a necessity test, which essentially requires that technical standards as well as licensing and qualification requirements and procedures be no more restrictive on trade than is necessary to fulfill a legitimate objective. Accordingly, under the accountancy disciplines it would be inadmissible for a Member that has scheduled commitments in this sector to make participation in a professional examination conditional on the applicant being resident or to charge fees not related to cost. However, there is nothing in these disciplines that would constrain the right of governments to determine the legitimate quality objectives within their jurisdiction.

The Agreement merely contains an illustrative list of such objectives, including the protection of consumers and the integrity of the profession. Work is under way with a view to extending such disciplines to other sectors. It is difficult to anticipate their precise content but it is clear that the ensuing disciplines would not affect the right of Members to regulate. Moreover, a general exception clause in Article XIV allows Members to depart from any obligation under the Agreement if this is necessary to protect human, animal or plant life or health, subject to the proviso that there be no arbitrary or unjustified discrimination or disguised restriction on trade. The clause might provide legal cover, for example, for a prohibition on over-the-counter sales of potent pharmaceuticals or for travel bans in the event of epidemics. As a general rule, however, protection from substandard medical services and service providers does not depend on this exception but can be ensured under normal GATS provisions, i.e. Article VI.However, there is one wholesale exemption. Pursuant to Article I:3, the Agreement does not apply to services provided in the exercise of governmental authority. The relevant definition of such services rests on two elements: they must be provided neither on a commercial basis nor in competition with one or more suppliers.

References

Janjaroen W, Supakankunti S. 2000. *International trade in health services in the millenium: a case of Thailand.* Bangkok: Centre for Health Economics.

Lodha R, Bagga A. 2000. "Traditional Indian systems of medicine". *Annals of the Academy of Medicine, Singapore*;29(1):37-41.

Mishra L, Singh BB, Dagenais S. 2001. "Healthcare and disease management in Ayurveda". *Alternative Therapies in Health and Medicine*; 7(2):44-50.

Morgan, Derek. 2003. "Medical Tourism: Ethical Baggage and Legal Currencies." *Medical Ethics Tomorrow* 63.1:1-5.

13

Tourism Marketing: Emerging Trends

The tourism market comprises three general classifications:

— the independent travel market,
— the speciality activity market, and
— the general package-holiday market.

Independent travellers are not part of organised groups but travel alone or in small groups of friends. They travel either out of a general interest or because they want to practise a certain activity in a new and different environment. Most independent travellers are young, adventurous, willing to use rustic accommodations, eat traditional foods, and take public transport.

Independent travellers get much of their information on a tourist destination either from friends who have visited the area or through guidebooks, newspaper and magazine articles, or, increasingly, from the Internet. Many in the tourism industry discount these tourists because they tend to travel cheaply, falling into the category of the budget-conscious "backpacking crowd". In reality, independent travellers are "explorers" who are often responsible for popularising a destination.

Their financial input is often enough to enable local businesses to expand and improve rustic accommodations for more demanding tourist groups. Such travellers, often young, are more willing to use local goods and services, and interact more with the community outside the supervision of an organised tour, which unfortunately may cause negative social impacts.

Speciality tourism firms organise trips for clients wishing to participate in a specific activity such as bird-watching, wildlife viewing, photography or archaeological, historical and cultural tours. Also in this category are adventure travel firms offering activities such as backpacking/ trekking, white water rafting, kayaking, canoeing, rock climbing and sport fishing. Other speciality firms organise field research trips for scientists. These firms attract groups of paying volunteers who sign up to work as field assistants on projects such as archaeological digs and wildlife monitoring programmes. In addition, this market includes organisations and universities with special interest travel programmes. For example, the World-wide Fund for Nature and many museums organise tours for their members. These tours generally help to raise funds for a particular cause or project. These groups generally sub-contract to other tour operators to handle the travel arrangements.

Speciality tour operators commonly use host-country ground operators for in-country logistics. These national firms, based in the country in which the tour is operating, provide all services (transportation, hotel accommodations, guides, etc.) from arrival to departure. Some speciality firms in North America and Europe handle ground operations in a foreign country for themselves, but they tend to be exceptions to the rule. Managers should be aware that many speciality companies are small and go in and out of business rapidly.

The general package-holiday market attracts groups wishing to see an area and its culture but without a specific interest in a defined activity or subject matter. These tourists tend to be interested in general sightseeing and shopping, and may be interested in cultural attractions such as museums, ruins or other well-known or documented historical sites. Tourists in this market tend to want the standard services and amenities offered by most general tours. They will probably not be satisfied with the services that a rural community can offer; more often than not, general international tour groups want comfort, ease of access, security and more upscale accommodations and food.

13.1. Speciality of Tourism Markets

Tourism is more than ever before divided into market segments defining different types of experiences. Specialised holidays cater to people's particular interests, such as sailing, bird-watching, photography or archaeology. Markets or market segments have been developed around the different activities. Specialised holidays have become so popular that whole new categories of travel have emerged, including ecotourism, adventure travel, heritage tourism and cultural tourism. A trek in the Himalayas is now likely to be considered adventure travel, and a week visiting cultural sites in India as cultural tourism.

Eco-tourism is one of the most frequently cited categories of the "new" tourism: It is defined by the International Ecotourism Society as, "responsible travel to natural areas that conserves the environment and sustains the well being of local people." A number of activities have been labelled eco-tourism, including bird- and whale-watching, helping scientists conduct conservation research, snorkelling off coral reefs, game viewing and nature photography. Eco-tourism is linked to and overlaps with heritage tourism and cultural tourism. Surveys show that eco-tourists tend to be young and highly educated, with professional and managerial occupations.

Eco-tourism trips tend to be longer, with fewer people in the typical tour group. Researchers report that eco-tourists are more likely to use small independent hotels, as opposed to mass tourists, who tend to stay at chain hotels. As would be expected, the eco-tourist is interested in a more natural environment, preferring less crowded destinations that are off the beaten track and that offer challenging experiences.

At the site level, the demands of eco-tourists and mainstream tourists may overlap and be difficult to differentiate. Some eco-tourists, for example, may demand condominiums, not campgrounds, for lodging. People on a bird-watching cruise to Patagonia could be considered eco-tourists but may have demands similar to those of tourists on an expensive Caribbean islands cruise. In practice, eco-tourism connotes a travel ethic, promoting conservation behaviours and certain economic policies. Examples are, an emphasis on low-impact techniques for viewing wildlife and a preference for hiring local guides.

Adventure tourism includes a wide range of outdoor activities: Adventure tourists engage in activities that are physically challenging and sometimes dangerous, or perceived to be so. Examples are sports such as trekking, mountaineering, white-water rafting and scuba diving. Adventure tourism does not necessarily require expensive facilities and infrastructure, but it does require good organisation, guides, transportation services, basic accommodation in the field, and opportunities for more comfortable accommodation at the end of the tour. Adventure travel is a rapidly growing sector of the speciality tourism market.

Cultural tourism is frequently used to describe certain segments of the travel market: It may be associated with visits to historical, artistic and scientific or heritage attractions. The World Tourism Organisation (WTO) has two definitions of cultural tourism. In the narrow sense, cultural tourism includes "movements of persons for essentially cultural motivations such as study tours, performing arts and cultural tours, travel to festivals and other cultural events, visits to sites and monuments, travel to study nature, folklore or art, and pilgrimages."

In the broader sense it is defined as "all movements of persons, because they satisfy the human need for diversity, tending to raise the cultural level of the individual and giving rise to new knowledge, experience and encounters." Because culture is subjective, definitions of cultural tourism tend to be either too wide or too narrow, limiting their practical use in the field.

Heritage tourism is a broad category that embraces both eco-tourism and cultural tourism, with an emphasis on conserving natural and cultural heritage: It is a category or market segment that includes visits to historic sites, museums and art galleries, and exploring national and forest parks. Heritage tourism, because of the large number of activities it covers, is difficult to define and measure. In recent years city planners interested in urban regeneration have adopted the term to describe many tourism programmes, a strategy that has received support from business and banks.

Many other tourism terms reflect environmental ethics and local interests. Environmental preservation concerns have given rise to what is known as green tourism, conservation-supporting tourism, and environmentally aware or environmentally sound tourism. Generally, such tourism favours minimal environmental impact and emphasises concern over environmental issues. Urban and rural tourism categories have also been created. However, since few countries have made the distinction, quantification has been difficult.

13.2. Tourist Types

Seeking definitions that would be more useful in practice, researchers have concentrated on tourists' behaviours and preferences. Definitions and their related market segments, such as adventure travel or cultural tourism, tend to group people into broad categories based on a range of activities. These definitions and activities necessarily overlap, making it difficult at the site level to differentiate between types of tourism.

For example, eco-tourism and heritage tourism combine aspects of both culture and nature, as do most speciality tours. So for instance, trekking in the Himalayas is considered an adventure travel activity, but most trekkers visit Buddhist or Hindu cultural sites at the same time. Bird-watchers visit archaeology sites and frequently engage in trekking.

The broad definitions of the international markets are too comprehensive to be used for site-specific decisionmaking. An effective way of addressing this overlap for research, policy and site management purposes is to classify tourists according to their motivations, behaviours and desired experiences. Researchers have developed several categories of tourist behaviours and preferences. For example, tourists may be classified according to the intensity of experiences they are seeking or the ruggedness of the conditions they desire or will accept, including the kind of accommodations expected. Thus:

— Hard-core tourists join tours or groups travelling specifically for educational purposes and/or to take part in environmental or cultural projects, such as wildlife monitoring.

— Dedicated tourists want to visit protected or cultural areas and understand local natural and cultural history.

— Casual tourists consider natural and cultural travel as an incidental component of a broader trip.

Another system that is useful for classifying preferences differentiates between "hard-class" and "soft-class" travel. This classification relates to the ruggedness factor, mostly concerning the degree of challenge involved and the comfort level of accommodations. These categories include:

— A hard-class experience that is physically difficult with an element of danger. For example, it may require walking miles into the back country, climbing a technically difficult mountain, or sleeping in rudimentary shelters.

— A soft-class experience means lower risk and more luxurious accommodations. For example, a tented safari may involve physically challenging conditions while offering amenities such as gourmet meals and comfortable transport.

13.3. Tourism : Consumer Trends

Consumers are increasingly considering environmental quality as well as the quality of services as factors in their selection of tourist destinations. More and more consumers want a high standard of environmental conservation coupled with simple, efficient and pleasant service. It appears that many tourists now prefer unspoiled and uncrowded destinations. A related trend is that, before they travel, many tourists inform themselves about environmental problems at individual sites.

They want destinations to be clean and environmentally sound. Tourists will avoid places that are perceived to fall short of this image. More than ever this information is obtained through the internet. Environmental degradation can lead not only to declining tourism rates but also to changes in the types of tourists that travel to a site. Examples of this cycle are found in the Mediterranean, where the pattern has led to continued degradation and urbanisation of beach resorts.

Interest in cultural tourism seems to be expanding, but the rate of growth is unclear: More quantitative data is needed to verify the trend. For example, attendance at cultural attractions in Britain and the Netherlands over the last five years indicates that cultural tourism has kept pace with the overall tourism market. Because the cultural tourism market is difficult to quantify, experts suggest that more research would help to identify broad groupings of cultural tourists based on their motivations. Establishing categories such as arts, archaeology, language learning and so on may be the most practical way to address this issue.

Tourists increasingly want "real" experiences with other cultures and lifestyles: A study of massmarket tourists and eco-tourists found that both groups felt that knowledge of folk arts and handicrafts, as well as knowledge about the destination's history, was important.

Consumers are seeking more active and educational holidays: Specialised markets are experiencing a trend towards energetic, environment-oriented tourism, with healthy menus and plenty of opportunities for exercise. Although mass-market tourists are less active and adventuresome, and less focused on one activity, active holidays at a lower level of intensity are also a growing trend in this market segment.

Visits to protected areas are on the rise: In developed countries, tourists tend to travel in smaller groups for shorter time periods. For example, visits to Australian national parks have increased substantially in the last ten years, but often for shorter periods. The two trends together-smaller group sizes and shorter stays- have created a need for greater individual space and more facilities designed to accommodate intense use, with extra services added during certain times of the year.

The tourism industry is expected to take more responsibility for sustainable development: Professionals working in conservation are beginning to ask the industry to be more involved in site management activities. Often this involves assuming a degree of financial responsibility for the long-term maintenance of the resources they profit from. Financial support can be in the form of direct or voluntary subsidies to management agencies or NGOs. Involvement may also mean accepting practices that limit the negative impacts of tourism.

An example is at the Great Barrier Reef Marine Park in Australia where operators have become increasingly selfregulating and accountable through the establishment of codes of conduct and guidelines for minimal impact practices. Operators at the Great Barrier Reef are also involved in the monitoring of their sites. The fact that operators are prohibited from relocating their facilities and activities once an existing site is affected by natural or unnatural environmental degradation has reinforced these actions.

— Tourism definitions can give direction to broad policy guidelines used in the development of goals and objectives for site management. For example, the International Eco-tourism Society's definition of eco-tourism states that tourism should maintain the integrity of an ecosystem and generate economic opportunities that make conservation beneficial to local people. This type of a statement can be incorporated into a policy statement defining the type of tourism a site will promote.

— Tourism definitions, such as that of eco-tourism, can be used in reports or proposals seeking funding for future projects. They can give documents a positive image and strengthen their attractiveness. Overall development concepts and definitions should match the audience for whom the proposal is being written.

For example, the term eco-tourism should be used in place of tourism when writing to nature conservation organisations; cultural tourism when writing to organisations concerned with the restoration of monuments, and so on. Market definitions can then be used in promotional materials. For example, a brochure may mention that eco-tourism is encouraged at a particular natural or mixed site.

— Operators' promotional materials give clues as to whether their products are compatible with site objectives. Tour operator literature can also help managers determine whether operators contribute locally to protec-tion efforts such as educating clients in low-impact practices.

Promotional literature will also reveal the types of clients they are targeting, what kind of experiences they value and their particular needs. For example, an operator may specialise in tours geared to a serious, single-minded bird-watching group or an amateur archaeology group.

— While knowledge of tourism definitions and speciality tourist markets can help managers set policy guidelines and understand visitor interests, the categories are general and tend to overlap. For management purposes it is useful to classify and analyse tourists according to their preferences and behaviours.

Categories such as "hard" and "soft" class provide a helpful start. These categories, which focus on visitor needs and expectations, are important for elaborating management plans and setting objectives including infrastructure development.

— Knowledge of the different market segments and the general behaviours and preferences of tourists can help managers decide which segments to promote. Different tourists present different management opportunities and requirements. For example, tourists seeking more demanding or "harder" experiences are more likely to be content with a minimal infrastructure than those seeking a "softer" experience.

Tour operators such as those working with keen bird-watchers or clients interested in archaeology may have special market demands. These specialised operators may want strict regulation of tourist numbers and noise to permit them to practise their activities undisturbed by other groups. In view of the range of preferences among nature-oriented people, the market should offer a range of accommodation.

— An analysis of the structure of the tourism industry surrounding a site can reveal opportunities for involving stakeholders in management. NTO officials could be involved in future promotional efforts. Tour operators and hoteliers who may also help with monitoring activities or establishing codes of conduct and minimal impact practices. They may also make direct financial contributions for on-site projects. Interviews with tour operators and hotel directors could determine what mechanisms, administrative and financial, would facilitate their contributions to conservation and protection efforts.

— A proactive approach will yield benefits if market trends are addressed. Continued growth in international tourism is predicted, particularly in special interest tourism. The growing concern over environmental and socio-cultural issues suggests the existence of a large potential source of support for the site.

Socio-economic profiles suggest that more and more tourists will have the means to contribute financially towards protection of the site. Consequently, if a site is planned and managed well, within defined limits, an increase in arrivals can potentially bring new financial rewards.

— Because tourists are more conscious of, and interested in, the protection of the natural, historical, cultural and social environment, it will be increasingly important to inform tourists and tour operators, through site interpretation and promotional activities, of the efforts that management is making to maintain the site.

— A preference for protected areas is a growing trend in tourism. Managers must be increasingly cognizant of these visitors' profiles and of visitation trends specific to each site.

13.4. Planning of Tourism Marketing

Since tourism is primarily a service based industry, the principal products provided by recreation/tourism (R/T) businesses are recreational experiences and hospitality. These are intangible products and more difficult to market than tangible products such as automobiles. The intangible nature of services makes quality control difficult but crucial. It also makes it more difficult for potential customers to evaluate and compare service offerings.

In addition, instead of moving the product to the customer, the customer must travel to the product (area/community). Travel is a significant portion of the time and money spent in association with recreational and tourism experiences and is a major factor in people's decisions on whether or not to visit your business or community. As an industry, tourism has many components comprising the overall "travel experience." Along with transportation, it includes such things as accommodations, food and beverage services, shops, entertainment, aesthetics and special events. It is rare for one business to provide the variety of activities or facilities tourists need or desire. This adds to the difficulty of maintaining and controlling the quality of the experience. To overcome this hurdle, tourism related businesses, agencies, and organizations need to work together to package and promote tourism opportunities in their areas and align their efforts to assure consistency in product quality.

13.4.1. Marketing Plan

One of the most important steps a business or community can take to improve the effectiveness and efficiency of their marketing efforts is to develop a written marketing plan. This plan will guide their marketing decisions and assist them in allocating marketing resources such as money and personnel time. The plan should include:

— the overall business objectives-what you want to accomplish;
— an assessment of the market environment-what factors may affect your marketing efforts;
— a business/community profile-what resources are available,
— market identification (segmentation)--the specific groups or clientele most interested in your product;
— the marketing objectives for each segment;
— the marketing strategies (or mixes) for different markets you target-the best combination of the 4 Ps (product, price, place, promotion) for each segment;
— an implementation plan-how to "make it work;"
— the marketing budget-how much you have to spend; and
— a method for evaluation and change.

13.4.1.1. Business Objectives

Businesses, agencies, and communities should develop overall objectives and regularly monitor their progress. The objectives should provide guidance for all decisions including finances, personnel and marketing. They should be quantitative and measurable statements of what the business or community wants to accomplish over a specified period of time.

Business objectives are often stated in terms of sales, profits, market shares and/or occupancy rates. Communities frequently establish objectives relating to such things as increasing the number of tourists, developing or changing their image, facility and activity development, cooperation among tourism related businesses and increasing length of stay and local expenditures. It is important that the objectives be reasonable given the market conditions and the firm's or organization's resources. Establish a few reasonable objectives instead of a long, unrealistic "wish list." This is especially true for new businesses or communities which do not have much experience in tourism development and/or marketing.

13.4.1.2. Market Environment Analysis

The next step in developing a marketing plan is to assess the impact of environmental factors (such as economic, social and political) on present and future markets. Changes in these factors can create marketing opportunities as well as problems.

13.4.1.3. Demographic and lifestyle trends

Changing demographics and lifestyles are having a major impact on R/T participation. An assessment of these trends is important to understand how they will likely affect your business or community. Some of the important trends that bear watching:

— population growth and movement;
— rural community growth compared to metropolitan areas;
— number of adult women employed outside the home;
— the number of households is growing, especially non family and single parent households, but family size is decreasing;
— the impact of two wage earner households on real family income;
— the number of retired persons with the financial ability to travel;
— better health to an older age; and
— continued aging of the population (we are becoming a middle aged society).

13.4.1.4. Economic conditions

Overall economic conditions can have significant impacts on recreation and tourism markets. A marketing strategy that is effective during periods of low unemployment rates may have to be significantly adjusted if unemployment increases. Businesses and communities should monitor and assess the likely impact of factors such as unemployment rates, real family income, rate of inflation, credit availability, terms and interest rates. Consideration should also be given to the prices of complementary products, such as lodging, gasoline and recreation equipment.

13.4.1.5. Laws and government actions

As a complex industry, tourism is significantly affected both positively and negatively by laws and by actions of governmental agencies. For instance, rulings on such things as liability issues or decisions regarding building and health codes may change or possibly prevent the construction of a proposed facility. If a public facility changes the prices of its services, this could affect the service offerings of associated private businesses. These actions may have both positive and negative effects on the marketing efforts of the business and community. To avoid wasting valuable resources it is important that R/T businesses, agencies, and communities continually monitor and evaluate governmental actions.

13.4.1.6. Technology

Technological developments are increasing rapidly. New recreation products, such as all-terrain vehicles and wind surfers, provide new ways for people to satisfy their recreational preferences. New production technologies and materials offer recreation and tourism businesses ways to reduce costs and improve the quality of their products/services. Advances in telecommunications have and will continue to create new promotional opportunities. Technological innovations, in relation to jobs and the home, have resulted in increased leisure time for many people.

13.4.1.7. Competition

Businesses and communities must identify and analyze existing and potential competitors. The objective of the analysis is to determine the strengths and weaknesses of the competition's marketing strategies. The analysis should include the competition's:

- product/service features and quality;
- location relative to different geographic markets;
- promotional themes and messages;
- prices; and
- type of customer they are attracting.

13.4.2. Community Profiles

Too many communities attempt to market themselves as tourist destinations without accurate information about their resources (facilities, services, staff), image, and how well their customers are satisfied. Without this information, it is difficult to make other decisions in the planning process. Included should be such things as recreational and entertainment facilities, cultural and historic sites, overnight accommodations, restaurants, shopping opportunities, special events and activities, staff size, and transportation. Each item of the "inventory" should also be assessed in terms of quality and availability.

13.4.3. Market Segmentation

Recreation and tourism businesses and communities often make the mistake of attempting to be all things to all people. It is difficult, and risky, to develop marketing strategies for the mass market. Strategies designed for the "average" customer often result in unappealing products, prices, and promotional messages. For example, it would be difficult to develop a campground that would be equally attractive to recreational vehicle campers and backpackers or promote a property to serve both snowmobilers and nature oriented cross country skiers. Marketing is strongly based on market segmentation and target marketing. Market segmentation is the process of:

— taking existing and/or potential customers/visitors (market) and categorizing them into groups with similar preferences referred to as "market segments;"

— selecting the most promising segments as "target markets;" and

— designing "marketing mixes," or strategies (combination of the 4 Ps), which satisfy the special needs, desires and behavior of the target markets.

There is no unique or best way to segment markets, but ways in which customers can be grouped are:

— location of residence—instate, out-of-state, local;

— demographics—age, income, family status, education;

— equipment ownership/use—RV's, sailboats, canoes, tents, snowmobiles;

— important product attributes—price, quality, quantity; and

— lifestyle attributes—activities, interests, opinions.

To be useful, the segment identification process should result in segments that suggest marketing efforts that will be effective in attracting them and at least one segment large enough to justify specialized marketing efforts. After segments have been identified, the business or community must select the "target markets," those segments which offer them the greatest opportunity. When determining target markets, consideration should be given to:

— existing and future sales potential of each segment;
— the amount and strength of competition for each segment;
— the ability to offer a marketing mix which will be successful in attracting each segment;
— the cost of servicing each segment; and
— each segment's contribution to accomplishing overall business/ community objectives.

It is often wiser to target smaller segments that are presently not being served, or served inadequately, than to go after larger segments for which there is a great deal of competition. Marketing objectives which contribute to the accomplishment of the overall business objectives should be established for each target market. Objectives serve a number of functions including:

— guidance for developing marketing mixes for different target markets;
— information for allocating the marketing budget between target markets;
— a basis for objectively evaluating the effectiveness of the marketing mixes (setting standards); and
— a framework for integrating the different marketing mixes into the overall marketing plan.

The target market objectives should:

— be expressed in quantitative terms;
— be measurable;
— specify the target market; and
— indicate the time period in which the objective is to be accomplished.

For example, increase the number of overnight stays by people from the Chicago market over the next two years by five percent. Remember, rank objectives by priority and carefully evaluate them to ensure that they are reasonable given the strength of the competition and resources available for marketing.

13.4.4. Marketing Strategy

The marketing strategy, or mix, should be viewed as a package of offerings designed to attract and serve the customer or visitor. Recreation and tourism businesses and communities should develop both external and internal marketing mixes for different target markets.

13.4.4.1. External Mix

The external marketing mix includes product/service, price, place/location, and promotion.

Product: Earlier we said the principal products that recreation and tourism businesses provide are recreational experiences and hospitality. The factors that create a quality recreational experience often differ among people. A quality experience for one skier might include an uncrowded, steep slope. To another it might be a good restaurant and a chance to socialize.

Decisions on what facilities, programs and services to provide should be based on the needs and desires of the target market(s). They should not be based on the preferences of the owner/manager or necessarily on what the competition is providing. Recognize that a recreational/tourism experience includes five elements: trip planning and anticipation; travel to the site/area; the experience at the site; travel back home; and recollection. Businesses should look for ways to enhance the quality of the overall experience during all phases of the trip. This could be accomplished by providing trip planning packages which include maps, attractions en route and on site, and information regarding lodging, food and quality souvenirs and mementos.

Recreation and tourism businesses should also view their service/product in generic terms. Thinking of products/services in this manner helps focus more attention on the experiences desired by customers and also the facilities, programs and services that will produce those experiences. For example, campgrounds are the business of providing recreational "lodging" not just campsites to park an RV or set up a tent. Marinas should provide recreational "boating" experiences, not just slippage.

Location and Accessibility/Place: Too many tourism businesses and communities fail to recognize their role in improving travel to and from their areas. They focus instead on servicing the customer once they arrive at the site/community. A bad experience getting to or leaving an R/T site can adversely affect a person's travel experience. Ways to help prevent this include:

— providing directions and maps;
— providing estimates of travel time and distances from different market areas;
— recommending direct and scenic travel routes;
— identifying attractions and support facilities along different travel routes; and
— informing potential customers of alternative travel methods to the area such as airlines and railroads.

Potential businesses should also carefully assess alternative locations for:

— distance and accessibility to target markets;
— location of competitors with respect to target markets;
— modes of travel serving the area; and
— other attractions and activities that might induce travel to the area.

Pricing: Price is one of the most important and visible elements of the marketing mix. When setting prices it is important to take into consideration all of the following:

— business and target market objectives;
— the full cost of producing, delivering and promoting the product;
— the willingness of the target market to pay for the product or service you provide;
— prices charged by competitors offering a similar product/service to the same target market(s);

- the availability and prices of substitute products/services (for example, campgrounds, motels, and bed and breakfast are all substitutes for lodging);
- the economic climate (local and national); and
- the possibility of stimulating high profit products/services (such as boats) by offering related services (such as maintenance) at or below cost.

When establishing prices, R/T businesses should give attention to pricing strategies which may encourage off season and non-peak period sales, longer stays, group business, and the sale of package plans (combination of room, meals, and recreational facilities).

Promotion: Promotion provides target audiences with accurate and timely information to help them decide whether to visit your community or business. The information should be of importance and practical use to the potential or existing visitor and also accurate. Misrepresentation often leads to dissatisfied customers and poor recommendations. Don't make claims you cannot live up to.

Developing a promotional campaign is not a science with hard and fast rules. Making decisions regarding which type or combination of promotion types to use (personal selling, advertising, sales promotions, or publicity) is not always easy. If, however, you follow a logical process and do the necessary research, chances for success will be improved. It will be necessary to make decisions regarding:

- Target audience—the group you are aiming at;
- Image—that which your community or business wants to create or reinforce;
- Objectives–those of the promotional campaign;
- Budget—the amount of money available for your promotion;
- Timing—when and how often should your promotions appear;
- Media—which methods (television, radio, newspaper, magazine) will most effectively and efficiently communicate your message to the target audience; and
- Evaluation—how can the effectiveness of the promotional campaign be determined.

13.4.4.2. Internal Mix

As stated, marketing services such as recreation and tourism differ from marketing tangible products. Recreation and tourism businesses must direct as much attention at marketing to customers on site as they do to attracting them. In this respect, internal marketing is important because dissatisfied customers can effectively cancel out an otherwise effective marketing strategy.

The success of internal marketing is dependent on creating an atmosphere in which employees desire to give good service and sell the business/community to visitors. To create such an atmosphere requires the following four important elements:

— *Hospitality and Guest Relations*—An organization wide emphasis on hospitality and guest relations, including a customer oriented attitude on the part of the owners and managers as well as the employees. If the owner/manager is not customer sensitive, it is unlikely the lower paid employees will be.

— *Quality Control*—A program which focuses on improving both the technical quality (the standards associated with what the customer receives) and the functional quality (the standards associated with how the customer receives the service). All employees who come into contact with customers should receive hospitality training.

— *Personal Selling*—Training the staff in the selling aspects of the property (business) or community. This also includes rewarding them for their efforts. By being informed about the marketing objectives, and their role in accomplishing those objectives, they can help increase sales.

— *Employee Morale*—Programs and incentives aimed at maintaining employee morale. The incentives can be both monetary and non-monetary.

A customer oriented atmosphere usually results in customers that are more satisfied, do less complaining and are more pleasant to serve. This helps build employee morale, their desire to provide good service and their efficiency.

13.4.4.3. Marketing Budget

Successful marketing requires that sufficient money and personnel time be made available to implement activities comprising the marketing strategy. A marketing budget is a financial plan which shows the total amount to be spent on marketing during different times of the year and how it is to be allocated among alternative activities. Separate marketing budgets should be developed for each marketing mix strategy. The separate budgets should then be aggregated to develop an overall marketing budget.

If the total amount is too great it will be necessary to modify the overall objectives and the target market objectives, narrow down or drop target markets, or adjust marketing mixes. The final budget should be realistic given your objectives. When deciding on a marketing budget, consideration should be given to the job that needs to be done as defined by the objectives.

Basing marketing budgets on some percent of sales or what the competition spends usually leads to over spending or under spending. Decisions should also be based on the costs, projected revenues, and desired profitability of different activities, not just costs alone. Successful marketing activities will generate additional revenues which can be projected based on the marketing objectives (such as increase off season stay by 5%).

Although budgets should be viewed as flexible plans, every effort should be made to adhere to them. Revisions in the budget should only be made after careful consideration of the likely impact of the change on the marketing mix and accomplishment of your objectives.

13.4.4.4. Implimentation

Many well designed marketing plans fail because they are poorly executed. Businesses, agencies, and communities can increase the likelihood of successful implementation if they:

— identify specific tasks which must be accomplished;

— assign people or departments specific responsibility for different tasks;

— provide employees with information on the marketing plan (rationale, objectives, strategies);

— develop time lines and deadlines;
— adhere as much as possible to the budget; and
— regularly monitor and evaluate progress.

13.4.4.5. Evaluation

It is important that marketing efforts be continually evaluated. This will improve the effectiveness of marketing strategies by quickly identifying differences between actual results and expected performance and determining likely reasons for the success or failure to realize objectives. A framework for evaluation would include:

— *determining which elements of the different marketing mixes are most important to evaluate.* It is rarely possible or cost effective to evaluate all elements;
— *establishing performance standards to compare against actual results.* Marketing objectives, if properly formulated, should serve as performance standards;
— *development of formal and informal methods for collecting data on actual results.* There are many ways different elements of the marketing mix can be evaluated. For example, promotions can be evaluated with money off coupons. Special information request forms, telephone numbers to call or post office box numbers to write to can identify the area the request is coming from.

13.4.5. Effective Tourism Marketing Program

Step-by-step instructions describe how to inventory attractions, assess current marketing efforts, find existing market research, determine target markets, determine tourist motivators, develop promotional goals, determine campaign themes, find an advertising media, develop public relations and gather the correct data for an evaluation.

13.4.5.1. Inventory of Attractions and Accommodations

The first step in developing effective marketing plans is to inventory the attractions a community has to offer tourists. A community must know what it has to offer or sell before plans can be laid for marketing the product. These can include natural, manmade, historical, cultural or ethnic, festivals, special events and recreational attractions.

13.4.5.2. Assessing Current Marketing Efforts

Listing current advertising efforts for all attractions is necessary to assess the present promotional campaign's successfulness, and to develop new campaigns.

13.4.6. Market Research

Market research is an important part of developing a market plan. Several important pieces of information are needed to develop a market plan. These include:

- An inventory of tourist attractions in the area, region, or destination
- Market trends
- Tourist motivations
- Tourist profiles, including expenditures

It helps to review other successful marketing plans, remembering that a marketing plan should meet the individual needs of the area, region or destination for which it was developed. Learning from previous mistakes is a key to developing better programs.

There are two types of research data that can provide this information. The first is primary research gathered through phone calls, surveys, or other interviewing techniques. Secondary data has been compiled by outside organizations. Be careful when using secondary data; confirm the reliability of the source.

13.4.7. Target Market

Trying to appeal to everyone is a common mistake made in marketing. Not everyone looks for the same thing in a destination, and every destination cannot be all things to all people. Target marketing, focusing on a particular segment or segments of the market,allows for a more effective marketing plan. Market research will define the market segments, which will find those tourists most interested in what a community has to offer. Data on past visitors can indicate the type of tourist or the geographic region on which to focus. A target market can be a geographic region, a type of tourist, a combination of the two or any grouping that makes sense.

13.4.7.1. Determine Tourist Motivators

The fifth step is detemine tourist motivetors. Tourist motivators should be studied once a target market has been defined. Discovering where and why tourists travel is important when focusing advertising. Enticing the tourist to chose a historical destination because of its mystique, or choosing a full-service resort where every need can be catered to requires different motivational factors.

13.4.7.2. Developing Promotional Goals

Establishing goals provides the basis to determine what a community wants its marketing and promotion program to accomplish. Goals should be well thought out and be measurable, and can also serve as controls. Writing down goals provides directional guidelines. It can be difficult to get feedback on promotional goals, but with specific goals set, an evaluation and feedback plan can be implemented. This will gather the necessary data for the evaluation process, which can determine the successfulness of a community's plans and program.

13.4.8. Determining a Campaign Theme

A campaign theme should emphasize the image aimed at tourists in a given area. Remember, always capitalize on the positive aspects in the area, region or destination. Campaign themes should be developed for a clearly defined target market. For example, New Mexico's promotion, "More to Explore... New Mexico USA," targets nonresidents, and capitalizes on the fact that New Mexico is a part of the United States, although many tourists think it is a part of Mexico.

A campaign focusing on New Mexico residents, on the other hand, would emphasize what their home state has to offer. It could incorporate a theme of "Travel Close to Home."

13.4.8.1. Advertising Media

Determining which advertising media to use should not be done until after the target market is identified. Once the market has been determined, the tourist profile of the target market can be matched to the audience profile of specific advertising media. Most advertising media can provide an accurate profile of their audience.

13.4.8.2. Public Relations

Public relations can be an excellent way to promote a community or attraction. Public relations activities are uniquely different from advertising. Advertising is paid, but public relations uses free public exposure to ensure goodwill. Public relations can use radio,television or newspapers. Public relations efforts not only can be used to promote the destination to tourists, but also to promote the community itself. It can help create a feeling of pride in the community by educating the local community about what it has to offer tourists. This can develop a feeling of pride for the residents when they are asked to describe their community to tourists. Instead of seeing tourists as invaders, they will be seen as an economic boost to the local economy.

13.4.8.3. Developing an Evaluation Plan

An evaluation plan requires detailed planning during the initial stages of a marketing plan. Establishing measurable goals in a marketing plan is the first step in this evaluation. From this step, decide what information is needed to prove or disprove the accomplishment of the goal. If methods to gather the information are established at the beginning, all needed information for evaluation will be available at the end.

One of the most difficult parts of an evaluation is uncovering all the information that is needed, especially if an organized system is not included at the beginning. The second most difficult part is convincing everyone of the importance of such an evaluation. It is the key to the entire marketing plan that says, "Yes, it worked" or "No, it didn't work." An evaluation can show if the wrong audience was targeted or the plan conveyed the wrong message. Evaluation also provides the information needed to improve marketing. Great care should be taken to incorporate an evaluation plan into the marketing plan.

Another important part of an evaluation is the conversion study, which compares the number of inquiries to the number of people who actually visit. The conversion study is conducted by using the list of inquiries generated over the specified time frame, randomly choosing a sample, then performing a follow-up telephone or mail survey. Other information that can be collected along with a conversion study, when it is determined that the inquiring person has actually visited, is:

— Place of residence
— What time of year visited
— Transportation
— Estimated expenditures during trip
— Purpose of trip
— Would you visit again

These questions help establish a tourist profile. Information that needs to be collected for a proper evaluation of a marketing plan is:

— Advertisement cost
— Advertisement dates
— Number of times an advertisement was run
— Advertisement agency costs (if any)
— Media in which advertisement was placed
— Number of inquiries received from each advertisement
— Request fulfillment costs (mailing costs, envelopes, mailing brochures)
— Follow up information

Gathering this kind of data provides information to determine the effectiveness of advertising. When follow-up information on actual visitation and expenditures is obtained, advertising effectiveness can be further evaluated.

— *Number of Inquiries*—The number of people who requested information through the advertisement.
— *Ad Costs*—The cost of placing an advertisement in the advertising media.
— *Ad Cost Per Inquiry*—Ad cost divided by number of inquiries.
— *Request Fulfillment Cost Per Inquiry*—Request fulfillment cost divided by number of inquiries: includes mailing, brochure, and envelope costs.
— *Ad Agency Fixed Cost Per Inquiry*—Ad agency fixed cost divided by number of inquiries.
— *Total Cost Per Inquiry*—Total costs divided by number of inquiries.

Data collection methods should be decided on and in place before any advertising is done. Thus, all needed information will be available when evaluation procedures start. Suggested advertisement monitoring methods include:

— A phone answering script that determines the caller's name, address, phone and type of information requested.

— Coding advertisements so inquiries received are easily tracked to a specific advertisement.

— Monitoring guest registrations for visitor's points of origin.

13.4.8.4. Funding

Once the marketing plan has been developed, there must be funding to support the implementation of the plan. Learning to budget the expenses that will be incurred with the marketing plan is the first step. Funding sources want to know from the beginning how the money will be spent.

Determining how much money to spend is not the hard part; determining where to get the money is. Non-profit organizations such as Convention and Visitors bureaus and Chambers of Commerce may have access to the Cooperative Advertising Program offered through the State Travel and Tourism Department, which provides matching funds. Lodgers' taxes are another source of funding. This money is usually administered by local government. Other funding sources at the local level are member fees, banks and utilities.

13.5. Supply Chain Management

Tour operators can integrate economic, environmental and social sustainability criteria into their choices of service suppliers and their contracts with those suppliers. From establishing a sustainability policy and action plan and developing a baseline assessment of tourism service suppliers to enabling suppliers to meet set targets and reviewing and reporting on progress made, the document maps out a methodology for improving the sustainability of the tour operator's supply chain.

A wide range of possible actions that tour operators can take, each company should select the actions that are most appropriate to its organization and the types of destinations and suppliers with which it works. It is not necessary to try to implement all the actions at once; indeed, it is often better to start with a few achievable actions and then build on those in the future. What is important is that a company start to take action.

As intermediaries between tourists and tourism service providers, tour operators bring together a variety of tourism-related services to form a complete holiday package, which is then marketed to customers either directly or through travel agents. Each package generally consists of accommodation (often including some food provision), transport both to and from the destination, ground transport within the destination, and events or activities such as excursions and social activities.

Because most of the goods and services included in a holiday package are provided by a supply chain of subcontracted companies, organizations and agents, tour operators are not always in direct control of the environmental and social impacts of those products. Yet, consumers increasingly expect the companies they buy from to ensure that their products provide not just quality and value-for-money, but also safeguard environmental and social sustainability.

Companies must take responsibility for ensuring the sustainability of all the inputs that go into their products. For tour operators, who offer products comprised almost entirely of contracted goods and services, this means that effectively implementing sustainability policies requires working closely with suppliers to improve sustainability performance in all the components of a holiday - throughout the life cycle of a holiday package. "Consumers are increasingly interested in the world behind the product they buy. Life cycle thinking implies that everyone in the whole chain of a product's life cycle, from cradle to grave, has a responsibility and a role to play, taking into account all the relevant external effects."

The actions presented are applicable to tour operators of any size, from the smallest to the largest. Although the way each company is organized can differ - thus affecting the staff who will need to be involved in various actions - here outlines the different roles that need to be brought together to develop and implement a sustainable supply chain policy and action plan.

13.5.1. Developing Sustainable Supply Chain

Working with suppliers to integrate sustainability into the supply chain can benefit tour operators, suppliers, customers and destinations. From a financial standpoint, improved sustainability can lower costs through greater operating efficiency, reduced waste generation, and reduced consumption of energy and water. Sustainability practices can also lead to increased revenue and shareholder value by generating more repeat business and attracting new business from customers who value good environmental and social performance.

A strong positive reputation as a company that cares about sustainability issues, coupled with improvements to the quality of the tourism experience provided to clients, can result in increased customer satisfaction and loyalty, strengthened brand value, enhanced publicity and marketing opportunities, and better acceptance by local communities in destinations. Good performance and a high-quality, sustainable product can also help a tour operator reduce the risk of conflict or problems with suppliers, governments, staff and local communities, and improve its status as a respected partner in destinations.

This may mean enhanced access to key business resources such as capital, the ability to develop products to meet growing market demand, improved relationships with governments, and a motivated and loyal staff. The costs and benefits of integrating sustainability criteria into the supply chain will vary for each company, depending on:

— Purchasing and contracting arrangements with suppliers;
— Availability of alternate suppliers in key destinations;
— Suppliers' current levels of sustainability performance and potential for change;
— Barriers to sustainability, such as external factors;
— A company's main sustainability and operational concerns; and
— Resources available to implement and promote sustainability throughout the supply chain.

For a tour operator, effectively integrating sustainability into its supply chain will require the establishment of a coherent company policy and accompanying management system that set out clear targets and actions on economic, environmental and social performance. Building this system on already existing internal processes will help keep down the costs of implementation and promote integration within a company's overall operations.

To establish this policy, a company needs to conduct a baseline assessment of its tourism service suppliers' current performance on sustainability, in order to determine priority targets and actions. The management system should include procedures for monitoring, reviewing and reporting on progress made in integrating sustainability principles into the company's supply chain. This helps to ensure transparency and allow tour operators to adapt any policies or actions that are not achieving their stated goals. Progress can be measured against the initial baseline assessment.

13.5.1.1. Create A Policy

13.5.1.1.1. Goal

Develop a coherent policy for improving the economic, environmental and social sustainability performance of suppliers, and for integrating it into existing company management systems.

13.5.1.1.2. Actions

- Build a team to develop and implement the policy
  - Bring together representatives of each area or department in the company that may have a role in implementing the overall policy, or which may be affected by it.
  - Create a management team to develop and implement the policy at each stage, drawing on expertise from all departments.
  - Consider inviting your company's suppliers to participate in the policy and planning process.
- Assess the company's strengths and opportunities
  - Assess the company's current position and policies and how they relate to sustainability issues.

— Consider trends and potential developments, including product quality, supplier performance and markets, as well as the way the company interacts with its suppliers.
— Identify opportunities to improve the sustainability performance of suppliers.

— Develop a policy
— Elaborate a common vision that can be shared by all departments in the company, based on the results of the strengths and opportunities assessment.
— Discuss the common vision with key staff, and invite their suggestions for policies and actions to implement this vision.
— Based on these discussions and the common vision, develop and agree on a policy and strategic goals for improved supply chain sustainability, and on the types of methods that could be used to meet these goals.

13.5.1.2. Baseline Assessment of Suppliers

13.5.1.2.1. Goal

Assess suppliers' current sustainability performance and their strengths and weaknesses, to generate data for designing a sustainability action plan, and to provide a baseline against which to measure progress over time and review and modify the sustainable supply chain policy and actions.

13.5.1.2.2. Actions

— Prepare an approach for assessment
— Develop assessment tools for measuring the sustainability performance of suppliers.
— Select a sample of suppliers to involve in the assessment.
— Consider prioritizing certain supplier groups, based on ability to influence them and the ease of addressing any identified impacts. Trying to tackle every type of service and every supplier or contractor at the same time can be very resource intensive.

— Assess suppliers' current performance
  — Use questionnaires, personal meetings and/or workshops to assess suppliers' current sustainability performance, strengths and weaknesses, their main concerns and the key areas requiring improvement.
  — Determine suppliers' general levels of awareness, technical capacity and desire to be involved in a sustainability program. In particular, it is important to understand their motives and values, and to identify any potential challenges or barriers to sustainability.
  — Identify any opportunities for additional cooperation with external stakeholders, in particular local authorities or NGOs.
  — Ask suppliers for information on how they select their own suppliers.

13.5.1.3. Prepare an Action Plan

13.5.1.3.1. Goal

Prepare an action plan for implementation of policies for improving the economic, environmental and social sustainability performance of suppliers, taking into account suppliers' strengths and weaknesses and existing company management systems.

13.5.1.3.2. Actions

— *Define actions and set targets:*
  — Define and agree on actions and targets to be achieved, based on the company's sustainable supply chain policy.
  — Ensure that targets are SMART (Specific, Measurable, Achievable, Realistic and Time-specific).
  — Set standards by which to measure suppliers' performance.
  — Ensure that standards are achievable. It is better to set standards that are achievable and can provide real satisfaction for suppliers and staff, rather than set over-ambitious standards that are unlikely to be achieved.
  — Develop an action plan to implement the strategy and meet set targets

- Agree on specific responsibilities for each department and the resources they will need to implement them, such as training or technical information. Incorporate departmental action plans in regular company procedures for reviewing progress and staff appraisal.
- Prepare a timetable for implementation of the overall plan and for each individual action.

— *Get the word out:*

- Inform suppliers about the sustainability policy and action plan, and the benefits of improved environmental, social and economic performance, through normal company communication channels, dedicated workshops and personal meetings between suppliers and company representatives.
- Inform staff about the sustainability policy and action plan through training workshops, briefings and feedback materials, and internal capacity-building on how to raise awareness of the policy and provide support to suppliers.
- Establish a system to keep staff informed of progress, for example through staff newsletters and the intranet.

— *Put the plan into action:*

- Consider prioritizing suppliers for involvement in the first stages of the program, based on economic and managerial considerations. It may be more practical to begin with just a few destinations and/or selected suppliers, rather than trying to introduce the program everywhere at once.
- Recognize that suppliers may have different priorities for improvements and are likely to make progress at different rates.
- Understand that change takes time. It is important to focus on achieving continuous improvements, rather than trying to achieve everything all at once. The key is to initiate programs with all suppliers to improve their performance and see measurable improvement over time.
- Consider working with other partners, including public authorities, NGOs and other tour operators operating in the same destination, to help encourage sustainability

performance improvements amongst all suppliers, for example by developing a common approach in certain geographic or supplier areas.

13.5.1.4. Monitor and Report on Progress

13.5.1.4.1. Goal

Monitor and report on progress made in integrating sustainability into the company's supply chain, to ensure that goals have been achieved and to identify any potential problems.

13.5.1.4.2. Actions

- Create and implement a monitoring system
  - Select appropriate indicators for monitoring performance.
  - Hold regular meetings with relevant individuals, to review progress and help sort out problems as they arise. Key staff in each area often understand best where and how improvements can be made, and involving them in the process helps to build and maintain their commitment to sustainability.
  - Ensure that monitoring is frequent enough to detect problems at an early stage, so that corrective action can be taken if needed.
  - Identify and refine the most successful approaches to improvement of sustainability performance across the company's supply chain.
  - Store information collected through monitoring in a central database.
  - Learn from successes and difficulties in implementing planned actions and modify plans accordingly; use the results of a progress review to plan for the year ahead.
- Report on performance
  - Report internally by communicating the results of monitoring back to staff, to show what has been achieved, recognize their commitment to the project and remind them of the program's objectives and targets.

— Agree on the format for a public report on supply chain sustainability, for example as a separate report or a section of the company's annual report.

— Consider using a third party to review the company's sustainability report before publication.

— Disseminate regular reports on progress to demonstrate a commitment to improving overall sustainability performance in the supply chain to key stakeholder groups, including suppliers, staff, customers, media, destinations and others in the tourism industry. Reporting also helps to foster openness and discussion about problems and successes and enables companies to more effectively prioritize future activities.

13.5.2. Reaching Sustainability Goals

Tour operators are well-placed to support suppliers in improving their economic, environmental and social performance. As tour operators interact directly with potential customers, they understand their clients' growing demands for high quality and sustainability. They also often have access to technology and information that smaller suppliers may have difficulty obtaining on their own. Because tour operators deal with a wide range of different suppliers, they can more easily gather information on a variety of best practices and facilitate the sharing of experiences amongst suppliers.

There are a number of ways that tour operators can enable their suppliers to improve their sustainability performance and meet set sustainability criteria and targets. Three of these measures - awareness raising, technical support and the provision of incentives. The appropriate mix of support measures for each company and supplier will depend on the results of the baseline assessment and the approach that the company has chosen to adopt for implementing its sustainable supply chain strategy.

13.5.2.1. Awareness on Sustainability Issues

13.5.2.1.1. Goal

Raise awareness amongst suppliers on relevant sustainability issues and demonstrate why sustainability performance is important.

13.5.2.1.2. Actions

- *Develop awareness-raising messages on sustainability*
  - Take into account feedback from suppliers, existing relationships with targeted supplier groups, the level of interest amongst suppliers in participating in the program, and suppliers' current capacity and priorities for performance improvement.
  - Design messages based on the dissemination channels that will be used to raise awareness, such as mailings, personal visits, workshops, etc.
  - Identify potential partners and support. Local partners, such as business associations or training institutes, can help open communication channels with local suppliers, especially amongst smaller enterprises, and may be influential in reinforcing awareness-raising efforts.
  - Focus on key issues that are important to the company's situation and its suppliers.
  - Provide information in the awareness-raising materials on the overall strategy and time frame for the company's sustainability program.
- *Communicate sustainability messages to suppliers*
  - Identify the characteristics of each group of suppliers, including their values and concerns, and select appropriate tools, media and styles to best reach these target groups. Tools might include workshops, bilateral meetings or dialogues, briefing materials and feedback forms for staff, checklists and questionnaires, or printed materials, such as leaflets, posters and manuals.
  - If questionnaires or checklists are used, indicate clearly what the information gathered would be used for. Consider preparing a summary report on the results, for example highlighting sustainability issues identified as priorities by suppliers and illustrating the general level of performance for each of the issues addressed.
  - Use personal communication wherever possible. Staff in contact with suppliers can provide up-to-date information on

sustainability issues and the company's progress. Trained staff should be available to inform suppliers about environmental and social issues, provide contact phone numbers, make personal visits, etc.

— Ensure that sustainability issues are followed up and discussed regularly with suppliers. Encourage feedback from suppliers to help evaluate the effectiveness of awareness-raising activities and provide important information on the attitudes of target groups to sustainability issues. This feedback can be used to refine awareness-raising activities and plan future developments.

— Monitor the response to the awareness-raising actions. Check how suppliers and staff respond to the project, recognize and appreciate results, and support continuous improvement.

13.5.3. Provide Technical Support

13.5.3.1. Goal

Support suppliers in improving their sustainability performance, particularly in areas that have been identified as priorities.

13.5.3.2. Actions

— Assess where support is needed

— Determine where technical support is needed amongst suppliers and establish targets for improvement.

— Identify the most appropriate technical support and capacity-building actions to match the suppliers' and company's targets.

— Identify, develop and deliver the most appropriate and effective technical support tools for suppliers, including printed material, workshops, bilateral meetings or dialogues, briefing materials and feedback forms for staff, training sessions, checklists and questionnaires, and telephone and on-line information and support services.

— Provide training and practical education opportunities to suppliers' staff at all levels, including managers, engineers, hotel maids, catering staff, guides, etc., on reducing resource use and procedures for waste separation and recycling.

- — Offer links to networks of local, national and international advisers on sustainability and business issues who can provide on-line and on-site assistance to suppliers - for example local experts on environmental and socio-economic issues, possibly in collaboration with local trade associations and non-governmental organizations.
- — Consider promoting the use of eco-labeling schemes to support improvement and provide information on technical issues tailored to a specific destination.
- — Identify external sources of information and support. Numerous technical materials on environmental management and solutions are already available through international and national hotel associations, international organizations and NGOs.

13.5.4. Incentives to Sustainable Suppliers

13.5.4.1. Goal

Build support for the sustainable supply chain strategy by recognizing and rewarding suppliers for improvements on key environmental, social and economic issues.

13.5.4.2. Actions

- — Create an incentive scheme
  - — Establish sustainability performance standards for the sustainability priorities set by the company's policy, to identify which suppliers will be offered additional promotional opportunities and/or other incentives.
  - — Identify the most suitable incentive measures to reward suppliers making significant improvements, such as preferential contracting, promotional opportunities, awards and events, for example:
  - — Indicate that suppliers who demonstrate improved performance will be the company's first choice when decisions are made on whom to contract in any destination or

category. Preferential contracting offers a major incentive to suppliers to improve their performance.

- Highlight good performers in catalogs and brochures with a special logo, making sure to provide clear information to customers about what the logo denotes.
- List specific sustainability actions that each supplier has adopted in the catalogs.
- Present certificates to suppliers who demonstrate the best sustainability performance.
- Organize events - in a destination or at company headquarters - for groups of suppliers who are making good progress in implementing sustainability performance improvements.
- Develop and agree on the internal procedures for providing the identified additional promotional opportunities and incentives.

- Get the word out
  - Inform suppliers about additional promotional opportunities and other incentives and the criteria that the company will use to allocate them.
  - Ensure that available recognition and reward opportunities and incentives are discussed with each supplier in personal meetings with a company representative.
- Verify supplier performance
  - Define mechanisms for collection of data on suppliers' performance in the identified action areas, such as questionnaires, personal visits, etc., and train staff to implement these procedures.
  - Create a monitoring and assessment system and procedures to verify suppliers' declared sustainability performance.
  - Establish a database to record information on suppliers' sustainability performance and ensure that the database can be easily used by all staff who need to access the information it will hold. Where appropriate, integrate the database with existing systems, such as health and safety databases.

13.5.4.3. Integrate Sustainability Criteria

Full integration of sustainability issues into a tour operator's business practices will require alterations to the way purchasing choices are made and suppliers' contracts are written. Inclusion of sustainability criteria in suppliers' contracts highlights the importance of sustainability issues to the tour operator's core business and ensures that priority issues are addressed with suppliers from the start. Sustainability criteria can be incorporated into suppliers' contracts to set both minimum performance standards that all suppliers of a particular type must meet and further optional criteria that they are encouraged to achieve. Performance against sustainability criteria will need to be monitored and assessed as part of regular reviews of suppliers.

13.5.4.3.1. Goal

Integrate environmental, social and economic criteria into suppliers' contracts and reward performance improvements by preferentially contracting suppliers that meet those criteria.

13.5.4.3.2. Actions

- Set sustainability contracting standards
  - Establish the minimum sustainability performance standards to be included in suppliers' contracts, and link them to the performance standards set as part of an incentive scheme.
  - Set standards sufficiently high so that they represent good performance and real improvements, but also ensure that they will be realistic and achievable for suppliers.
  - Allow flexibility to accommodate varying local socio-economic and environmental conditions among different destinations and different types and sizes of suppliers.
  - Seek guidance on standards for different types of suppliers from relevant national or international bodies.
  - For each destination, review the sustainability performance of the full range of suppliers for each service or item and identify alternate supply options.

— Set a sustainable contracting system

  — Develop and agree on an internal approach and procedures for implementation of sustainability performance as a contracting criteria.

  — Draft contractual clauses to reflect minimum performance requirements on key issues and consider legal matters arising from incorporation of sustainability standards into suppliers' contracts.

  — Establish procedures to deal with suppliers that fail to meet minimum set standards or that have submitted false information. In serious cases and on specific issues, companies may decide to suspend contracts with suppliers who are in breach of contract conditions.

  — Consider appointing an individual staff member or a small team to develop and update standards and support materials, coordinate training for suppliers and staff, manage informational databases, coordinate monitoring, auditing and verification, and provide progress reports.

— Get the word out

  — Run workshops to train staff on contracting procedures for sustainability issues and procedures for monitoring and auditing suppliers' sustainability performance.

  — Set up a communications program to inform suppliers about the new contract clauses and contracting policy.

  — Consider developing a parallel voluntary program with additional sustainability performance standards.

  — Offer assistance to help get suppliers back into compliance, for example by making suggestions for improvements and sources of technical assistance.

— Monitor and evaluate the system

  — Set up assessment and monitoring procedures to evaluate supplier sustainability performance in relation to standards set in contracts. For example, arrangements could be made for sustainability performance to be audited as part of existing health and safety audits.

— Arrange for this assessment and monitoring to be conducted by the supplier, the company or a third party, using checklists, questionnaires, site visits and staff interviews as appropriate. Customer feedback through surveys or informal comments can also be an important source of information.

— Establish a database to record information on suppliers' sustainability performance and ensure that the database can be easily used by all staff who need to access the information it will hold. Where appropriate, integrate the database with existing systems, such as health and safety databases.

— Ensure the confidentiality of any sensitive or confidential data in the database.

References

Gardiner, Rosalie. 1998. *A Review of Codes of Practice for Sustainable Tourism.* London: UNED-UK.

United Nations. 1999. Economic and Social Council. Commission on Sustainable Development, Seventh Session. *Tourism and Sustainable Development.* E/CN.17/1999/L.6, 29 April.

Wagner, Lynn. 1999. Personal communication and observation at the Seventh Session of the UN Commission on Sustainable Development, New York, NY.

World Tourism Organization (WTO). 1999. Web site: http://www.world-tourism.org/, including *Tourism Highlights 1999 (Revised preliminary estimates, 19 May 1999).*

Bibliography

Bar kin, D. 2002. *Eco tourism for sustainable regional development*. Current Issues in Tourism. pp. 5(3–4):245–253.

Baum, T. 1995. *Managing Human Resources in the European Hospitality and Tourism Industry – A Strategic Approach*, Chapman and Hall.

Beirman, D., 2003, *Restoring Tourism Destination in Crisis: A Strategic Management Approach,* Allen & Unwin, Crows Nest, Australia.

Buhalis, D & Laws, E. (eds). 2001. *Tourism Distribution Channels-Practices, Issues and Transformations*, Continuum Publishing, London.

Carter R & Bedard, F. 2001. *E-Business for Tourism-Practical Guidelines for Tourism Destinations and Business,* WTO Business Council, Madrid.

Cheng, A. and Brown, A. 1998. 'HRM strategies and labour turnover in the hotel industry: a comparative study of Australia and Singapore', *International Journal of Human Resource Management*, 9(1),136–154.

Conservation International. 2003: "Tourism and Biodiversity: Mapping Tourism's Global Footprint". http://www.conservation.org

Costa, Frank J. and Allen G. Noble. 1999. "Sustainable Tourism: An Overview," in Allen G. Noble and Frank J. Costa, editors, *Preserving the Legacy: Concepts in Support of Sustainability*. Boulder, CO: Lexington Books.

D'Annunzio-Green, N., Maxwell, G. and Watson, S. 2002. *Human Resource Management: International Perspectives in Hospitality and Tourism,* Continuum.

Department for International Development (DFID). 1999. *Changing the nature of tourism: developing an agenda for action*. DFID. London, UK.

Douglas, M., 1994, *Risk and Blame: Essays in Cultural Theory*, London: Routledge.

Drabek, T. E., 1995, "Disaster Responses within the Tourist Industry". *International Journal of Mass Emergencies and Disasters*, 13(1), 7–23.

Elsubbaugh, S., R.Fildesn and M.B.Rosenn, 2004, "Preparation for Crisis Management:A Proposed Model and Empirical Evidence", *Journal of Contingencies and Crisis Management*, 12(3),112-127.

Faulkner, B., 2001, "Towards a framework for tourism disaster management", *Tourism Management*, 22, 135–147.

Gardiner, Rosalie. 1998. *A Review of Codes of Practice for Sustainable Tourism.* London: UNED-UK.

Gupta, S & Bansal, S.P. 2001. *Tourism Towards 21st Century,* Deep and Deep. New Delhi.

Harrington, D., Lenehan, T., 1998, "*Managing Quality in Tourism; Theory and Practice*", Oak Tree Press, Dublin.

Harris P., J. & Brown Jackie Brander, 1998, Research and development in hospitality accounting and financial management, *Hospitality management*, 17, pp. 161-181.

Honey, Martha. 1999. *Ecotourism and Sustainable Development: Who Owns Paradise?* Covelo, CA: Island Press.

Ingram Hadyn, 1995, "Hospitality and tourism: international industries experiencing common problems", *International Journal of Contemporary Hospitality Management,* University Press Limited, 0959-6119 7(7), pp. 44-54.

Inkpen, G. (1998. *Information Technology for Travel and Tourism*, Addison Wesley Logman, Essex UK.

Isaacs, J.C. 2000. *The limited potential of ecotourism to contribute to wildlife conservation.* The Ecologist. pp. 28(1):61–69.

Janjaroen W, Supakankunti S. 2000. *International trade in health services in the millenium: a case of Thailand.* Bangkok: Centre for Health Economics.

Jayawardena, C., 1993, "Harmonising the tourist needs and country's expectations from tourism industry", *Tourism, Hoteliering and Hospitality Education*, pp. 28-31.

Johnson, Stanley P. 1994. *The Earth Summit: The United Nations Conference on Environment and Development.* Boston: Graham and Trotman.

Kadison, H., Weismann, J.E., Modahl. M., Lieu, K.C. and Levin, L 1998, *Online Retail Strategies*, Forrester Report 1/1, http://www.forester.com, April 1998.

Leatherman, JC. 2000, *Internet-based commerce: Implications for rural communities*, U.S. Economic Development Administration, viewed 15 April 2005.

Lepp, A., and H. Gibson, "Tourist Roles, Perceived Risk and International Tourism", *Annals of Tourism Research*,30(3),606–624

Lodha R, Bagga A. 2000. "Traditional Indian systems of medicine". *Annals of the Academy of Medicine, Singapore*;29(1):37-41.

Marcussen, C. 1999. *Internet Distribution of European Travel and Tourism Services*, Research Centre of Bornholm, Denmark.

Mishra L, Singh BB, Dagenais S. 2001. "Healthcare and disease management in Ayurveda". *Alternative Therapies in Health and Medicine*; 7(2):44-50.

Morgan, Derek. 2003. "Medical Tourism: Ethical Baggage and Legal Currencies." *Medical Ethics Tomorrow* 63.1:1-5.

Palmer, A & McCole, P. 2000, 'The role of electronic commerce in creating virtual tourism destination marketing organisations', *International Journal of Contemporary Hospitality Management*, vol. 12, no. 3, pp. 198-204.

Phillips, P.A. and Moutinho, L. 1998. *Strategic Planning Systems in Hospitality and Tourism*. CABI: Wallingford.

Porter, M.E., 2001, *Strategy and the Internet*, Harvard Business School Publishing Corp, Mass, USA.

Rita, P. 1993.*A Knowledge-Based System for Promotion Budget Allocation by National Tourism Organizations*. Doctoral thesis, University of Wales, College of Cardiff.

Sheldon, PJ. 1998, *Tourism information technology*, CABI Publishing, New York.

Sitarz, Daniel, ed. 1993. *Agenda 21: The Earth Summit Strategy to Save Our Planet*. Boulder, CO.

United Nations. 1999. Economic and Social Council. Commission on Sustainable Development, Seventh Session. *Tourism and Sustainable Development.* E/CN.17/1999/L.6, 29 April.

Vivanco, L. 2002. *Ecotourism, Paradise lost - A Thai case study*. The Ecologist. pp. 32(2):28–30.

Wagner, Lynn. 1999. Personal communication and observation at the Seventh Session of the UN Commission on Sustainable Development, New York, NY.

Werthner, H. and Klein, S. 1999. *Information Technology and Tourism – A Challenging Relationship*. Springer: Wien-New York.

World Tourism Organisation 1999, *Marketing tourism destinations online: Strategies for the information age*, Madrid.

World Tourism Organization (WTO). 1999. Web site: http://www.world-tourism.org/, including *Tourism Highlights 1999 (Revised preliminary estimates, 19 May 1999)*.

World Tourism Organization, 1998, *"Tourism: 2020 Vision", Madrid: WTO.*

Index